MANAGING STRATEGICALLY FOR SUPERIOR PERFORMANCE

THIRD EDITION

Donald O'Neal, Ph.D.
University of Illinois at Springfield

american press

BOSTON, MASSACHUSETTS

Copyright © 2003, 2005, 2008 by American Press.
ISBN 978-0-89641-453-2

All rights reserved. No part of this publication may be reproduced, stored in a retrieval system, or transmitted, in any form or by any means, electronic, mechanical, photocopying, recording, or otherwise without the prior written permission of the copyright owner.

Printed in the United States of America.

ACKNOWLEDGEMENTS

This project began as a personal quest to provide students, particularly non-traditional students who continue working while they complete their education, with a textbook that concentrates as much on the practical application of organizational theories as it does on the theories themselves. Its use in the field since 2003 has demonstrated the book's value, both as a strategic management textbook and as a management handbook. Although a second edition, incorporating a number of revisions and additions, was published in 2005, my editor, Marci Taylor, and I agree that now is the time to expand its content. This, the third edition, includes five new chapters: Chapter 4, *Competitive Analysis*; Chapter 8, *Global Strategies*; Chapter 12, *Time Management*; Chapter 16, *Boards of Directors*; and Chapter 17, *Decision Making*.

I must first acknowledge my students, past, present, and future. They are the inspiration for what I do; they help me understand how they learn; they provide invaluable feedback on what works and what doesn't, even long after they've graduated; and they continue teaching me how to teach them.

I owe a lasting debt of gratitude to the professors who have taught and guided me and continue to do so, and the colleagues with whom I have had the good fortune to work and study.

My wife, Nancy, is a great proof-reader, particularly when it comes to grammar and sentence construction, and I have her to thank for dozens (maybe hundreds) of excess commas that no longer clutter these pages. But most of all, thanks, Nancy, for your support and understanding, which have been essential to bringing this project from a rough idea to its current state.

Finally, reading the book or scanning the References section should give the reader some idea of the number of other writers who have influenced my thinking. This book is an integration of thoughts and ideas selected from many sources, as well as from my own experience in the classroom, in corporate management, and in consulting with a variety of organizations. I am grateful to all whose writings have influenced my thinking.

Following are some writings from which I have reproduced or adapted specific figures to illustrate the discussions:

Figure 4 (Chapter 4), The Five Forces of Industry Competition, is adapted with the permission of *The Free Press*, a Division of Simon & Schuster Adult Publishing Group, from *Competitive Strategy: Techniques for Analyzing Industries and Competitors*, by Michael E. Porter. Copyright © 1980, 1998 by The Free Press.

Figure 6 (Chapter 4), Industry Life-Cycle, is reprinted by permission of *Harvard Business Review*, from "Exploit the Product Life Cycle", by Levitt, Nov-Dec, 1965. Copyright © 1965 by the Harvard Business School Publishing Corporation; all rights reserved.

Figure 11 (Chapter 7), Growth/Share Matrix, is adapted from *Long Range Planning*, 1977, "Strategy and the Business Portfolio," Hedley, Copyright © 1977, with permission from Elsevier Science.

Figure 12 (Chapter 10), Maslow's Hierarchy of Needs, is adapted from *Maslow on Management*, Maslow, Copyright © 1998 by Ann R. Kaplan. Reprinted by permission of John Wiley & Sons, Inc.

Figure 21 (Chapter 15), Wheel of Learning, is adapted from *Organizational Psychology: An Experiential Approach* 3/E by Kolb/Rubin/McIntyre, © Reprinted by permission of Pearson Education, Inc., Upper Saddle River, NJ.

No matter how conscientious I may have been, this book is, and will continue to be, a work in progress, and I welcome any suggestions for correction or improvement, or for additional topics or examples.

Don O'Neal
Professor of Management
University of Illinois at Springfield
(oneal.don@uis.edu)

PREFACE

The subject of strategic management, which is about the things managers do to enable their organizations to establish competitive advantage in their industries, has been directed almost exclusively toward top-level executives: those who set the direction for their organizations. Yet I found, first as a mid-level manager and later as a corporate officer, that the concepts of strategic management could be utilized advantageously by individuals at *all* levels of the organization, including those who aren't yet in supervisory positions.

As a graduate student (while still functioning as vice president of a business organization), I was impressed with the number of business theories that seemed to make good sense, but surprised at how few of them I had ever seen applied successfully in business organizations. I finally concluded that part of the reason, perhaps a major part, was that business-school professors and business professionals don't speak the same language. Most of what business-school academics write is written for and to their colleagues, rather than for business people. Nowhere is this more evident than in business textbooks which, like academic journals, are written *by* professors, appear to be written *for* professors and, without translation by someone who knows both the theory and how to apply it, are of limited use to either undergraduate students or business practitioners.

After earning a Ph.D in Strategic Management, I began teaching the subject in a business school using traditional strategic management textbooks. But a high percentage of my students were "non-traditional:" full-time workers who take classes in the evening and on weekends, and many were already in management positions. This type of student viewed traditional textbooks as "necessary evils" rather than useful reference books, and invariably sold them back to the bookstore once the class was over. I noticed, however, that many students kept my handouts, and used them as on-the-job reference material. To them, the handouts contained a condensed version of the strategic management concepts that seemed most likely to be useful in the business world.

I believe my subsequent success in the classroom has been due to the manner in which I translate textbook theory and information into practical contexts. It is important to understand that this is *not* "dumbing down," of either the information or the classes, but making the best use of busy peoples' time by getting to the heart of the important concepts with a minimum of confusion. And that's why I decided to write this book, which is based largely on information that I have synthesized from a wide range of sources over more than 30 years of managing, teaching, and consulting.

This volume is intended as a practical guide to strategic management, designed for the classroom, but also useful as a reference manual by individuals and professionals at all levels. It is based on a proven framework that allows students to learn, understand, and apply the principles of strategic management in a practical manner. The success of this method has been repeatedly verified by students, alumni, and clients, who emphasize the value of being able to immediately apply these concepts to their jobs, and even to their personal lives.

Beyond the traditional classroom, I see at least two additional opportunities for this book. First, in seminars and workshops on strategic management that I, and others, lead and facilitate for a variety of organizations (business, government, and not-for-profit). Second, for participants in "certificate" programs, which range from a few days to a few weeks, concluding with the awarding of a certificate in a particular subject. Strategic management may be the subject of the program, or it may be just one of several subjects in an integrated (e.g., business management) program.

CONTENTS

Preface v

Introduction xi

PART I — PLANNING 1

Chapter 1 — **Leadership and Management** 3
    Leadership vs. Management 5
    Strategic Thinking 9
    Summary 10

Chapter 2 — **Mission (Purpose)** 13
    What Needs? 13
    Whose Needs? 14
    How? 15
    Mission Statements 16
    Summary 16

Chapter 3 — **Goals (Objectives)** 17
    Strategic Issues 18
    Setting Goals 19
    Prioritizing Goals 19
    Major Goals 20
    Measurable Goals 21
    Timing of Goals 23
    Levels of Goals 23
    Tradeoffs 24
    Summary 25

Chapter 4 — **Competitive Analysis** 27
    Industry Analysis 27
    Industry Structure 29
    Industry Life-Cycle 30
    Learning-Curve Effects 33
    Competitors 34
    Summary 35

Chapter 5 — **Internal Analysis** 37
- Strengths 37
- Weaknesses 38
- Stakeholders 39
- Distinctive Competence 42
- Gap Analysis 43
- Summary 43

Chapter 6 — **External Analysis** 45
- Opportunities and Threats 46
- Managing the External Environment 47
  - Adapting to the External Environment (Internal Strategies) 47
    - Boundary Spanning 47
    - Buffering 48
    - Rationing 48
    - Smoothing (*Demand* Smoothing) 48
  - Changing the External Environment (External Strategies) 49
    - Advertising 49
    - Contracting (*Supply* Smoothing) 49
    - Co-opting 50
    - Lobbying 50
    - Strategic Alliances 50
- Summary 51

Chapter 7 — **Competitive Strategy** 53
- Competitive Advantage 53
- Fundamental (Basic) Competitive Strategy 54
  - Low-Price Leadership 54
  - Differentiation 55
- Contingent Strategies 58
  - Focus (Niche) Strategy 58
  - Offensive Strategy 60
  - Defensive Strategy 60
  - First-Mover Strategy 60
  - Follower/Imitator Strategy 61
  - Vertical Integration 62
  - Strategic Alliances 65
  - Diversification 68
  - Divestiture 69
- Portfolio Strategy 70
- Customer Service 72
- Summary 73

Chapter 8 — **Global Strategies** 75
    International Market Differences 75
        Exchange Rates 76
        Trade Policies 76
        Cost Variations 78
    International Strategies 79
        Licensing 79
        Export 79
        Multi-National 80
        Global 80
        Strategic Alliances 82
    Summary 83

PART II — PEOPLE 85

Chapter 9 — **Organizational Culture** 87
    Social Responsibility 88
    Values 88
    Summary 91

Chapter 10 — **Incentives and Rewards** 93
    Incentives 94
    Rewards 96
    Employee Satisfaction 99
    Summary 100

Chapter 11 — **Conflict, Power and Politics** 103
    Conflict 103
        Resolving Conflict 104
        Stimulating Conflict 105
    Power 107
    Politics 109
    Summary 110

Chapter 12 — **Time Management** 113
    Time-Wasters 113
        Wasted Talents/Abilities 113
        Routine Tasks 114
        Meetings 114
    Time-Savers 114
        Highest and Best Use 114

        Routine Tasks 115
        Effective Meetings 115
    Summary 116

PART III — ORGANIZATION 117

Chapter 13 — **Designing the Organization** 119
    Functional Structure 121
    Decentralized Structure 122
        Geographically Decentralized 122
        Product/Market Decentralized 123
    Matrix Structure 125
    Which Organization Form is Best? 128
    Summary 130

Chapter 14 — **Innovation and Technology** 133
    Technology 133
        Product Technology 134
        Service Technology 136
    Innovation 138
    Summary 139

Chapter 15 — **Knowledge and Learning** 141
    Knowledge 141
    Learning 143
    Information 145
    Summary 146

Chapter 16 — **Boards of Directors** 149
    Board Responsibilities 149
    Board Composition 150
    Board Effectiveness 150
        CEO Duality 151
        Stockholder Apathy 151
        The Proxy System 152
    Governance Failure 153
    Not-for-Profit Boards 153
        Size 153
        Composition 153
        Operation 154
    Board Issues 154
    Summary 154

PART IV — STRATEGIC RESPONSIVENESS 157

Chapter 17 — **Decision Making** 159
    Rational Decision-Making 159
    Individual Decision-Making 160
        Programmed Decisions 161
        Non-Programmed Decisions 161
        Intuitive Decisions 161
        Bounded Rationality 161
    Organizational Decision Making 162
        Management Science Approach 163
        Carnegie Model 163
        Incremental Model 163
        Garbage Can Model 163
    Escalating Commitment 163
    Summary 164

Chapter 18 — **Resource Allocation/Budgeting** 167
    Summary 169

Chapter 19 — **Performance Evaluation (Feedback)** 171
    Summary 175

Chapter 20 — **Managing Change** 177
    Resisting Change 177
    Leading Change 179
    Summary 184

REFERENCES 185

INDEX 189

INTRODUCTION

*"You may not have been responsible for your heritage,
but you are responsible for your future."*
(Author unknown)

Success, for organizations or individuals, is measured by *accomplishment*, by *results*, by *outcomes*, *not* by the amount of work done or by the effort expended.

Although a willingness to work hard is certainly a virtue, and usually necessary for success, it is not *sufficient* to ensure success. Today's organizations, be they business, not-for-profit, or governmental, are in intense competition, not only for their immediate success but also for their ultimate survival, and in this competition success is measured by *results*. Success comes from efforts directed toward specific *outcomes*; toward achieving planned *goals*.

Consider, for example, the mission of a typical college student: to further her education and earn a degree that will serve as evidence of her commitment and the knowledge she has acquired. Since she knows she is required to complete a set of prescribed courses to accomplish that mission, each course becomes a specific goal; something she must achieve, often in a prescribed sequence, before she can graduate. Pursuing those goals will keep her efforts focused on that one purpose: completing her degree. Without that sense of purpose and concentration of effort, a student might work diligently for years without ever completing a degree or accomplishing any other tangible result.

Of course, if one has no need to demonstrate accomplishment, either to himself or to others, he may see no value in having a sense of purpose or in achieving specific results. But for those of us who *want* to achieve or *need* to achieve, or both, the message is clear: *focused* efforts get results, achieve goals and, ultimately, accomplish purpose.

Which leads to the purpose of this book: *to help you get the maximum results from your efforts and become more effective as an executive, manager, professional, or as an individual.* This book is based on the concepts of corporate strategy and strategic management.

Corporate strategy has been defined, as "the pattern of decisions in a company that (1) determines, shapes, and reveals its objectives, purposes, or goals; (2) produces the principal policies and plans for achieving those goals; and (3) defines the business the company intends to be in, the kind of economic and human organization it intends to be, and the nature of the economic and noneconomic contribution it intends to make to its shareholders, employees, customers, and communities" (Christensen, et al., 1982:93).

Strategic management is the process through which management "...charts the company's long-term direction, develops competitively effective strategic moves and business approaches, and implements what needs to be done internally to produce good day-in/day-out strategy execution." (Thompson and Strickland, 1998:2,3)

In other words, strategic management is a process through which firms attempt to consistently outperform their competitors in satisfying customers and in achieving financial success. Although the concepts of strategic management have been directed primarily at top-level executives, experience has shown that these principles can be successfully applied to any organization, or any part of an organization, at any level, from those who lead the entire organization to those who supervise only themselves. This book is designed to clearly explain the principles of strategic management, in terms that make them easy to understand and apply in any situation in any organization. No matter who you are, where you are, or what you are currently doing, managing strategically can help you focus your performance to get the best results from your time and effort, both on and off the job.

This book is written to bridge the gap between the academic world, with its theories of how to manage more effectively, and the world of working managers, professionals, and individuals who can *apply* those theories in ways that will utilize their time, effort, and resources more efficiently. Unlike most textbooks on strategic management, this book discusses ideas and information in contexts that are likely to be more useful to practitioners, and downplays those aspects that tend to be primarily of interest to academics and their graduate students. It is intended to be useful not only as a classroom text but also as an ongoing reference manual for organizational managers and professionals

"Superior performance" has a dual meaning. On one hand, it refers to the primary purpose of strategic management: to encourage managing organizations proactively rather than reactively. If you develop a viable strategic plan, including a mission, specific goals, and a clear-cut strategy for achieving those goals, and if you execute that plan effectively, you will be better able to anticipate the uncertainties that inevitably occur and deal with them in an organized manner. Managing strategically will minimize the time you spend reacting to unanticipated events (i.e., fire-fighting), which is one of the biggest time-wasters in any organization, and allow you to direct the majority of your time and effort toward achieving *planned* goals. The primary difference between average performance and superior performance is that one focuses on the amount of work that gets done, while the other concentrates on getting *results*.

Applying the concepts of strategic management to organizing and directing your own (individual) efforts will have a similar effect, with two major benefits: increased job security and improved marketability.

Most organizations would probably consider a majority of their people good performers because they consistently meet the expectations of their supervisors. However, in these same organizations there are always a few people who are considered *outstanding* performers because they *exceed* their supervisors' expectations. It is important to note that the difference between "good" performance and "outstanding" performance is seldom how *hard* a person works, but how much he accomplishes; the *results* he achieves. A key to getting results, and a major difference between *good* performance and *outstanding* performance, is knowing *what* to do and concentrating on getting *that* done rather than anything else. Strategic planning, by helping you determine, in advance, *what* needs to be done, can help make you a superior performer; one whose performance is considered "outstanding." It can help you concentrate your efforts on achieving the most important things that need to be accomplished, rather than squandering them on fire fighting (i.e., responding to the crisis-of-the-moment).

Being considered one of the best performers can have a major influence on your job security, particularly when your organization faces the prospect of cutting its workforce, which can put even the "good" performers at risk. But you, as one considered "outstanding," are much more likely to be spared, because any organization, even one in crisis, *must* keep its top performers; they are the key to its future.

Another personal benefit is when executive recruiters (corporate "headhunters") come looking for key employees for their clients. They are seldom looking for average performers; they want people who get results; the top performers. So being a superior performer enhances your job security by making you more attractive to other companies.

But the best part is that you don't have to be a "superstar" to be an outstanding performer. You can do it by simply being more effective; by managing *yourself* strategically. Doing that will help you stand out in any organization, because there are so few who understand the difference between managing to get the work out and managing for results.

Strategic management, shown as a sequential framework in Figure 1, is a process, or method, for formulating and executing the actions and activities necessary to accomplish a pre-determined purpose. For managers and executives, managing strategically is a proven process for competitive success, at any level in any type of organization. But it is equally effective in helping individuals who are not yet managers, and even those who have no intention of becoming supervisors, improve their individual performance.

This book has been developed in four parts: Part I, Planning, includes Chapters 1-8, covering the *formulation* of strategy, often referred to as *strategic planning*. Parts II, People, and III, Organization, include Chapters 9-16, which describe how to *implement* strategy, once it has been formulated; and Part IV, Strategic Responsiveness, includes Chapters 17-20, which discuss decision making, resource allocation, performance assessment, and managing change.

Although the book is written from an organizational perspective, most of the concepts discussed can be applied at any *level* of analysis: the organization as a whole; organizational elements (e.g., departments, work groups); and individuals (as workers in organizations and as private individuals).

In addition, the concepts of strategic management can be effective in any *type* of organization: private-sector companies (both product and service); not-for-profit organizations; and governmental organizations (local, municipal, state, federal), as well as organizations of any *size*, from those that employ only a few people to those with thousands.

In other words, strategic management can make *any organization* more effective, at any level, and can make *any individual* more effective, both inside and outside of formal organizations.

PART I—PLANNING

Part I covers the elements of strategic management that are concerned with *creating* a strategic *plan*, including leadership, mission, objectives, internal analysis, external analysis, and competitive strategy. This is the process generally referred to as *strategy formulation*.

Chapter 1 discusses and describes *leadership* and *management*: what they are; what are their similarities and differences; why they are important; and where and when each is most appropriate and most effective. Also discussed is the role of leadership in planning, and why planning is so important to organizational success.

Managing successfully, whether it is a business, a department, a single employee, or one's self, begins with a *mission*. Every organization exists for a reason. its mission, or purpose, and all of its activities should be directed toward that purpose. The same should be true for every person. Every activity of every person should have a purpose—we should always know *why* we are doing what we are doing. This is what gives meaning to our actions, and ultimately to our lives. Chapter 2 describes and explains the process of developing a mission.

Once we have a mission, there are certain things we must do to pursue it, to make it happen, certain activities that are necessary to keep us on course. These are our *goals*, or *objectives*. Although these two terms can be used interchangeably, in this book we will primarily use "goals." All of our actions should be directed toward meeting a few carefully-selected goals which, when achieved, will be replaced by other goals. In this way, the achievement of goals keeps us continually progressing in pursuit of our mission. *Goals* are the focus of Chapter 3.

Once goals have been set, we need to develop *strategies* for reaching them; the actions we plan to take to accomplish them. But before we choose strategies we'll need thorough understanding of three major forces that are likely to affect them:

1. *competitive* forces—who will be our strongest competitors, and how they're likely to compete;
2. *internal* forces—the organizational resources that will be available for use in executing our strategies; and
3. *external* forces—obstacles, often beyond the organization's control, that we may need to overcome in order to reach our goals.

Chapter 4 discusses competitive analysis, Chapter 5 internal analysis, and Chapter 6, external analysis.

After we've gained a clear understanding of how to utilize our internal resources to overcome competitive and external forces, Chapter 7 leads us through the process of determining which *strategies* are likely to give us the greatest competitive advantage. Chapter 8 then discusses the ways in which *global strategies* are likely to differ from those we use in domestic competition.

When we've developed strategies for achieving our goals, we will have completed the planning part of strategic management, *strategy formulation*, and are ready to begin *strategy implementation*, the process of putting the strategic plan into action. The key elements of strategy implementation are *people*, and *organization*. *People* are the focus of Part II, and *Organization* is covered in Part III.

PART II—PEOPLE

Everything an organization accomplishes is the result of its people. Everything organizations do is done with, for, or by people, which is why understanding people is critical to achieving an organization's goals, and ensuring its success. The chapters in this section discuss how people act and interact, particularly inside organizations.

The ability to achieve and maintain effective relationships requires knowing how organizational *culture* (Chapter 9), *incentives* and *rewards* (Chapter 10), and *conflict, power* and *politics* (Chapter 11) influence our actions, interactions, and communication. Chapter 12 discusses the importance of *time management*, and how we can use it to improve both personal and organizational effectiveness.

PART III—ORGANIZATION

We discuss "organization" first as a noun—*an* organization (e.g., a business or social entity); then as a verb—*to* organize. As we discuss organizations and organizing, we are primarily concerned with how responsibilities are assigned, authority is divided, activities are coordinated, information and communication flow, and how resources are allocated.

Chapter 13, *Designing the Organization*, discusses various ways of structuring an organization to allow people to coordinate their work as effectively as possible. Chapter 14, *Innovation and Technology*, describes how the tools and methods we use to accomplish our goals affect, and are affected by the organization. Chapter 15 discusses one of the most significant changes of our time: the accelerating shift from organizations based primarily on labor to those in which *knowledge* is the critical element in adding value to products, services, organizations, and individuals, and where *learning* is essential to keeping that knowledge current.

Chapter 16 discusses *boards of directors*: their purpose, roles, responsibilities, and how they operate.

PART IV—STRATEGIC RESPONSIVENESS

Chapters in this section describe sometimes overlooked elements that help make the difference between conventional management and strategic management, and between success and failure.

Chapter 17 discusses the importance of *decision-making*, and the primary considerations in making timely and effective decisions.

Chapter 18 discusses how effective *allocation of resources* (e.g., material, equipment, money, people, and time) can make the difference between the success and failure of a strategy.

Chapter 19 discusses the importance of constantly assessing the organization's *performance*, so we know how well the strategy is being executed and so we can quickly make whatever changes may be necessary. Even the best strategic plan can quickly become ineffective without ongoing feedback, evaluation and fine-tuning. In closing, Chapter 20 discusses *change*: why it happens, why it is necessary, how to manage it, how to lead it, and how to use it to your strategic advantage.

OVERVIEW

Although the topics in this book are arranged in a linear sequence, generally following the flow in Figure 1, it is important to recognize that strategic management (both planning and implementation) is most effective as an iterative, or circular process, in which activities, particularly those involving some degree of trial and error, may begin early in the process, even before the plan has been fully developed. This provides early and ongoing feedback on the performance of the plan, allowing the plan to be improved as it matures.

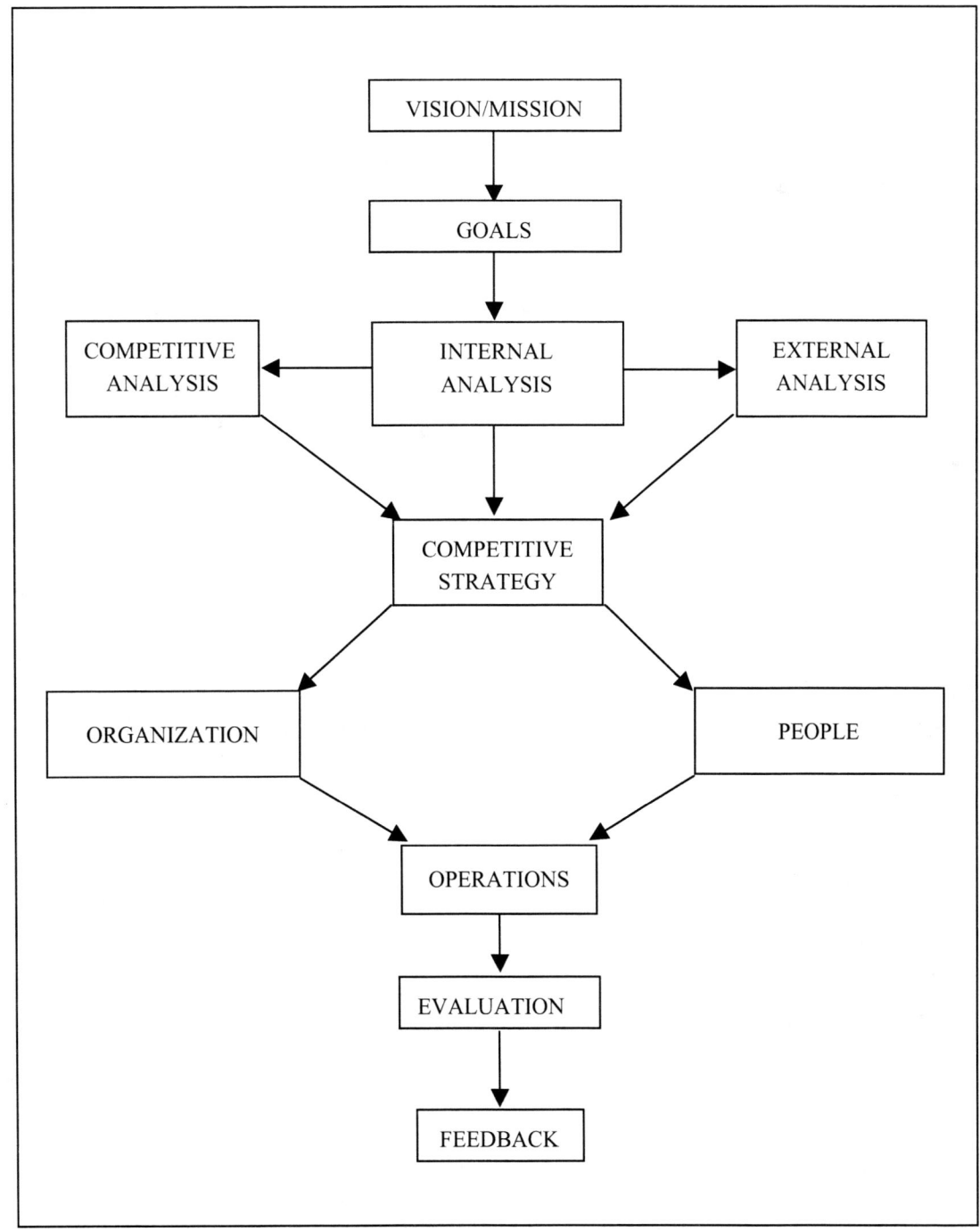

Figure 1. The Strategic Management Process

PART I
PLANNING

We plan so that we can decide, in advance, how we can best use our knowledge, talent, money, time, and energy to achieve the goals and objectives that are most important to us, rather than wasting those resources *reacting* to whatever circumstances may overtake us. Planning allows us to influence our own destiny instead of leaving our future to the whims of fate.

The chapters in this section discuss the elements that we should consider when we *formulate* a plan for the future—a *strategic plan*.

Chapter 1

LEADERSHIP AND MANAGEMENT

"Leadership is the lifting of a man's vision to higher sights, the raising of a man's performance to a higher standard, the building of a man's personality beyond its normal limits."

(Peter Drucker, 1986:159)

Throughout history, few subjects have inspired more books than leadership, and every author seems to have his own idea of what a leader is, or should be. As a result, there may be as many definitions of leadership as there are books on the subject. In some sense, it suggests the dilemma faced by those struggling to measure *quality*: "I can't define it but I know it when I see it." So the definition of leadership probably varies from one person to another; your idea of a leader and mine may be quite different. Although leadership may be defined by how we view an individual (e.g., "she is a leader"), it may more often be situational: a person takes on a leadership role in a particular situation due to the circumstances of the moment.

As a teacher and student of leadership, I have read countless books and articles, and spent endless hours trying to develop a better understanding of the subject. When I began I had a long list of characteristics (perhaps 25 or 30) that I thought might be inherent in leaders; a list I intended to narrow down to a few that I found to be common characteristics of all leaders, regardless of their times in history or the arenas in which they led. To help assess these characteristics, I began requiring each of my students to research a leader who was born before 1900, and write a report analyzing his/her background, influences, leadership characteristics, strengths, weaknesses, etc. The pre-1900 requirement was to eliminate current high-profile public figures who, although they may be perceived today as leaders, might not stand the test of time.

Having continued this process for several years I have, by now, heard and read about the backgrounds of hundreds of leaders, from all walks of life and from a wide range of circumstances. And throughout the process, I have marked off my list, one by one, the leadership characteristics that weren't common to all leaders.

It is interesting to note that one of the first to go was "charisma," the first word that many people use in describing a leader. Defined as "A quality attributed to those with exceptional ability to secure the devotion of large numbers of people." *(American Heritage Dictionary,* 1983). While charisma may very well apply to leaders like Abraham Lincoln, Winston

Churchill, General George Patton, and even Adolph Hitler, it would hardly be appropriate in describing leaders like Harriet Tubman or President Harry Truman. So charisma was crossed off early, as not being common to all leaders; in fact it wasn't even common to *most* leaders.

And so it went for most other characteristics, until the original list had been winnowed down to just four characteristics that seem to be common to all leaders: an unwavering *vision*, a *commitment* (in some cases, an *obsession*) to making the vision a reality, an *understanding* of *people*, and the *persuasiveness* to convince (or inspire) them to follow.

At this point it is interesting to consider the reaction of one of the earliest readers of this chapter. Contrary to my theory that charisma was *not* common to all leaders, he (an experienced business executive) suggested that the four final characteristics on my list could, in fact, be considered the four qualities of charisma. When a leader is seen as charismatic, it may very well be because of the image projected by his unwavering commitment to a lofty vision and his persuasiveness in inspiring others to join in following that vision. Whether or not these are the qualities that generate charisma, they are unquestionably important to leadership.

Of these four qualities, *vision* is the most important. It provides direction: which way to go; which hill to climb. A corollary to vision is visioning: the ability to see a bigger picture; to envision what might be. Visioning is essential to knowing when to change the vision; where we go from the top of the hill, especially when the view from the top of the hill isn't quite what we had expected.

Next is *commitment*: the drive to make the vision a reality; the stamina to make it up the hill regardless of the obstacles encountered. Without commitment, the vision may remain an unfulfilled dream. For some leaders, the word commitment would be too tame; too benign; *obsession* might be more appropriate. But whichever term we use, a major requirement of successful leadership is the determination to pursue the vision no matter what obstacles are encountered or how long it takes, and doing whatever is necessary to achieve it.

People will only follow a leader if they are inspired by the vision; convinced of its value and worthiness. This kind of inspiration comes from a leader's *persuasiveness*: his ability to describe the vision convincingly. And persuasiveness is based on the leader's ability to *understand people*: what their needs are and what inspires them.

Charisma aside, there are many great leaders who led by personal example rather than by inspiring people to follow them. Albert Einstein and Eleanor Roosevelt were outstanding leaders not because they understood and could persuade others—they may have had no need or desire to do that—but because their actions and activities served as examples that inspired others to follow. They were recognized as leaders because of what they accomplished; not for their charisma. Leaders of this type may share only two characteristics: *vision* and *commitment*. They begin by leading themselves toward a vision of what might be done, and achieve their vision through total commitment; with every thought and every ounce of energy focused on that pursuit. In a sense, they are "thought leaders," whose views and ideas are well ahead of their times, and of their peers; sometimes so far ahead they are initially viewed as "oddballs" or "crackpots."

For someone who is deliberately striving to be a leader of people, the first four characteristics are absolutely essential, although they may not be sufficient. Most of us have high expectations for our leaders; certain qualifications that we expect someone to have before we are willing to follow them. And the higher our expectations, the longer the list of qualities we expect them to have.

On the other hand, some of history's most famous leaders have been not just famous, but infamous. Would we ever deliberately select a Hitler, or a Stalin, or a Saddam Hussein to lead us? Since they do not fit our ideal of a "good" leader, our initial response to that question would probably be, "never!" Yet, in their times, in their particular circumstances, their followers may have perceived them as better than the alternatives; better than what they had had before. However, most of us would want our leaders to have characteristics, in addition to *vision, commitment, understanding,* and *persuasiveness,* that will ensure they are "good" leaders, more like Churchill or Roosevelt. So what *are* the characteristics of a "good" leader; a moral leader?

Aside from the four previously mentioned, surveys of business executives have consistently ranked *integrity* as the most important leadership characteristic, followed by *decisiveness* and a sense of *responsibility*. Adding these to the previous four, it seems as though a solid set of leadership characteristics for an ideal organizational leader should include at least: *vision*, *commitment*, *understanding* of *people*, *persuasiveness*, *integrity*, *decisiveness*, and a sense of *responsibility*. But what about *intelligence*? Research has shown that, although a reasonable level of intelligence is desirable, effective leadership does not require superior intellect. In fact, in many situations common sense may be more valuable than above-average intelligence.

Now that we have a clearer picture of *leadership*, what about *management*? How is it different?

LEADERSHIP VS. MANAGEMENT

Whereas the dictionary defines *lead* as, "To guide, conduct, escort, or direct. To influence; induce. To be ahead, or at the head of;" it sees *manage* as "To direct, control, or handle. To administer or regulate. To make submissive." (American Heritage Dictionary, 1983) Figure 2 compares some of the differences that these definitions suggest.

Management is based on controlling the *means*—*how* things are done—to ensure that people do things in a prescribed way, and is most appropriate where processes need to be carefully controlled, to assure consistency of output, or to gain economies of scale. These processes usually involve unskilled or semi-skilled manual laborers, working in jobs that are relatively routine and repetitive, and in which they seldom have to make decisions. The objective is to control the process and every operation in the process, so that everything happens in the same way every time, thus eliminating uncertainty.

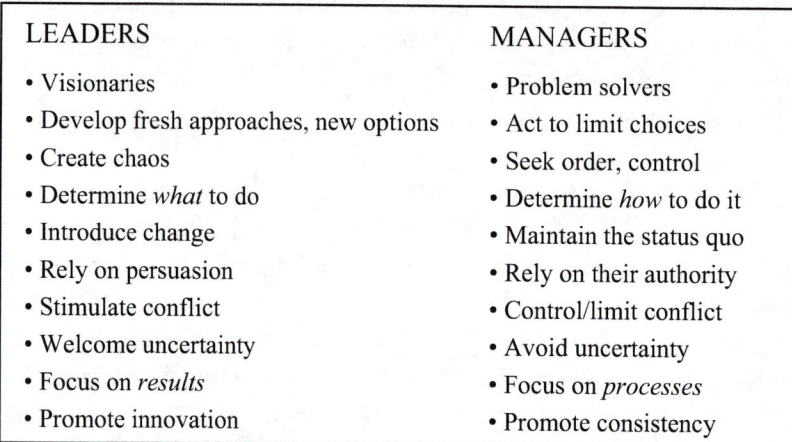

Figure 2. Leadership vs. Management

Leadership, in contrast, is more subtle and involves influencing and guiding the efforts of people toward specific *ends*. It focuses on *what* needs to be accomplished, by providing a clear vision of the goal and helping people in their efforts to achieve it, but not making them do it in a certain way; not telling them *how* to do it. Leadership is appropriate when it doesn't matter *how* something is done, as long as it achieves the desired outcome. This is often the case in jobs that require some degree of expertise gained through apprenticeship programs, specialized training, or education. As a result of their specialized knowledge these workers usually know, better than their supervisors, how to do their jobs, and what they need most is guidance and support, rather than specific procedures, processes, or methods.

Leadership is most effective when direction (e.g., vision, mission, and goals), and facilitation (e.g., influencing, guidance, encouragement) are needed more than control. The role of a leader is to provide direction and ensure that the organization's goals are achieved. Leaders control *what* needs to be done, not *how* it's done. Therefore, leadership is most appropriate when outcomes are important but we don't care how they are achieved, or when those performing the processes are sufficiently knowledgeable to be able to provide the necessary process control without guidance from above.

Yet, an effective leader may lead as much by example as by anything she says, or by any orders she gives. And, in this sense, she may actually influence *how* her followers do what they do; they may be inclined to do things in much the same way as they have seen their leader do them.

A major difference between leadership and management is in the area of authority. Traditionally, a manager has governed by the authority of his *position*; authority granted from above. A leader, on the other hand, governs by authority granted by his *followers*: authority granted from below. This is the concept outlined in our Declaration of Independence: "...governments are instituted among men, deriving their powers from the consent of the governed;..." Leadership is most effective when a leader gains his authority the same way—from

Chapter 1—Leadership and Management 7

the consent of his followers. A clear understanding of the differences between leadership and management is becoming increasingly important as the nature of work changes, and as the organizations that coordinate the work change.

The types of industries in which people work and the percentage of jobs provided by each industry have changed significantly over the past 150 years, sometimes gradually and sometimes quite dramatically. Figure 3 shows the evolution of jobs in three major employment sectors, from the end of the Civil War to the present time.

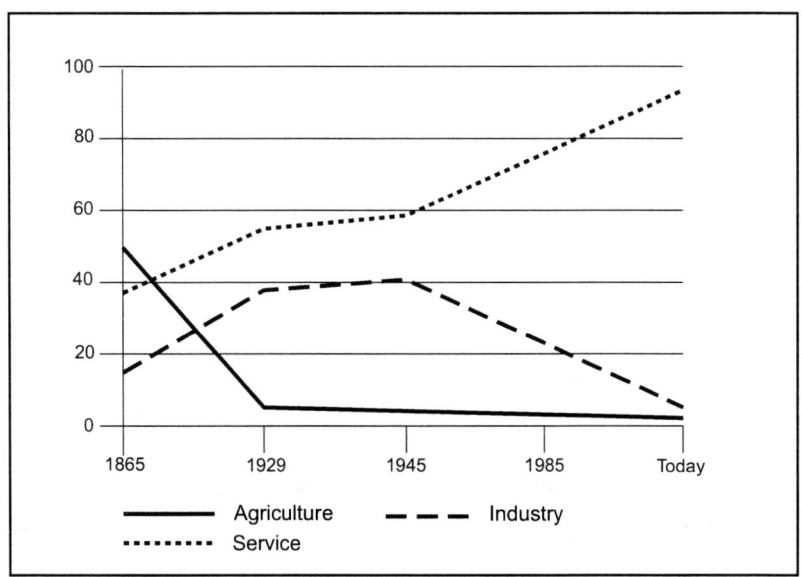

Figure 3. Percent of U.S. Employment by Sector

The percentage of American workers employed in the agricultural sector, which was the dominant sector in 1865, had dropped dramatically by 1929, from 48% to just 8%, no doubt due to the advent of the industrial revolution. And agricultural jobs have continued to decline, to just 2% of the workforce today.

The industry sector, accounting for only 14% of jobs in 1865, was up dramatically by 1929 (to 37%) and continued to climb until 1945, when it reached a peak of 39% of the workforce. Since 1945 the percentage of industrial jobs has been in a gradual decline, to a total of only 5% today; not much more than agriculture.

But the real eye-opener is the service sector. At 38% in 1865, its share of the workforce was more than 20% higher than the industry share and it maintained approximately that same lead until 1945, when it began moving sharply higher, while industry jobs began a faster downward trend. Today, a surprising 93% of all jobs in this country are in the service sector. Other than being interesting, what does this have to do with leadership and management?

Initially, the majority of available jobs, in all three employment sectors, were unskilled or semi-skilled. Most jobs involved physical labor, either on farms or factories, or as clerks in stores or servants in homes. For these types of jobs, management was the order of the day. People had to be told what to do and how to do it, and the perception was that if they weren't constantly watched they might slow down, not do it right, or not work at all.

And this remained the dominant logic for many years, until organization theorists began to understand the social nature of organizations and how it might influence work. One of the early proponents of a different approach to management was Douglas McGregor (1960), who observed were two different types of managers: theory X managers, who saw workers as lazy and unlikely to work unless they were constantly watched and prodded, and theory Y managers, who believed that most workers were willing to work hard and would respond better to encouragement and support than to being controlled.

Researchers also emphasized the importance of recognizing that, whereas some workers seemed to perform better with *minimal* supervision, others appeared to be more effective when they were *closely* supervised. A worker of the first type was described as having an *internal* locus of control, in that she was capable and willing to direct herself, while the second, with an *external* locus of control, needed, perhaps even preferred, to be directed by someone else.

It follows that a self-directed person will likely respond better to leadership, while a person with an external locus of control would prefer, in fact may need, to be managed. Therefore, an organization with a majority of externally-focused people is likely to be more effective if managed, in which case it would require more managers than leaders. On the other hand one with a majority of goal-oriented (internally-focused) people would probably respond better to leadership and would require more leaders than managers.

What this means is that both leadership and management are important to most organizations; and the key is understanding where each can be utilized most effectively. We can't provide a formula that fits all organizations, because each is different, but we can offer a rule of thumb: as an organization becomes more knowledge-based, that is when more of its distinctive competence is based on the *knowledge* of its employees (i.e., on what it *knows*) than on what the organization *does* or how it does it, leadership will become more important, and management less important.

This is because people who are valued for what they know are more likely to be self-directed, type Y workers who will flourish in an open environment, but will resent excessive interference in how they perform their jobs. And it is these knowledgeable people on whom organizations are becoming increasingly dependent as we move from product manufacturing toward service-based organizations, and their knowledge becomes increasingly important to the organization's competitive advantage.

It stands to reason, then, that the trend to knowledge as an organization's distinctive competence will make attracting, hiring, and retaining knowledgeable people a primary objective of organizations. Making the organization attractive to employees, both current and potential,

Chapter 1—Leadership and Management

and assuring that their work is satisfying for them, will be more likely to happen through leadership (vision, guidance, support) than management (control).

In short, although we can continue to *manage things*, we will increasingly have to *lead people*, and the essence of leadership is *developing people*, to help them reach their highest potential.

STRATEGIC THINKING

Another key element of leadership, which may not be as necessary for a manager, is the ability to think strategically. As we discussed earlier, without a vision there is no leadership, and strategic thinking is the driver of vision.

Thinking strategically is about looking ahead; planning the organization's future; and leading the organization into that future. It is based on the belief that creating the organization's future allows you to *control* what happens to the organization, rather than just responding to whatever the future brings. But *how* organization leaders do that, how they think strategically, can be dramatically different, depending on their points of view.

One school of strategic thinking focuses on getting the most from the organization's current resources. This is a relatively conservative approach; sort of a *"this is what we have to work with; what can we do with it?"* perspective. It revolves around the idea of doing more with less, which can be appropriate for some situations, but as a primary strategy would limit an organization's long-term potential.

Another approach, also based getting the most out of *current* resources, is to leverage those resources to the maximum extent, to gain competitive advantage and put competitors at a disadvantage. While also conservative, in that it operates within available resources, this approach utilizes the organization's resources more aggressively than the previous approach; an offensive, vs. passive, strategy.

A third way of thinking is based on developing the organization's mission and vision without considering how they might be limited by a lack of resources. This approach focuses on dreaming big; setting high expectations; focusing on what the organization *could* do; what it *could* be. This perspective requires believing that if you want something badly enough, you will find ways to obtain the necessary resources. While some may see this as a high-risk way of planning, it need not be. Having high expectations and acting responsibly are not mutually exclusive.

Whichever approach is used, the core of strategic thinking is being seen as *different* by customers; different in the sense that the organization's approach to meeting its customers' needs is valued by customers, and not easy for competitors to duplicate. Whether the organization does that with products or services, or how they are delivered, doesn't matter as much as how the customer feels about what he or she receives for her money.

Mintzberg, Quinn, and Voyer (1995) offer a six-step formula for thinking strategically:

1. **Open up thinking**—think more freely about what the organization is facing—question current wisdom.
2. **Realize where problems come from**—most are the result of the firm's own actions.
3. **Think long-term**—anything done now will have long-term consequences, but when those consequences finally occur, nobody remembers the actions that made them happen. Therefore, when you take an action now, think through the consequences that action might yield in the future.
4. **Keep active and keep learning**—learn to innovate continuously, and look for opportunities to apply what has been learned and created.
5. **Manage culture and process**—let the innovative energies of the firm's members roam freely.
6. **Open up who does the thinking**—thinking is much more effective when done by many minds, not just one. Thinking and learning are more powerful when they harness the energies of everyone in the organization.

SUMMARY

Although recognizing the difference between management and leadership is important, keeping them in perspective is even more important. It isn't as simple as the choice between becoming a leader and a manager; in many jobs we must be effective at *both*, so we have to be able to recognize when to lead and when to manage. In many ways, management is easier than leadership; if we control the process the outcome will be predictable. And leadership is more abstract, because it requires trusting that a predictable outcome will be achieved *without* controlling the process.

In that sense, in addition to being able to think strategically, a leader must have faith in his ability to select and inspire people. Leadership is a capability so important and so powerful that we can all benefit from developing it, no matter what our occupation or our goals.

Following are some concluding thoughts on leadership.

Great leaders:
- surround themselves with great people
- encourage their followers to "surpass me in every way"
- know their weaknesses and continually try to minimize their effects

Perhaps one of the best examples of how to deal with personal weaknesses is Benjamin Franklin's process for self improvement. To establish himself as a leader in his community, Franklin created a list of thirteen virtues and kept a daily log of how faithfully he followed them. His virtues were:
- Temperance—moderation in food & drink
- Silence—mentioning only important matters

- Order—proper organization of time and space
- Resolution—accomplishing one's responsibilities
- Frugality—purchasing only worthwhile items and wasting nothing
- Industry—making the most of one's time and energy
- Sincerity—being honest and forthright
- Justice—practicing impartiality and refusing to wrong others
- Moderation—avoiding extremes
- Cleanliness—using good hygiene under sanitary conditions
- Tranquility—remaining calm and composed despite life's obstacles
- Chastity—refusing to allow sex to interfere with one's life
- Humility—avoiding excess pride and haughtiness

What Franklin accomplished during his lifetime is a testament to self-improvement, and offers excellent examples of self-leadership and leadership by example.

Chapter 2

MISSION (Purpose)

*"Far away there in the sunshine are my highest aspirations.
I may not reach them, but I can look up and see their beauty,
believe in them and try to follow where they lead."*

(Louisa May Alcott)

As individuals, our missions define *who* we are, *what* we do, and *where* we are headed. They give meaning and direction to our jobs and our lives. Without a clear sense of mission we are likely to wander aimlessly, guided more by circumstances than by our own objectives, needs, or desires. And, in this sense, organizations are no different than individuals—an organization's identity is shaped by its mission; its sense of purpose. Without a mission an organization is also likely to wander aimlessly and react to circumstances as they occur, rather than actively pursuing a pre-determined course of action.

Although many organizations develop *written* mission statements, whether or not the mission is paper is less important than *having* a mission; a clear sense of purpose. A mission focuses our attention and forces us to prioritize our efforts; to concentrate on those activities that will lead to the outcomes that are most important to us. Having a clear sense of mission requires finding the answers to three important questions:

1. *What needs* are we trying to satisfy?
2. *Whose needs* are we trying to satisfy?
3. *How* are we trying to satisfy these needs?

These three questions help define the business or purpose of the organization and are the starting point of strategic planning.

WHAT NEEDS?

The key word is, of course, *needs*. Everything we do is, or should be, directed at satisfying specific needs, either our own or those of someone else. Although many organizations think primarily in terms of the products or services that they offer, we should think in terms of customer service: what *needs* do customers have that our products or services can help satisfy? The difference in these two viewpoints is subtle but important.

For many years Ford Motor Company's primary focus was designing and manufacturing automobiles, then selling them to customers, whoever and wherever they might be. If a person needed an automobile, and if Ford made one that fit that person's needs and pocketbook, the person was a potential a customer. Understanding the *individual* needs of its customers was not essential; the company was in business to manufacture and sell cars.

But a few years ago Ford developed a new mission; one that viewed customers not merely as car buyers, but in terms of life-long relationships. The company redefined its business as meeting customers' *personal transportation needs*, as those needs change throughout the customer's lifetime. As customers mature, get married, raise families, become more affluent, and ultimately retire, their personal transportation needs are continually changing and may, over their lifetimes, include owning or leasing a wide variety of cars, trucks, and recreational vehicles. Operating from this perspective, Ford changed its focus to meeting needs, rather than selling cars and, in the process, became more likely to benefit from increases in both customer satisfaction and repeat customers.

Focusing on satisfying needs, rather than providing products or services, will lead to closer relationships with customers and a better understanding of their needs, and of how we can provide products or services that are designed to meet them. This perspective will lead to higher levels of customer satisfaction than can be reached by merely selling customers whatever products or services we already offer (regardless of how well they may or may not actually meet customers' needs.)

WHOSE NEEDS?

Once we have a clear picture of *what* needs we intend to fulfill, we must determine *whose* needs we will be trying to satisfy. This means identifying, as precisely as possible, our intended market, and who will be our customers.

The customers who buy our products and services are so essential to our success that without their money, which they pay for the satisfaction they *expect* to receive, our organization could not survive. But customer satisfaction is not automatic, nor is it guaranteed. It comes only from products or services that are closely matched to the needs of customers. So, to be successful, we must carefully select our customers and take great pains to understand their particular needs and to meet their individual expectations. Some organizations make the mistake of assuming that *everybody* is a potential customer, and then learn the hard way that one size does *not* fit all; that only the largest organizations are likely to have the resources necessary to satisfy the needs of everyone. That's why successful organizations focus on selected market segments. A consumer-focused organization, for example, may define its target market by demographics such as age, gender, education level, income level, or geographic location.

Whereas our primary focus will be on customers who are *outside* of the organization, those of us who work for organizations have another set of customers: our co-workers. Satisfying our outside customers begins with each member of the organization satisfying his/her *internal* customers. The process of producing a product or providing a service usually requires a series of activities performed in a specified sequence, involving a number of different people. As participants in this process, our immediate customers are those who, in the next step in the sequence, add to the work that we have completed as *our* part of the process. And once our customer has completed her step in the sequence, she will pass the product on to the next person in the sequence, who is *her* customer.

Our most important inside customers are usually our immediate supervisor and the other members of our work group. To them we are responsible for doing the right *things* (i.e., providing the outputs they need), in the right *way* (i.e., making sure that our outputs meet pre-set standards for quality, quantity, and timeliness). How effectively we meet the needs of our internal customers has a major impact on *their* performance and on their evaluation of our performance. As a result, our self-esteem, pride, sense of accomplishment, and reputation are largely dependent on how well we satisfy the needs of our internal customers. And, ultimately, how well we each of us satisfies our internal customers determines how well the organization, as a whole, satisfies its outside customers.

It is important to remember that, in serving customers we can seldom, if ever, satisfy *everybody*. In fact, it is often the case that when we attempt to please everybody we risk pleasing *nobody*. So we must clearly define our customers, both internal and external, make sure that we understand their needs, and then direct all of our efforts toward satisfying those, and only those, needs. For it is only through knowing our customers and their needs that we can effectively determine *how* we can best meet those needs.

How?

Having defined *what* needs and *whose* needs we are trying to satisfy, our next challenge is to determine *how* can we satisfy those needs? Answering this question means identifying our organization's *distinctive competencies*. Although this term will be discussed in greater detail in a later chapter, a short definition is: *capabilities, knowledge, or resources that are valuable to our customers, and which cannot be easily, quickly, or inexpensively duplicated by our competitors*. In general, a distinctive competence is a unique capability; one that will clearly distinguish one organization, or individual, from all others.

Our customers value us by how well we satisfy their needs, and whether or not they can get this same satisfaction at a comparable cost from someone else. This applies equally to internal and external customers, so we should never take either of them for granted. We should always assume that customers will come to *us* only as long as we provide better value than they can get from someone else. So if we hope to achieve and maintain a competitive advantage, we must have, or must develop, a distinctive competence.

Therefore, answering the question "How?" requires identifying how we will provide superior value to our customers. Will it be because we offer lower cost, distinctive product or service features, superior service, a more attractive design, greater convenience, better location, or what?

MISSION STATEMENTS

Once the three key questions have been answered, it is useful to draft a mission statement that describes the organization and its uniqueness.

A good mission statement should be brief, to the point, and distinctive. Brevity is important, to make the statement easy to remember, especially for employees. While it doesn't have to include the answers to all three questions, it should be specific enough to make the organization easily recognizable by customers. Two good examples are:

> *"One mission—low fares." (Southwest Airlines)*

> *"To best satisfy America's snacking needs
> by providing fun foods within arm's reach." (Frito-Lay)*

A useful guideline for the length of a mission statement is that we are able to recite the entire statement without taking a breath.

SUMMARY

A clear sense of mission serves as a cornerstone; a constant reminder of our primary purpose, and should keep our efforts focused in that direction. Lack of a mission makes it too easy for an organization to waste time, effort, and resources wandering aimlessly, responding to the crisis-of-the-moment, following the path of least resistance, or even following somebody else's mission.

The final result of a successful mission is the achievement of the goals that are most important to the organization. Absence of a mission usually leads to waste: time and effort expended with no clear accomplishment to show for it.

The primary role of every member of an organization should be to help the organization achieve its mission. But the most successful organizations are those who also make it possible for their members to meet their individual needs in the process. This outcome, of course, requires careful selection of organization members and effective job/role placement within the organization. Both are discussed in later chapters.

Chapter 3

GOALS (Objectives)

*"Did you ever hear of a man who had striven all his life
faithfully and singly toward an object
and in no measure obtained it?"*

(Henry David Thoreau)

Setting goals is one of the most essential ingredients of success; it may, in fact, be the *most* important ingredient. A goal, which is a commitment to produce a specific result in a specified time, gives focus to our efforts and activities; makes us work *toward* something specific. Without specific goals we risk wasting time and energy on those tasks that are easiest, most enjoyable, or most pressing, rather than those that are most important. Or worse, we spend time working on bits and pieces of several different projects, trying to get *something* done on *each* project. And that's a sure-fire formula for failure; for accomplishing little or nothing. We may do a lot of work but we are unlikely to get anything *completed*, at least in a timely manner. Setting goals forces us to prioritize our efforts, and direct them toward achieving the *outcomes* that are most important. For the purposes of this book we will be discussing goals primarily in an organizational context, although all of the principles of goal-setting can also be applied to individuals, both within and outside of organizations.

It is important here to clarify a semantic issue: the difference between goals and objectives. Some business texts use "goals" as top-level objectives of the organization, and "objectives" as lower-level objectives that are derived from organization-level goals. Others use "goals" for non-measurable objectives and "objectives" for any that are measurable. The dictionary doesn't discriminate; it defines "goal" as "A desired result or purpose; objective." and "objective" as "Something worked toward or striven for; goal." *(American Heritage Dictionary,* 1983) In other words, they mean the same thing, so although in this book we will generally stick with "goal," I will not distinguish between the two terms, and may occasionally use them interchangeably. I will also continually emphasize the importance of stating goals in *measurable* terms.

STRATEGIC ISSUES

Identifying and resolving strategic issues are keys to the success of the strategic planning process. *Strategic issues* are important issues or critical challenges that are likely to affect our ability to fulfill our mission or achieve our goals. They often involve conflicts of one sort or another, and they might be viewed as either threats or opportunities, depending on the strategies that we develop to address them. Although strategic issues can be identified at any stage of the planning process, the most effective time is usually *after* our mission/purpose has been determined but *before* our goals have been set, for a number of reasons.

Strategic issues will vary significantly from one company to another, depending on a variety of factors, but most importantly on what business the company intends to be in, including what products or services it intends to provide (i.e., what *needs* it intends to meet); what customers it intends to serve (i.e., *whose* needs); and *how* it intends to serve those customers. Since all of these issues are addressed by a mission, it follows that strategic issues can not be accurately identified until the organization's mission has been clarified.

Although organization-level goals *could* be set without considering strategic issues, when those issues are critical to the future success of the organization (which is often the case,) they should be an important consideration in determining how the organization will focus its efforts and prioritize its resources. Therefore, it is usually more useful to identify strategic issues *before* setting organization-level goals.

A useful way of identifying strategic issues is to ask each participant in the planning process to list his/her thoughts on what are the top three strategic issues facing the organization. Such a request will usually result in a fairly comprehensive list of issues, with a small number (perhaps 3 or 4) that appear to dominate. Questions that can be useful in addressing strategic issues include:

- What is the issue?
- Why is it a strategic issue?
- What are the consequences of failing to address it?

Some strategic issues will arise due to circumstances or events that occur at a particular time or place that demand immediate attention and action. Although they command our attention at that moment, they may be only temporary; here today and gone tomorrow. Other issues, often those that are more strategic but less sensational, tend to be more ongoing in nature; always there, and always important, but since they are less dramatic they may seem less commanding. They include:

- the quality of customer service;
- attracting and retaining key employees;
- introducing, leading, and managing change;
- increasing demands for fewer resources;
- government (federal, state, and local) regulation.

Chapter 3—Goals (Objectives) 19

Since they are not as obvious, this type of issue may seem less demanding, but will often be more important to the success or failure of the organization than many of the issues that capture our immediate attention. Therefore, these five issues should always be primary considerations in our strategic planning, regardless of what other issues may arise.

SETTING GOALS

Setting goals should begin with listing *everything* the organization wants to accomplish. *Everything*, in this sense, means the major outcomes that we feel must be achieved to pursue the mission, and to ensure our ongoing success. It is important to keep in mind that goals should always be mission-driven, that is the purpose of every goal should be to help accomplish the mission. And of course, strategic issues should be a prime consideration in setting goals: are there any issues that are so critical to future success that they should be high-priority goals?

PRIORITIZING GOALS

Once our primary goals have been set, they should be prioritized: ranked in order of their importance. Prioritization is absolutely essential, as it will ultimately influence things like the sequence of activities, assignment of responsibilities, and allocation of resources. Failure to consciously prioritize can lead to prioritization by default, as illustrated by the example of the executive who gives a subordinate several assignments at the same time and, when asked to prioritize them in terms of urgency, responds "They're all number 1."(meaning "I want them all done—now!") The subordinate, realizing that attempting to work on all of them simultaneously will likely mean that none of them will get done in a timely manner, will be forced to prioritize them himself. So, instead of impressing his subordinate with the urgency of *all* of the assignments, the executive has essentially abandoned his responsibility and passed the buck for prioritization to his subordinate.

This happens because, when it comes right down to it, most of us are able to do *just one thing at a time*, particularly if we intend to do a quality job of it. Sure, we see examples of "multi-tasking" every day, like the people who carry on phone conversations while driving (sometimes while eating or smoking, as well.) Although they may see this as a good use of time, statistics show that people who talk on the phone while driving have significantly higher accident rates, which should make us think seriously about the hidden costs of trying to do too many things at one time. In reality, much of the multi-tasking we think we are doing involves rapidly shifting our attention from one task to another, sometimes unconsciously. As a result, although we may keep several projects going at the same time, we only do so by switching back and forth from one project to another.

But remember that success is *not* measured by how hard we work, or by how many projects we keep going at the same time, but by what we *accomplish*. Toward that end, prioritizing is not only important to effectiveness, but also makes much more efficient use of our time. It lets us work on one thing at a time, doing whatever is most important until it's done, and done right, before moving on to whatever is next in importance Or we work on the top priority project as long as we can, until it reaches a point where we need someone else's input before we can continue. Then, until we can get back to it, we shift to the second priority project.

Organizations can, of course, work on more than one important project at a time, by delegating projects, or parts of them, to more than one person. But if we're not careful this can be misused, and multi-tasking taken to a whole new level, with the same result: everyone in the organization has so many demands on their time that, unless they prioritize their own assignments, they will be working harder, and accomplishing less and, in the process, becoming increasingly frustrated. So, effective goal-setting must begin with prioritization.

MAJOR GOALS

Once our major goals have been identified and prioritized, the list should be shortened from the bottom up, to no more than 4-6 goals; the fewer the better. This is essential, to ensure that our activities are sufficiently focused that they provide the intense concentration of effort that is so important to getting things done. The more goals we set, the fewer we are likely to achieve. If we set only one goal, we are almost certain to concentrate on it until it has been achieved, and even five or six have a high probability of being achieved. But beyond that, the probability of completing *all* of them decreases dramatically and the probability of achieving *none* of them *increases*, particularly if we try to work on all of them at the same time. On the other hand, if we have the internal discipline to prioritize goals and work on them in priority order, the total *number* of goals becomes less intimidating.

Self-discipline is essential because, no matter how much we *think* we can ignore low priority projects, in reality they have a kind of magnetism that makes them almost irresistible. I suspect there may be three reasons for that: 1) we may be psychologically unable to ignore *anything* on our "to do" list, no matter how far it is down the list, simply because it's *there*; 2) we are tempted to do low-priority projects before those that are high priority, simply because they "won't take long" and then we can mark something off our list; or 3) we do it because somebody coaxes us with " it will only take a few minutes and then I'll be out of your hair," and many of us lack the fortitude to tell our friends and co-workers "NO." So, in reality, it's better to have a short list of goals than to depend on having the self-discipline to *always* do things in priority order.

The impact of concentrating organizational efforts is well illustrated by Daft's (1998) example of Marmot Mountain, a manufacturer of high-performance outdoor clothes and equipment. When its parent company filed for bankruptcy, Marmot's management team purchased the company and set about leading it to profitability. Convinced that the company's future success hinged on concentrating on only one or two major goals at a time, Marmot's management team made on-time delivery its number one priority for the first year, and were so intent

Chapter 3—Goals (Objectives) *21*

on achieving it they even restricted their sales force from opening any new accounts during that period. Once it was established as the company's number one priority, nothing was allowed to interfere with anything related to improving delivery. By delaying other projects, canceling meetings, and working nights and weekends, Marmot met its goal, then set a new priority for the next year, and another for each following year. The year after it was purchased the company saw the first profits in its 20-year history.

Perhaps the most remarkable thing about Marmot is not its focus on a single priority but the lengths to which it was willing to go to assure achieving that one goal. How many companies would be willing to deliberately *stop taking new orders* to concentrate on improving service to their *existing customers*? Many companies are so anxious to take *any* new orders that they sometimes do so even at the expense of their existing customers. But Marmot's strategy has paid off. At last report they had become the third largest-selling company in their industry, and had experienced several years of growth in excess of 40% per year.

MEASURABLE GOALS

Once we have agreed on which goals are most important, we need to define them in terms that will allow us to measure progress, and know when a goal has been achieved. So, to be consistent with our definition of a goal as a commitment to produce a specific result in a specific time, every goal must be *measurable,* and to be measurable it must be stated in way that answers three questions:

1. *How much?* quantifies the outcome—how much of the activity needs to be done?
   (e.g., how many products; how many candidates; how many lines of code)

2. *What kind of performance?* refers to the activity itself—what is it that needs to be done?
   (e.g., producing products; interviewing candidates; writing programs).

3. *By when?* asks for a deadline—by when will the activity be finished; the outcome achieved?
   (e.g., the end of the month, quarter, year)

Any goal that isn't stated in terms that provide specific answers to all three questions is not measurable, and any goal that isn't measurable is *useless*, because we have no way of knowing if, or when, it has been met.

If, for example, your boss says, "I want you to increase the market share of your product," and you agree, don't be surprised when she calls you in six months later and asks, "Why haven't you done what I asked?." You reply, "But I *did*. Our market share has increased from 17% to 19%" but your boss responds, "That's not enough! I expected more." This is an example of a common misunderstanding; different interpretations of an ambiguous goal, in this case "increase market share." This ambiguity could have been avoided if the goal had been stated in measurable terms; for example, if the boss had said "I want you to increase the market share of your product from 17% to 21% in the next 6 months." Then there would have been no question about her expectations. Stating goals in measurable terms ensures that everyone concerned will understand more accurately what the goal is, and will know whether or not it has been achieved.

Goals will ultimately be used to measure performance, not only of the organization as a whole, but also every level within the organization, including individual performance. Therefore, how we establish the measurements is important. Keeping in mind that all goals exist to satisfy someone, we should be continually aware of who that someone is. For individual goals that someone will be ourselves, in which case setting goals means agreeing with ourselves. But goals that have to satisfy someone else should be based on discussions with that person, and agreement on what is desired and what is realistic.

When we want to compare our performance with others (organizations or individuals), setting the level of a goal is likely to require making sure that we meet or exceed a specific standard against which our competitors measure their performance. Sometimes referred to as "benchmarking," this process involves learning which organizations are recognized for being the best at a specific activity, then studying their processes and methods to determine how we might bring our own performance up to that level. Benchmarking is a popular way of making sure that a company's processes are as efficient, and its costs as low, as those of competitors

The need to remain competitive will usually pressure us to make our goals *challenging*, but it important to remember that they must also be *achievable*. They should be *challenging* for the one responsible for meeting the goal, as a part of continuous improvement. Last year's performance should not be the standard for next year's. For ongoing success, we should always work toward continuous improvement, believing that everything can be improved; everything we do can be done better, continuously and indefinitely. For goals to be *challenging* they must always demand a higher level of performance than in the past.

Being *achievable*, on the other hand, means that goals should not be set so high that they seem impossible to reach. For these reasons, developing goals that are both *challenging* and *achievable* works better when measurements are arrived at through negotiation between the person who will be working to achieve the goal and the one whose expectations are to be satisfied. The latter should make sure that accomplishing the outcome will be challenging, and the former should assure that the goal is, in fact, achievable.

Returning to the issue of continuous improvement, it is important to understand that improvement need not always be incremental; we should not always expect it to be a gradual process. Sometimes, and in some circumstances, improvement will come in infrequent, and sometimes unpredictable, jumps. And preparing for these discontinuous changes, or compensating for them (after they occur), may require short-term sacrifices in other areas. Because following a long-term strategic plan is seldom a linear process, there will be times when it is hard to see any results at all, and other times when things are happening so fast the process may appear to be out of control. And that's why measurable goals are so important: they give us the means to know how we're doing at any stage of the process.

TIMING OF GOALS

From the perspective of time, goals are of two types: short-term and long-term. *Short-term* goals are concerned with the day-to-day things that must be accomplished in order for the individual or organization to survive. These are largely operational issues, often financial (e.g., cash flow, meeting payroll, human resource issues). *Long-term* goals are usually more strategic in nature and are essential to sustaining or improving our longer-term success. They tend to be directional, including such issues as where we intend to go from here; how we deal with the future; and in what businesses we intend to be in the years ahead. An organization's major goals will generally include some of each type, but they should be prioritized so that organizational activities are not allowed to focus entirely on short-term issues.

LEVELS OF GOALS

Achievement of the organization's goals requires translating them into goals at all levels of the organization, because all of us, every function, every department and every person in the organization, are there for the same purpose: to achieve the organization's goals. To make sure that this process (sometimes known as "cascading") happens, every corporate-level goal must be broken down into departmental, sub-departmental, and individual goals. Generally this process takes place through meetings among the leaders of the major organizational departments or functions, in which they collectively agree on what each must do to assure that the parent organization achieves its goals. These proposed departmental accomplishments become the *department's* goals. As we develop lower-level goals, we should attempt to apply the same basic rule of numbers that was emphasized for organization-level goals: no more than 4-6, because the same principle applies: the fewer the goals the better we can concentrate our efforts.

Let's use, as an example, an organizational goal of increasing the market-share of a product line, say from 25% to 32% by the end of next year. The functional departments ultimately agree that the best way to do this is by strengthening the company's presence in three heretofore undeveloped market segments. This will require engineering to come up with two new product variations, one to be available to customers by September of this year, the other by next March. To have the new products produced and in the field by those dates, manufacturing must have finished specifications from engineering no later than June 1 for the first version, and by December 1 for the second. Sales will need to have an advertising campaign in place beginning no later than July 1 for the first variation, and no later than next January 1 for the second, and service manuals available in time to pack with the products.

This example demonstrates the affect that a *single* organizational goal can have on just *three* functional departments: engineering, manufacturing, and sales. Other departments that will likely be affected in some way include purchasing, shipping, training (to teach sales people how to demonstrate and sell the products), accounting and, of course, as previously mentioned, marketing and advertising. In some way or another, this one organizational goal will require activities by nearly every function in the organization, involving dozens or even hundreds of individual employees. Just thinking about going through this same exercise for four or five additional organizational goals should make it clear that achieving the organization's major goals should be a full-time job for everyone in the organization.

The next step is to break down departmental goals, layer by layer, into *sub-departmental* and, ultimately, *individual* goals. Which people in engineering, for example, will be responsible for which of the activities involved in designing two new product versions? And who in manufacturing will determine where, how, when, and by whom the new products will be fabricated, assembled, and tested? And who in sales will oversee the design and execution of the advertising campaign, and who will hire and train the additional sales force? Once all of that (and much more) has been accomplished, everyone in the organization will know exactly what they have to do, to make sure the organization reaches its goals.

Finally, departments and people at all levels must determine precisely what *activities* will be necessary to reach their goals. This determination should involve step-by-step action plans, each of which should include specific designated responsibilities (i.e., who does what), and sequenced schedules and deadlines (i.e., what must be accomplished, in what order, by what time). These activities must then become the primary focus of *all* of the efforts of everyone in the organization.

At this point it is important to note that once organization-level goals have been translated into goals for everyone in the organization, every activity of every person and every department in the organization should work *only* toward those goals. No person, activity or resource should be wasted on anything else. The organization's commitment should be total and absolute. This means that everything that is important to the ongoing operations of the organization must, in some way, be included.

For example, when things like machine maintenance and skills training are important to organizational goals (as they invariably are), they must be included in the goals of some level of the organization. In short, when organizational goals are broken down more specifically at lower levels, they must cover not only new initiatives but also any *ongoing* needs. And the final checkpoint in making sure all efforts and resources remain concentrated on organizational goals should be the budget. Any cost that isn't, in some way, essential to achieving corporate goals, should be critically reviewed to see if it should be funded at all.

TRADEOFFS

It is important to remember that setting goals is a process of determining how we should invest our resources. Every organization and every individual has a limited supply of resources, and should attempt to utilize those resources in the most effective manner, to ensure getting the most from what the organization has to work with. What those outcomes should be will differ from one organization to another, one individual to another, and from one set of circumstances to another. Our job is to invest the organization's resources wisely, considering the circumstances at hand. This involves making choices that take into consideration what

Chapter 3—*Goals (Objectives)*

level of *risk* we are willing to take to achieve the *return* we want, and how much *pain* we are willing to endure to accomplish the *gains* we seek.

Making choices would be easy if we had all the resources we needed or wanted, but that will almost never be the case. We will seldom, if ever, have all of the *money* we would like, nor an unlimited supply of *energy* (i.e., people). And *time* and *attention* are the most scarce of all resources; we are allotted only a certain amount of time: 24 hours a day, and nobody knows how many days.

So a major part of our success will be the tradeoffs we make in setting goals; how we choose to invest our resources.

SUMMARY

The power of goals is often overlooked. It is amazing what can be accomplished when we convince ourselves that a particular thing not only *can* be done but *must* be done, and then we direct the full force of our efforts to making sure it *is* accomplished. And since organizational goals are achieved by the efforts of the individuals within the organization, ensuring the achievement of corporate-level goals depends on translating them into group and individual incentives at all levels of the organization. Incentives will be discussed in more detail in a later chapter.

A final note on goals: we should always consider them to be dynamic rather than static. Although we plan in terms of pursuing a goal until it has been achieved, in reality, a goal may change before it has been reached. We should always be aware of our goals, and the progress we're making toward reaching them, and anything that might affect our ability to reach them. And any time we see the situation changing, we should ask ourselves, "How does that affect our goal?" and "Do we need to re-set it?" then act accordingly. And every time we reach a goal, we should immediately build on it by setting the one, because goals, themselves, are only the means to an end: accomplishing the mission. They are "mile-markers" on the road to completing our mission. The mission may not change, but the goals through which it is accomplished will evolve throughout the process.

Chapter 4

COMPETITIVE ANALYSIS

The heart of strategic management is developing strategies that will achieve the organization's major goals, and ultimately accomplish its mission. But it's difficult, if not impossible, to know what type of strategy will effective without first considering three factors: our *organization,* our *competitors,* and our *external environment.*

So, before we attempt to develop strategies, we should conduct three types of analysis: a *competitive* analysis, to understand our *competition* (e.g., their strengths, weaknesses, distinctive competencies, and competitive strategies); *an internal* analysis, to understand our *organization,* and the things we *can* control (e.g., our strengths and weaknesses); and an *external* analysis, to understand our external *environment*, which we *cannot* control (e.g., opportunities and threats.)

This chapter focuses on the first of those—*competitive analysis*—while Chapter 5 covers internal analysis, and 6 external analysis.

INDUSTRY ANALYSIS

The first step in competitive analysis is making sure we understand the industry in which we intend to compete. An industry is a group of organizations that compete to supply the same needs for the same set of customers (i.e., the same market.)

Although no organization can control its external environment, an industry is a discrete piece of that environment which might, to some degree, be controlled by its member firms. In that sense, an industry is somewhat more predictable than the external environment as a whole.

A useful way of analyzing an industry is to view it through from the perspective of Porter's Five Forces Model, a framework for analyzing and predicting the economic attractiveness of an industry. See Figure 4.

Porter (1980) suggests 5 "forces" that are the primary determinants of competition within an industry, and which can be used to predict how difficult it will be to achieve profitability.

First, and most powerful, is the *rivalry* among competitors: how fiercely they compete. Rivalry in the industry will be affected by: the number of competitors and their arsenals of competitive weapons; the industry's current life-cycle stage; and supply vs. demand. In general, the more intense the rivalry the less attractive the industry.

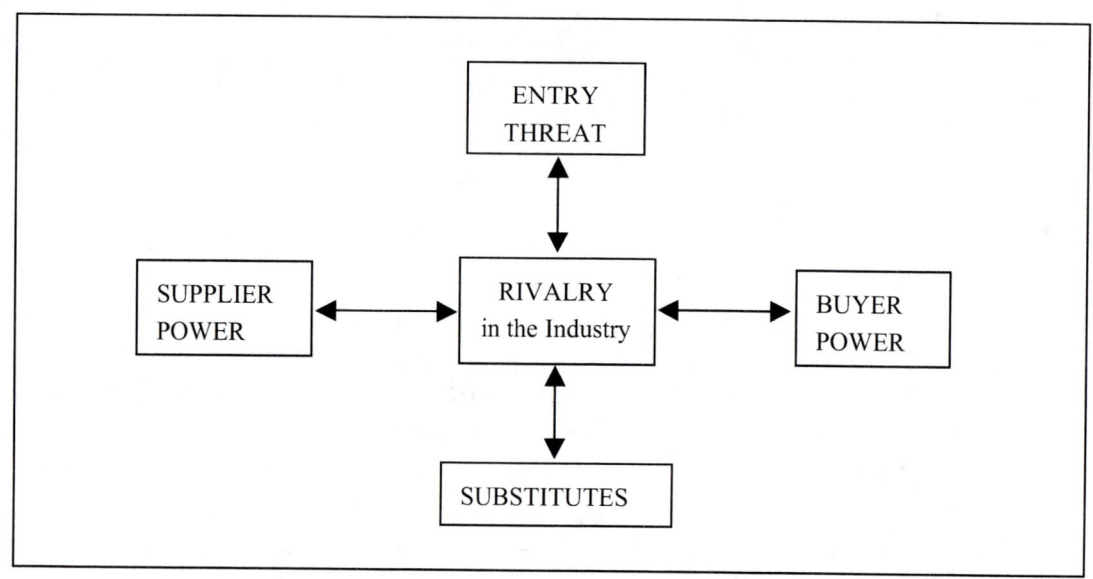

```
                    ENTRY
                    THREAT
                      ↕
SUPPLIER  ↔   RIVALRY   ↔   BUYER
POWER         in the Industry   POWER
                      ↕
                  SUBSTITUTES
```

Adapted with permission of The Free Press, A Division of Simon & Schuster Adult Publishing Group, from *Competitive Strategy: Techniques for Analyzing Industries and Competitors,* by Michael E. Porter. Copyright © 1980, 1998 by The Free Press

Figure 4. The Five Forces of Industry Competition

Next is *entry threat*: the likelihood that new competitors will enter the industry. The threat of entry will usually be a function of how attractive the industry appears to potential entrants, and how easy it is for them to enter. Ease of entry is strongly influenced by entry barriers: obstacles that a potential entrant must overcome to be successful. Examples of entry barriers include brand loyalty, which can make it difficult for new competitors to gain market share, and high capital costs, which require large initial investments in plant and equipment. The higher the entry barriers the lower the threat of new competitors, and the more consolidated, and profitable, the industry is likely to remain.

A threat of *substitutes* refers to the possibility of customers having their needs met by a product or service from an entirely different industry. Here, we are not concerned with competitive products but with the possibility of being surprised by something that we didn't consider a competitive product or service.

For example, the majority of steel produced in the U.S. is used in building automobiles. Although auto companies would prefer to use more aluminum, to reduce weight of cars and improve their fuel economy, aluminum is much more expensive than steel, so is used sparingly. However, steel companies should keep an eye on the price of aluminum because, should the price of steel go up, or the price of aluminum drop significantly (e.g., due to excess capacity in the aluminum industry), auto companies would be likely to jump at the opportunity to substitute lower-cost aluminum for steel. Therefore, aluminum is a potential substitute for steel.

Chapter 4—Competitive Analysis   29

Supplier power exists when a particular vendor is a company's only source for a critical input, which puts the company at the vendor's mercy, and gives it little recourse in the face of price increases, quality problems, or delivery delays. When we face supplier power, we have just two choices: meet that supplier's demands, or find another supplier. But supplier power does not always affect all companies the same way. It is possible for some firms to experience supplier power while others in the same industry don't.

If, for example, two companies purchase inputs from the same supplier, the one that purchases the largest quantity is likely to experience the least supplier power, and is likely to get preferential treatment, including lower prices and more timely deliveries. An extreme example is Wal-Mart, which purchases everything in such huge quantities that it experiences little or no supplier power, even from suppliers who are its only source.

Needless to say, when supplier power affects more than one competitor in an industry, it is likely to make that industry less attractive to potential entrants, and reduce the threat of entry. But any firm that experiences less supplier power than its competitors will be in a stronger competitive position.

Buyer power exists when one or more of a firm's customers buy large quantities of its products or services. High-volume customers may have the leverage to negotiate more favorable terms, such as lower prices, or just-in-time delivery. Firms that sell to the general public are usually not faced with buyer power, but those that depend on any single customer for a significant percentage (e.g., 10% or more) of their total sales, will generally give that customer special consideration. It should be apparent that buyer power is a double-edged sword: organizations go to great lengths to get and keep large customers, but once they have them they become dependent on them. And any firm that relies on just one large customer is placing a big part of its success in the hands of that customer.

As with supplier power, buyer power does not always affect all companies the same way. It is possible for some firms to experience buyer power while others in the same industry don't. Wide-spread buyer power in an industry tends to make it less attractive to potential entrants, but firms with lower buyer power than their competitors have a competitive advantage.

An effective analysis of those the five forces should provide a good idea of the overall attractiveness of an industry, and should be a primary consideration in developing competitive strategies.

INDUSTRY STRUCTURE

The structure of an industry depends on how many competitors it has and how fiercely they compete. We have defined an industry as a group of firms competing for the same group of customers. On a continuum with a monopoly (i.e., one firm) at one extreme and a free market (i.e., hundreds, or thousands of competitors) at the other, most industries will be somewhere between "consolidated" and "fragmented." See Figure 5.

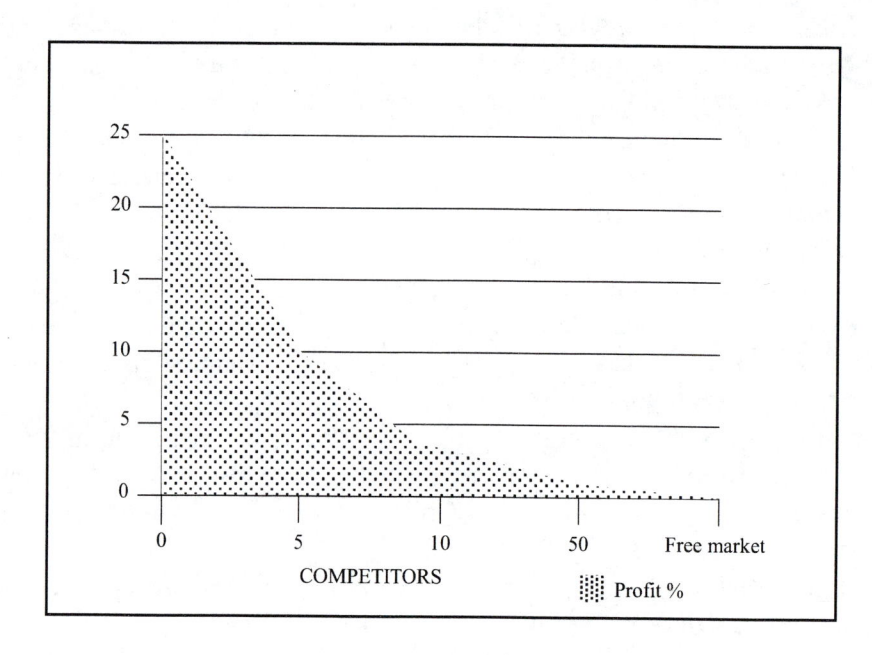

Figure 5. Profit vs. Number of Competitors

In a *consolidated* industry the majority of the market-share will be controlled by a few large firms, and competition driven by a competitor's ability to differentiate its products or services from those of other firms. In such an industry, competitors are inter-dependent: whatever one does will affect the others. Recognizing this, the attitude of major competitors is likely to be "live and let live" and "don't rock the boat," and competition will be neither cut-throat nor price-based. Competition is more likely to be based on building brand loyalty.

In a consolidated industry there may be an unwritten understanding among competitors that when one firm raises or lowers prices it's a signal to the others that they should change theirs accordingly. Sometimes called "tacit collusion," this is a legal way of getting around price-fixing laws.

A *fragmented* industry has many competitors, none of them dominant. Although competition may be based on differentiation, it is more often price-driven; customers base their buying decisions on who has the lowest price, rather than on brand name. As shown in Figure 5, the more fragmented the industry the lower its overall profitability. Whereas in a consolidated industry there is the potential for at least the dominant firms to make a profit, in a fragmented industry only the lowest-cost producers have much chance of profitability.

INDUSTRY LIFE-CYCLE

Every industry goes through a life-cycle, beginning with its birth and *infancy*, followed by a period of *growth*, then *maturity* and, ultimately, *decline*. See Figure 6.

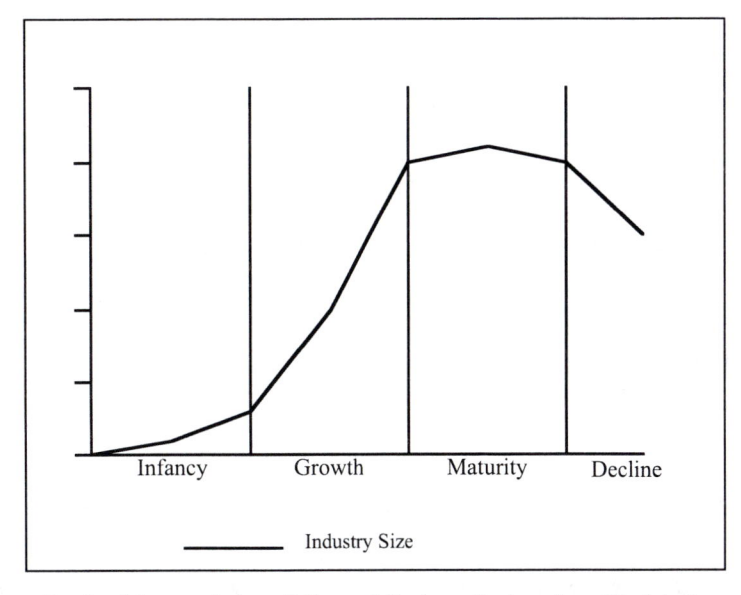

Reprinted by permission of *Harvard Business Review*, from "Exploit the Product Life Cycle," by Levitt, Nov-Dec, 1965. Copyright © 1965 by the Harvard Business School Publishing Corporation; all rights reserved.

Figure 6. Industry Life-Cycle

Knowing the current stage of an industry can tell us a lot about competition in the industry, including the number of competitors, how fiercely they compete, and how profitable the industry is likely to be.

In its *infancy* an industry will have a small number of competitors, who will usually be innovators: the first to develop new technologies, products, or services. During this stage, competition is likely to be a race to define and/or create the market, and industry profitability is likely to be very low or non-existent.

Dominant strategies are likely to trying to get a jump on the competition, to establish a significant lead in market-share, and be the first to benefit from experience-curve effects. These "first-movers" will be more concerned with trying to establish their individuality (i.e., differentiating), and less concerned with the price of their products/services.

During the *growth* stage, the number of competitors will increase, as "followers" attempt to gain a piece of the market, once its potential has been demonstrated by the first-movers. These imitators are not willing, or perhaps not financially able, to gamble on an uncertain market but will move quickly to grab market share as soon as the market's potential is evident. Although the number of competitors may be increasing at this stage, the industry will remain profitable as long as the market is growing faster than the number of competitors. This is often the most profitable stage of the industry life-cycle, and the dominant strategy will be trying to gain market share.

As it reaches *maturity*, the industry's competitive picture is likely to change substantially. Since, by definition, the market is no longer growing, any attempt to increase market share, by either an incumbent or a new entrant, can only be accomplished by taking it away from another competitor. As long as all competitors are content with their current share of the market, the industry can remain stable and reasonably profitable for everyone. Differentiation and brand loyalty can be the best ways of maintaining market share, but if just one firm decides to increase its market share at the expense of the others, the equilibrium will be broken, leading to price-driven competition.

Think of it this way: the majority of firms may be content to *keep* their current share, but none are likely to tolerate *losing* customers. So just one predator stealing market share will force everyone else to either become defensive, or go on the offensive to retaliate. Price-based competition will quickly lower the overall profitability of the industry, and the more fierce the competition, the lower the profits.

When an industry begins to *decline*, the dominant strategy is likely to be *survival*. By definition, decline means a shrinking market: fewer customers, and as the number of customers declines, *somebody's* market share has to go down. The more the market declines, the more it is likely to affect *all* competitors, and when that happens, competition changes dramatically. That's because once a firm has been organized to operate at a certain production level, its overall efficiency (i.e., cost structure) depends on maintaining that level, and any drop in production that results in excess capacity will mean a loss of revenue, and a loss of profit.

Realizing that, most firms will do everything they can to continue operating at full capacity, and do whatever it takes to maintain their market shares. With every competitor fighting to maintain market share in a declining market, something has to give, and that something will usually be *prices*. So the dominant survival strategy in a declining industry becomes cutting prices and trying to hang on until others drop out. At this stage, although there is little possibility of *any* firm "winning," there will be survivors; usually firms with the most cost-efficient operations, or those with the deepest pockets. In either case, it's not a pretty picture, and not an industry anyone would *choose* to be in.

Surviving in a declining industry often leads firms to consolidate, through mergers and acquisitions. If done with the right partners, for the right reasons, consolidation can be an effective survival strategy. But all too often consolidation is undertaken in desperation, and may ultimately put the combined firm at an even greater disadvantage.

By now it should be clear just how important it is to understand industry life-cycles. If, for example, we compete in an industry that is reaching, or has reached maturity, we should be asking ourselves questions like, "what can we do *now* to avoid having to compete in a declining industry?" and "should we get out now, while we're still profitable?" Obviously, it is much better to ask this kind of question *before* the organization gets to that stage than *after*.

One of the best ways to avoid being caught in a declining industry is to take an active role in either re-inventing the industry or joining an industry that is replacing yours. Manufacturers of black-and-white television sets, for example, knew for years that color television was

Chapter 4—Competitive Analysis

coming, but most of the industry leaders didn't do anything about it, and eventually found themselves fighting for survival in a declining industry. Today, history may be repeating itself, as manufacturers of traditional color television sets are threatened by high-definition and flat-panel television. Those who haven't had the foresight to start diverting their efforts to the new technology face the prospect of trying to survive in another dying industry. It's always interesting to see how current competitors seem more inclined to view this type of evolution as a threat, rather trying to see the opportunities it may offer.

LEARNING-CURVE EFFECTS

The proverb, "Practice makes perfect" aptly describes what is known as the "learning curve." Also known as an *experience curve*, the learning curve in Figure 7 shows that the more often we perform an activity the faster we are able to do it. If we do it enough times, we are able to do it in just a fraction of the time it originally took. This "learning effect" provides an opportunity to lower the cost of operations through reductions in labor, set-up, and material costs.

When we do things in multiples rather than one at a time, we gain the advantages of greater economies of scale, and lower labor costs. Economies of scale come from doing things in large quantities, which allows us to take advantage of volume discounts when purchasing materials, and the lower set-up costs of longer production runs. Economies of scale can also improve learning effects.

In the example in Figure 7, the cost of producing the first 1000 units is $1.00 per unit, but the second 1000 costs only 50c per unit, the fourth 1000 just 25c per unit, and so forth. In this example, each time cumulative production doubles, the cost per unit is reduced by another 50%, due to learning effects. This example is referred to as a "50% learning curve." The 50% number won't apply to all cases, but will vary from one activity to another and from one industry to another. In industries where production quantities are relatively small (e.g., aircraft manufacturing, shipbuilding,) the learning curve may not be a competitive advantage, but in industries where quantities are large, it can be a significant competitive advantage for those firms that can increase their production quantities faster than their competitors.

The length of the learning curve will vary from industry to industry. The shorter the learning curve, the faster firms can get down the curve to capitalize on the lowest possible production costs, which will give them a temporary competitive advantage, until competitors catch up. The longer the learning curve, the longer it takes to get the full advantage of it, but the greater competitive head-start it offers those who are first down the curve.

An example of a long learning curve is the pharmaceutical industry. It sometimes takes ten years or more to develop a new drug and get it tested and approved for sale. That's a significant investment in time and money, but imagine the advantage for a company that is first out with a blockbuster drug: a competitive advantage that may last for years.

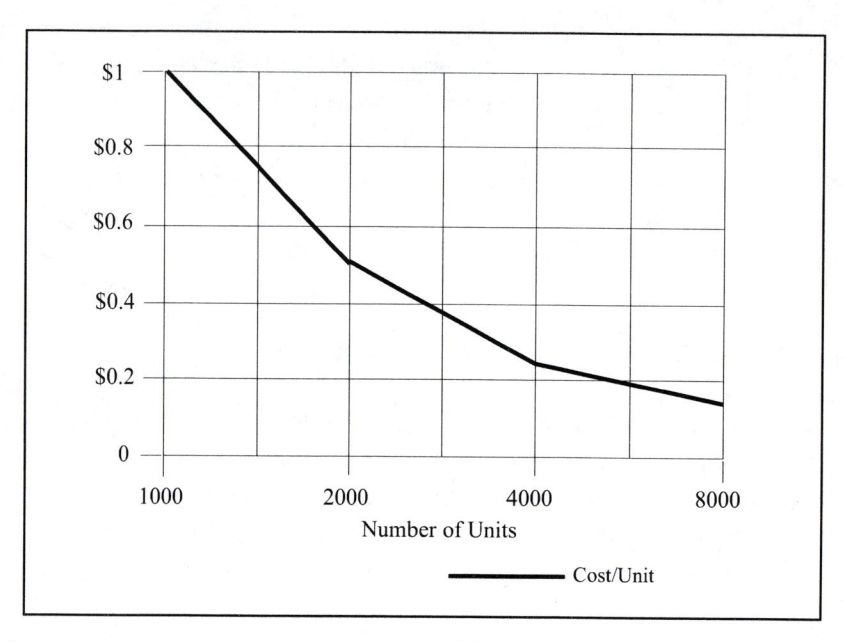

Figure 7. The Learning Curve

To make sure your company has the maximum opportunity to benefit from learning-curve effects, rather than being handicapped by them, it will be helpful to consider these questions:
- is there a learning-curve effect in our industry?
- if so, where and what is it?
- who currently has the greatest advantage of it?
- how will it affect us?

COMPETITORS

Up to this point, we've focused our competitive analysis on an entire industry, but now we need to look at our competitors as individual companies. Seldom will we need to analyze all of the companies in our industry. Usually, there will be just 2 or 3 who will be our strongest competitors. For example, some industries are made up of several "strategic groups": small clusters of companies that compete directly with each other, but not with the rest of the industry. The beer-brewing industry, for example, contains one group of major players, dominated by Anheuser-Busch, Miller, and Molson-Coors, which compete directly with each other but do not compete with micro-breweries such as Samuel Adams, and Anchor.

So we should focus our attention only on those companies who are likely to be our most challenging competitors, and examine their strengths, weaknesses, distinctive competences, and competitive strategies. While this may seem a daunting task, there are many sources of information about other companies, including published sources such as: annual reports, Standard & Poor, Value-Line Investment Survey, and industry trade-publications.

One of the best sources is people within our own company who deal with external stakeholders. Sales people, for example, will invariably be aware of how customers compare our products/services with those of our competitors, and will also see our competitors' strategies in action. Service people often have the opportunity to compare the quality of our products/services with those of our competitors, hear customers' comparisons of our outputs with those of competitors, and see competitors' service organizations in action. Purchasing people can provide valuable information on competitors' cost structures, based on the volume discounts of parts and raw materials.

While these are just a few examples of sources of competitive information, they illustrate the abundance of information that is available on almost any competitor. The more such information we can gather, the better we can analyze our competitors' competitive capabilities and competitive strategies, then determine how we can gain competitive advantage over them.

SUMMARY

The first step in developing competitive strategies is knowing our competitors. That requires an in-depth understanding of our industry, which of its competitors are likely to be of most concern to us, and their competitive capabilities: strengths, weaknesses, distinctive competencies, and competitive strategies.

Once we clearly understand what it takes to be successful in our industry, and have a good idea of how our competitors operate, we will have taken the first step toward developing strategies that will not only give us an advantage over the competition but a *sustainable* competitive advantage. The next step is to know *ourselves*, as an organization, as well as we know our competitors. While that may sound like an easy task, it is seldom as simple as it may appear. In the next chapter, we'll discuss why.

Chapter 5

INTERNAL ANALYSIS

"Know thyself" (Plutarch)

The purpose of internal analysis is to examine the organization's internal capabilities, to determine what resources and capabilities can be used to achieve its goals. The process should begin with an inventory of what we think are the organization's strengths and what should be considered weaknesses. A *strength* is something at which the organization *excels*, or a characteristic that gives it a competitive *advantage*, while a *weakness* is something it *lacks*, or *does poorly*, or a condition that puts it at a competitive *disadvantage*.

There are many possible strengths and weaknesses including:

current strategy	equipment	capabilities
resources	core values	people
performance	processes	image
facilities	knowledge	reputation
distinctive competencies	skills	culture
technology	methods	partnerships

We must have a clear understanding of both our strengths and weaknesses, for two reasons: 1) they are part of the organization's internal environment, which we *can*, and *should* control; and 2) they will be keys to the success of our competitive strategies. Successful strategies are built by capitalizing on an organization's strengths, and eliminating, minimizing, or defending against its weaknesses. This requires an *objective* analysis of both strengths and weaknesses.

STRENGTHS

Analyzing strengths begins with understanding the difference between something we do *well* and something that's a true *strength*. Something should only be considered a *strength* if it is something we do, or something we have, that our competitors *can't match*. In other words, it is only a strength if it gives us a *competitive advantage*. A true strength becomes part of our *distinctive competence*: something we do or something we offer that is preferred by customers, but cannot be easily, quickly, or inexpensively duplicated by our competitors.

One of the difficulties in identifying true strengths is recognizing that something that we do well is not necessarily a strength. Our measure of a strength should be "does it give us an advantage over our competitors?" If the answer is "no," it isn't really a strength. Although this may seem fundamental, a surprising number of organizations (and individuals) are unwilling to admit that, although they do something very well, somebody else does it better. And when we fail to recognize when a strength is not really a strength, we give our competitors the advantage: what we *think* is a strength, they *know* is actually a weakness. It is much more to our advantage to be realistic and recognize that, although something we do well is not currently a competitive advantage, it *could* be. It might have the potential to be developed into a true strength.

We can develop a sustainable competitive advantage by capitalizing on distinctive competencies in one of two ways: 1) providing lower-price products or services; or 2) differentiating our offerings from those of the competition, in ways that allow us to charge premium prices.

WEAKNESSES

A company's weaknesses may be even more difficult to identify, objectively, than its strengths, because there is a human tendency to defend anything *we* have done or created against all criticism. This tendency seems to be even stronger in the higher levels of organizations, and the executives of an organization are often the most defensive of all.

In fact, it isn't uncommon for executives to try to divert attention away from a discussion of their firms' weaknesses by disparaging the competition: "ACME's quality is much worse than ours". It is, of course, a matter of pride (sometimes called "management hubris"); an unwillingness to admit that the organization (*their* creation) could be anything less than perfect.

But every organization, like every individual, *has* weaknesses; areas that can make it vulnerable to competition; areas that could be improved. And if we don't recognize these weaknesses, as our competitors surely will, we will be operating at a competitive disadvantage, because our competitors will know us better than we know ourselves. If we want to be competitive we have no choice; we must be aware of our weaknesses, as our competitors surely will.

One of the most effective ways of learning our vulnerabilities is to ask those who are in closest contact with our external environment. What better place to start than with those who work with customers? They are invariably, and constantly, reminded of where we are *not* meeting customers' expectations. For example, people in sales, service, marketing, and human resources can tell us how we're doing; which stakeholders' expectations are being met and, more importantly, which are *not*.

Or we can learn our weaknesses in the most direct way, by asking the stakeholders themselves. They are continually comparing us with our competitors to determine which of us can best meet their needs, so who is in a better position to tell us where we don't measure up?

Chapter 5—Internal Analysis

STAKEHOLDERS

> *"An organization is an organ of society, and fulfills itself by the contribution it makes to the outside environment."*
> (Drucker, 1966:15)

A *stakeholder* is any person, group, or organization that has something to gain or lose from the organization's actions. These are individuals and/or groups who contribute important resources to the organization and depend on its success. Different stakeholders have different, often conflicting, expectations of what the organization should achieve, and they have different kinds of power that they will use, when necessary, to influence organizational outcomes.

With that in mind, it is important to understand:

- *Who* are our primary stakeholders?
  - What do they *expect* of us?
  - How do they *measure* our *performance*? (What *criteria* do they use?)
  - How well are we *meeting* their *expectations*?
- *Why* are they *important* to us?
  - How do they *influence* us?
  - What do *we need* from them?
- What can we do to *improve* their *satisfaction* with our performance?

An organization's stakeholders will generally include: owners/shareholders, customers, employees, unions, community, governments, suppliers, lenders, competitors, and board of directors. Some examples of stakeholder expectations include:

Stakeholder	Expectations
Owners/shareholders	Return on their investment
Customers	Value
Employees	Fair wages, fair treatment, opportunity
Unions	Voice, Respect
Community	Jobs, taxes, respect for environment
Governments	Compliance with laws
Suppliers	Fair profitability
Lenders	Interest, repayment
Competitors	Ethical/legal competition
Board members	Networking opportunities, prestige

It is important to recognize that, with so many conflicting expectations, it is nearly impossible to satisfy *all* stakeholders *all* of the time, or even *all* of the stakeholders *any* of the time. Moreover, we will seldom, if ever, be able to *completely* satisfy any group of stakeholders without dissatisfying others.

In fact, if we were to ask each group of stakeholders to describe its expectations of the organization, we would find that meeting the combined expectations of all stakeholders would take more resources than the organization has. This is illustrated in Figure 8, where the inner circle represents the total resources of the organization, and the outer circle the total expectations of its stakeholders.

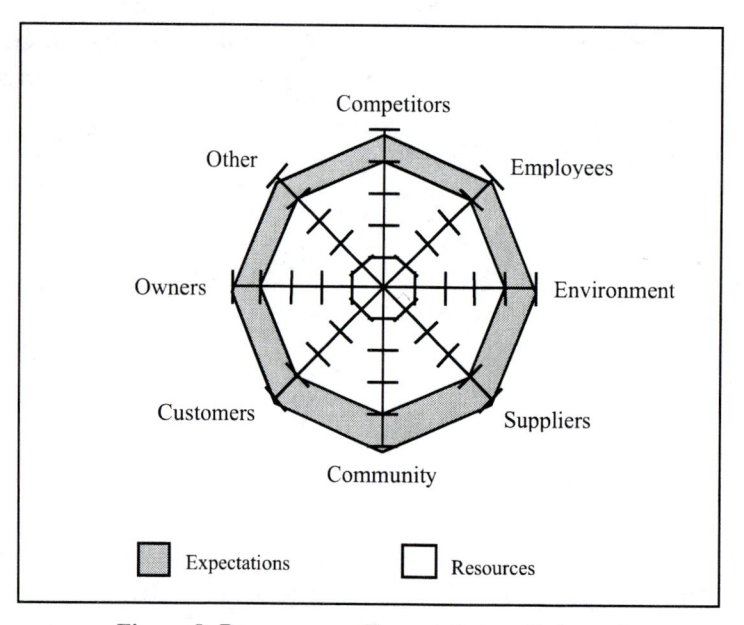

Figure 8. Resources vs. Expectations—Balanced

This represents a fundamental dilemma: how do we meet all of these stakeholder expectations? From the previous discussion, it should be apparent that we *can't*. Then what are our choices?

Well, we could determine who are our *most important* stakeholders and try to meet just their expectations. To do that, we would first have to define what we mean by "most important." After some consideration it would likely come down to the groups that have the most influence on the organization; those capable of providing the greatest rewards and/or the most severe punishment (e.g., top executives, large shareholders, the board of directors.) Now, suppose we do every thing we can to completely satisfy the expectations of just one of those favored stakeholder groups. Will it solve our problem? Not necessarily. If the remaining stakeholders feel they have been overlooked, or penalized in any way, they will be likely to punish the organization, because every stakeholder group has its own form of power.

Stockholders, for example, can sell their stock, replace the organization's management, or sell the company; customers can switch to competitors, or boycott; employees can strike,

Chapter 5—Internal Analysis

resign, engage in production slowdowns, or even sabotage; and the community can raise taxes, increase utility charges, enact new policies. In short, all stakeholders have the means to retaliate if they feel they are being treated unfairly.

To illustrate, let's use as an example a cyclical firm that is approaching its busiest season of the year, a six-week period that normally accounts for 40% of its annual sales. The bargaining unit that represents the majority of the firm's employees decides to use this critical time as leverage in bargaining for higher wages. To avoid a strike during its best sales season, the firm gives in to the union's demands for an immediate across-the-board wage increase. As a result, the firm has met the full expectations of *one* stakeholder group, but how will it fund the wage increase? We know the firm doesn't have the extra money, so who will pay the price? Which stakeholder group's expectations will be sacrificed?

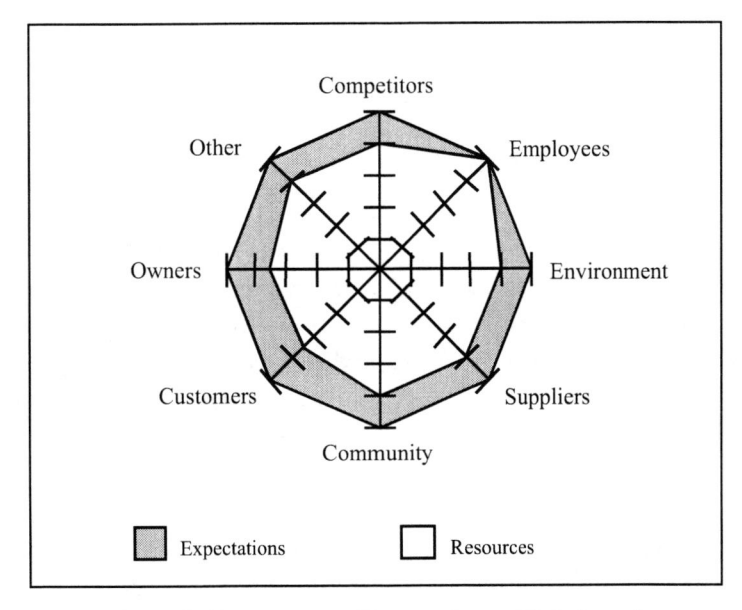

Figure 9. Resources vs. Expectations—Unbalanced

There are a number of things the firm can do: raise prices, cut or eliminate dividends, pressure suppliers to lower their prices, increase productivity, reduce costs, or lower profit margins. Figure 9 shows what would happen if we compensated for the wage increase by reducing the dividend paid to shareholders and increasing product prices. This way, the employees have had their expectations fully satisfied, but at the expense of the firm's owners and customers, both of whom are likely to be upset. This could result in shareholders selling their stock (which will likely drive the stock price down), as well as some customers choosing to buy from the competition.

But there is a way the company could pay for wage increase without penalizing innocent stakeholders: require those who receive the raise to increase their productivity accordingly. This would be logical, from the standpoint that any organization, particularly one whose costs of doing business are increasing, should be continually looking for ways to decrease its overall costs, and one of the best ways of doing that is by increasing productivity. And it would be fair, from the perspective that the stakeholder group whose increased expectations are being satisfied would be paying for its own satisfaction.

But even so, a productivity increase is likely to be a long-term solution, while the wage increase will create an *immediate* cash-flow problem, which will probably force management to consider short-term options for a temporary remedy. One would be to pressure suppliers to lower their prices, but that might be detrimental to future relationships with them. Another option would be to reduce or eliminate dividends, but that would be almost certain to alienate some shareholders, who might sell enough stock to drive down the price of shares, which might upset other shareholders.

So let's suppose that management decides their easiest and quickest solution is to do nothing; simply let the increased costs reduce the firm's profit margins temporarily, until improved productivity can increase them again. Those most affected by this strategy would be shareholders, and possibly lenders. How much they will be affected will depend on how long it takes to increase productivity and re-establish the original profit margins. With this approach management would be gambling that productivity can be increased before either shareholders or lenders become unduly concerned. So time becomes the enemy; the longer it takes, the more concerned both owners and lenders are likely to become, thus increasing the number of stock-sellers, and possibly driving up the cost of borrowing.

The point is: if an organization satisfies an increased demand by any stakeholder group at the expense of other stakeholders, the other stakeholders are likely to exact some form of penalty. But if we can find a way for the stakeholders whose increased expectations have been satisfied to, in some way, pay the price of the increase themselves, we may be able to avoid negative reactions from the other stakeholders.

DISTINCTIVE COMPETENCE

As explained earlier, a distinctive competence is something that we do that is valued by customers and that cannot be easily, quickly, or inexpensively duplicated by competitors. It can be the basis of a sustainable competitive advantage. Note the implication that there is a *single* distinctive competence; only one to a person, or to an organization. Although it is possible to have more than one, more often than not people or organizations who think they have multiple distinctive competencies are just kidding themselves; they may be examples of a "jack of all trades, and master of none." A better strategy is to concentrate on developing just one distinctive competence; one solid competitive advantage. If you can develop others later, fine, but start by concentrating all of your efforts on just one.

Distinctive competencies can be location, knowledge, patents, production capabilities, advertising expertise, or a multitude of other possibilities. Honda's expertise and experience in designing and building engines makes them the world leader; Sony's distinctive competence is in electronic miniaturization; Wal Mart's is distribution technology, and responsiveness to customer needs; Procter and Gamble's is advertising; and Rubbermaid's is rubber and plastics. Although some of these companies may have more than one distinctive competence, each has built its reputation by focusing on excellence in one primary area.

An important question to keep in mind when considering distinctive competence is "Why will customers choose me, or my product, over those of the competition?" If you can't clearly and confidently answer that question, you haven't yet identified, or developed, a distinctive competence.

GAP ANALYSIS

Now that we have a clear picture of our organization's strengths and weaknesses, and at least an idea of what might be its distinctive competence(s), it's time to conduct a gap analysis, to see the difference between where we *are* and where we *want to be*, and to help us determine how large a leap it will take to get from here to there.

Once we've analyzed how far our current capabilities and resources are likely to stretch toward reaching our goals, we'll also know which resources we *don't* have. We will have *realistically* examined what we need, rather than trying to achieve something that may be impossible with present resources. Once we understand what we *don't* have, we'll have two choices: 1) find a way to get the additional resources we need; or 2) change our expectations to goals that can be achieved with the resources that we currently *have*. Questions that are useful in gap analysis:

- What resources (e.g., skills, capabilities, equipment, space, time, money) will be required to achieve our major goals?
- Which of these resources do we *currently* have?
- What are the *gaps*—which resources will we need but do *not* currently have?

Although it is important to conduct a gap analysis as part of our internal analysis, it should be done again, or at least reviewed, after we have developed our competitive strategies (Chapter 7). Although we can *estimate* the resources required based on our goals, we can't be *sure* what resources will be needed until we have determined exactly *how* we'll achieve those goals; what specific strategies and actions we'll take.

SUMMARY

Accurate and objective internal analysis is absolutely essential to developing an effective competitive strategy. It should provide a clear perspective of the strengths on which an organization may be able to build a competitive advantage, the weaknesses that may offer advantages for the competition, and the stakeholder expectations that must be considered in the process. In the end, the stakeholders will be the final judges of the degree of success or failure of any organization's competitive strategy.

It is important to remember that, unlike the external environment, over which we may have little or no control, *internal* elements *can* be controlled. And we *should* control them, but not obsessively. Although our organizations will have weaknesses—they all do—it won't be necessary to eliminate them all; we won't have to be perfect in all areas. We should identify where we'll allow ourselves to be weak, to allow us to concentrate on where we need the greatest strength. It's ok to be weak in some areas, as long as we recognize those weaknesses, and as long as they are not in areas that make us vulnerable to our competitors.

Chapter 6

EXTERNAL ANALYSIS

"The only fence against the world is a thorough knowledge of it."
(John Locke)

Many organizations operate as, and think like, closed systems; s though they can control anything that might affect them. But in reality all organizations are open systems, operating in an external environment over which they have little or no control. Figure 10 is a diagram that shows an organization's relationships with its external environment.

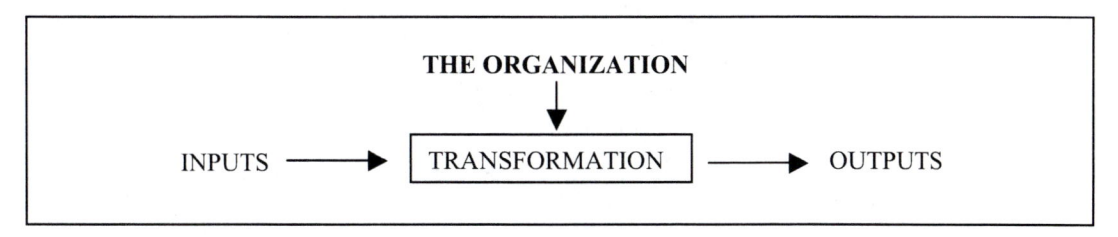

```
                    THE ORGANIZATION
                            ↓
    INPUTS   ────→   TRANSFORMATION   ────→   OUTPUTS
```

Figure 10.

The box labeled "Transformation" depicts the internal part of the organization; everything that takes place within the organization and is within its direct influence.

The "Inputs" arrow represents those resources the organization has to get from outside its boundaries; from its external environment. In the most basic level, inputs include labor (people) and capital (money) although, in practice, capital is merely a means to an end; to purchase the raw materials, equipment, information, and physical facilities that are necessary for the transformation process.

The "Outputs" arrow represents the products and/or services that the organization creates from its inputs. Once inputs have been transformed into outputs, the external environment again becomes important, this time as a market for those outputs. The organization cannot provide its own customers (at least not enough to purchase *all* of its outputs), so it must find them outside the organization.

For those reasons, every organization is dependent on its external environment, both as a source of the inputs necessary to do what it does, and as an outlet for its outputs. So the success of an organization can never be completely within its own control; how well it responds to or manages its external environment will also be a major factor. But before it can either respond to or manage its external environment, the organization must understand that environment, and what effects it is likely to have.

One of the most important responsibilities of any manager is reducing uncertainty; making things as predictable as possible, and predictability is, to a large extent, a function of control. If we can control something, we can influence what happens, thus reducing uncertainty. And this is what managers try to do *inside* their organizations; control what happens. But the external environment is something else. At first glance it appears to be pretty much beyond our control, representing mostly uncertainty. But that doesn't mean that it is totally unpredictable. As a matter of fact, if we know what to look for we can predict many things that happen in the external environment, *before* they happen.

For example, if I throw you a ball, you will see it coming and automatically "predict" what you have to do to catch it or to avoid being hit by it. You may not initially know exactly where it will arrive, but as you watch its progress you will automatically narrow the possible target area. In fact, we do this all the time, much of it almost unconsciously.

When driving a car, we frequently predict, based on how fast we and other drivers are traveling, whether or not we will have time to pass the car in front of us without colliding with an oncoming car. In this way, based on some combination of experience, perception, attention, and reaction-time, we are able to do a certain amount of predicting. And we do it based on the observation of *trends* and *events;* watching what *has* happened and what *is* happening, then estimating what *will probably* happen.

Doing this requires continually watching the external environment; looking for emerging trends: developing circumstances that may someday affect the organization. Once we have become experienced at trend-spotting, we can more easily analyze and identify them as either opportunities or threats.

OPPORTUNITIES AND THREATS

A *threat* can be defined as a possible *danger:* something bad that might happen to us, while an *opportunity* is a *favorable* set of circumstances: something that might be an advantage for us. Although we define them differently, threats and opportunities have many similarities, and they emerge from major trends and events in several areas:

demographics	the economy	education
technology	the workplace	the physical environment
health care	globalization	government/legislation/politics

Trends that most others see as threats can often be turned into opportunities through innovative, forward-looking strategies. The most important thing to understand about the external environment is that threats and opportunities are perceptual in nature: whether something is a threat of opportunity depends on how we look at it.

Chapter 6—External Analysis 47

A threat to one person or organization will be seen as an opportunity by another. Note how we tend to reinforce our mind-sets by the terms that we use; a threat *to* (i.e., something bad that is likely to happen *to* us), but an opportunity *for* (i.e., something good that is likely to happen *for* us; to help us). Perhaps a large part of the perceptual difference is in *preparation*: how well we are able to see current and future trends and anticipate how they are likely to affect us. What is seen as an opportunity by someone who is prepared is more likely to appear threatening to someone who is caught off guard. Why, then, do some organizations seem to prepare for the future, while others allow themselves to remain at the mercy of circumstances?

The difference is usually how strategically they are managed. Some organizations continually monitor their external environments so they can see trends as they develop and use those insights to act in *anticipation* of future events. In effect, they try to *manage* the external environment and how they respond to it. Others become so bogged down in *reacting* to the things that happen to them on a day-to-day basis, that they never take the time to look ahead. As a result, they wind up being *managed by* the external environment. Time after time I've heard busy executives say "We're too busy. We don't have time to plan." But a key to managing the external environment rather than being managed by it, is *believing* that you can do something about it. Then you have to *know how*. Since a big part of believing that you can do something is knowing how to do it, let's discuss some strategies for managing or influencing the external environment.

MANAGING THE EXTERNAL ENVIRONMENT

Robbins (1990) suggests two ways of dealing with the external environment: 1) developing *internal* strategies for *adapting* to it; and 2) developing *external* strategies for *changing* it. Following are discussions of several strategies in each category that almost any organization, regardless of size, can use to become less dependent on its external environment

Adapting to the External Environment (Internal Strategies)

Boundary Spanning

Boundary spanning is perhaps the most important strategy because it enables us to keep an eye on what is happening, or is likely to happen, in the external environment that may affect our organization or our strategies for gaining competitive advantage. Some of the most effective boundary spanners are people within the organization who are constantly in touch with the outside world. Examples are people in sales, service, purchasing, public relations, and human resources who, in the normal course of their work, have access to information from suppliers, customers, the community, the industry, and current and potential employees. The information they provide can help the organization anticipate what is likely to happen, and when, and allow it to plan accordingly, and to know which internal or external strategies may be most effective in reducing future uncertainty. Boundary spanning is our window on the world; it provides information that will help us spot future trends *before* they become threats, while they may still be *opportunities*.

Buffering

Buffering can be used to reduce uncertainty in two areas: the organization's ability to acquire the *inputs* it needs, when it needs them; and its ability to make *outputs* available when they are needed. Buffering, in this sense, means protecting against shortages; shortages of inputs (e.g., raw materials, people, equipment), or outputs (products and services). On the output side, buffering is primarily by building up inventories of finished goods. On the input side we can also build up inventories of raw materials. But we have several additional options, including multiple suppliers (to assure that material is always available, regardless of what happens to any single supplier), preventive maintenance (to ensure that work flow isn't interrupted by equipment failures), and recruiting and training employees (to make sure their skills are available *when* they're needed.)

Rationing

We begin to think about rationing a product or service when there isn't enough of it to meet the demand. During World War II, for example, everyone in the United States was affected by rationing; rationing of meat, sugar, butter, coffee, gasoline, and tires, to name just a few. The purpose was to make sure that those fighting in our armed forces had first priority on everything *they* needed. Whereas that form of rationing was directed mostly at *commodities*, many organizations today make rationing an integral part of their competitive strategies for different reasons.

For example, while any organization that produces *products* can meet increased demand by producing more products or by building up inventory, a *service* organization is limited because its services cannot be inventoried. Although it could increase capacity by hiring more people, that might require downsizing when business slows, which often happens when the demand for its services is cyclical. For that reason, service organizations often *ration* their services to allocate their output in a way that customers can understand. Customers know that, since restaurants have a certain number of tables available, getting seated during the busiest periods may require reservations in advance. Popular colleges and universities are limited in how many students they can accommodate, so they use some sort of priority or standards-based admission system to ration admissions.

Smoothing (Demand Smoothing*)*

Smoothing is designed to level out the demand for a product or service, and is an effective strategy when demand varies dramatically from hour to hour or day to day. Phone companies, for example, charge their highest prices for calls made during business hours, and much lower prices for evening and weekend calls. Why? To encourage customers to shift their calls from the busiest times to slower periods. Electric utility companies use a similar approach, with a process called "demand metering" determining which businesses demand the highest loads of electricity, then charging them a much higher rate for it, even though the largest demand may last for only a few minutes at a time. They charge more because they have to generate more electricity *all of the time*, to be able to satisfy the higher demand when its needed. That's because electricity can't be stored until it is needed; it is produced at the time it is used.

Due to limited seating and the uncertainty of how many people will attend each game, sport teams sell season tickets to guarantee a minimum amount of income; to smooth out their revenue stream. Magazines and newspapers apply the same method, by selling subscriptions to provide a much more predictable flow of income than newsstand sales would allow. Auto rental agencies are another example. They offer much lower rates on weekends, when their cars would otherwise be idle and bringing in no revenue at all.

Changing the External Environment (External Strategies)

Advertising

Organizations advertise to build brand loyalty, and brand loyalty increases their customers' switching costs. The more loyal customers are to one brand the more difficult it is for them to justify switching to a competitive brand. Brand loyalty, therefore, makes the demand for a product more constant; less variable. If we can convince our customers that the product or service offered by our company is superior in some way, through quality, service, features, image with peers, etc., they will be more likely to continue buying our brand and less inclined to switch to competitive brands, and they may also be willing to pay a premium price for our product. Advertising helps convince potential customers to try our brand and reinforces, for current customers, their belief that they bought the right product. And the more we lock in repeat business, the more we reduce the uncertainty of our revenue stream.

Contracting (Supply Smoothing)

It can be to an organization's benefit to reach agreements with major customers, in which the customer commits to purchase specified quantities of products/services over a specified time (e.g., 5000 units over the next 3 years), in exchange for guaranteed prices over that period. The seller is guaranteed a certain volume of business in exchange for not raising prices during the term of the contract, and the buyer benefits from stable prices. Although this example is designed to stabilize the output side of the business, contracts can also be negotiated on the input side, to guarantee the flow of raw material at a pre-determined price.

Co-opting

Robbins (1990) defines co-opting as absorbing those organizations or individuals who threaten the organization's stability. This is can be done through appointments to an organization's board of directors. For example, it is not uncommon for an organization to offer an executive from its lending institution a directorship; the same holds true for retired members of governmental agencies (e.g., the Environmental Protection Agency); or for retired military officers (by defense contractors). The principal idea of coopting is to get people on the side of the organization who know how to blunt or buffer issues that offer particular threats to the company, or who can assist in taking advantage of opportunities in their areas of expertise and experience.

Lobbying

A popular way of co-opting is to hire lobbyists to influence the passage of legislation that will be favorable to the organization, or to fight against legislation that may threaten it. For small organizations, this is often done through trade associations, whose lobbyists work on issues that are of vital interest to all members of the association. Lobbying is often done to reduce competition in an industry, by making it difficult for new entrants, through licensing requirements and regulation.

Strategic Alliances

Another way to reduce the uncertainty of the external environment is for one organization to enter into a strategic alliance with another, in order to develop synergies, to improve economies of scale, to increase the ability to influence the environment, to gain entry into new markets, or simply to eliminate the other company as a competitor. Strategic alliances include mergers, in which organizations permanently join forces; joint ventures, in which organizations enter into cooperative arrangements that are generally more limited in scope and time; and acquisitions, in which one firm purchases another. These types of alliances will be discussed in more detail in another chapter.

Ultimately, long-term success rests on how effectively an organization anticipates and acts on trends and events in its external environment. Those with the clearest windows on their worlds will be best able to develop competitive strategies that will turn potential threats into grand opportunities, and allow their organizations to operate proactively rather than wasting time and energy responding to unanticipated events. In the long run, the most successful organization is likely to be the one that is most effective in responding to unanticipated events in an organized manner.

SUMMARY

Although we cannot directly control the external environment, there are a number of ways in which we can either adapt to it or influence it. Although most organizations attempt to manage their *competitive* environments, they often ignore, or give only minimal attention to the part of the external environment that is *outside* of the industry, a larger area, and one from which major trends and events can evolve that may affect them in the future, as either threats or opportunities. So it is important that we make a concerted effort to continually monitor our *entire* external environment, not just our competitive arena.

Although we may not be able to predict the future, we can spot trends, sometimes years in advance, that may ultimately affect us. We are all aware of the many businesses that have been devastated by changing technologies (e.g., steam engine, telegraph, telephone, railroads, automobile, airplane), yet the vast majority of those innovations were under development, and visible, for years before they began to significantly affect organizations. The best way to manage the external environment is to watch those trends as they develop; then decide which might offer future opportunities for your organization, and prepare accordingly.

Chapter 7

COMPETITIVE STRATEGY

"The race is to the swift; the battle to the strong"
(John Davidson, 1857-1909)

After carefully analyzing our competition, assessing strengths and weaknesses, determining what will be our distinctive competencies, and gaining a clear perspective on the opportunities and threats presented by the external environment, we are prepared to move forward in developing the competitive strategies that will achieve our primary goals. We say "competitive" because seldom, if ever, can we expect to execute a strategy without opposition from competitors. Whenever *we* see a need that looks like a market opportunity, we can be sure that sooner or later *others* will see the same opportunity, and position themselves to compete to meet the needs of the same group of customers.

COMPETITIVE ADVANTAGE

So the primary purpose of a competitive strategy is to make our products or services more attractive to potential customers than the offerings of our competitors; to give us a *competitive advantage*.

But it's important that our competitive advantage is *sustainable*; that it will give us a competitive edge over a long period of time (e.g., years,) rather than just temporarily. The longer we can sustain a competitive advantage, the better we can chart our own course and control our destiny. If we can be the competitive leader and set the agenda for the competition we should be in the best position to compete according to our own plan rather than reacting to someone else's. There are many ways to gain a competitive advantage, but some are not sustainable. We might, for example, gain a competitive advantage by marking down the prices of our products or services so they are lower than those of our competitors, but we cannot usually sustain this type of advantage indefinitely, without seriously eroding our profitability. On the other hand, there are strategies, such as providing superior service or higher quality, can lead to longer-term competitive advantages.

It's also important to recognize that not all strategies are *deliberate* (planned). There are also those, called *emergent* strategies, that are developed outside of the formal planning process. They *emerge* from within the organization, for a variety of reasons. Being constantly aware of the possibility of emergent strategies, whenever and wherever they may develop, is essential to the strategic management process, for two reasons. First, an emergent strategy may offer improvements on the current plan, or be better than the current plan and, if so, we may want to incorporate them into our plan. Second, because some emergent strategies are designed to pursue separate agendas: goals that are different from those we have designated as our highest priorities. When this happens, the emergent strategy should be nipped in the bud; shut down before it can divert our resources to non-strategic purposes. Remember that competitive strategy is, above all, about how to most effectively allocate resources to achieve the organization's major goals.

Finally, it is important to remind ourselves that our strategy will not be executed in a vacuum. What we do will affect others and they, particularly our competitors, will respond accordingly. So as we develop strategy we should think beyond what *we* plan to do and ask ourselves, "What will *they*, our competitors, do in response?" Then, "How should we react to their response?" and so on. Like a game of chess, we must be thinking several moves ahead, as we can be reasonably sure our competitors will.

And as we consider possible strategies, it is important to ask ourselves: "What will make the customers buy *our* product or service rather than our competitor's?" Unless we come up with a compelling answer to that question, we will not yet have identified a true competitive advantage.

Identifying competitive advantage for any customer involves, first, determining *why* the customer buys a particular product or service; what needs (or wants) will it fill for him? Understanding *why* is essential to the development of products or services, and should guide us in determining how to best meet those needs. Determining *how* requires knowing how the customer chooses which products or services will best meet his/her needs. Once we know that, we will understand what has he biggest influence on the customer's buying decision: *price*, or *distinctive features*.

FUNDAMENTAL (BASIC) COMPETITIVE STRATEGY

There are two fundamental competitive strategies: *Low-price leadership* and *differentiation*. Our choice of which one to pursue will have a major influence on who we hire, and how we structure our organization.

Low-Price Leadership

When their buying decision is based on price, it usually means customers see the product as a commodity and don't really care who they buy it from. They buy the product or service from whomever offers it at the lowest price, assuming, of course, it is of acceptable quality. This strategy is known as *low-price leadership*, and to be competitive an organization will have to be designed to operate at maximum *efficiency* and lowest cost. In this arena, competi-

Chapter 7—Competitive Strategy

tion is driven strictly by price, and competitors with the lowest internal-cost structures have the advantage. Competitive success depends largely on continually improving the organization's cost structure, and producing and selling in large volumes.

Of course a major factor in determining the price of a product or service is its *availability*. If more is available than customers are willing to buy (i.e., supply is greater than demand), sellers will lower the price until they have sold their inventory. On the other hand, if buyers want more than is available (i.e., demand is greater than supply), buyers will bid the price higher as they attempt to get what they want before the supply runs out. In this situation, scarcity has the effect of differentiating even a commodity product or service.

Differentiation

But if customers base their buying decisions on anything *other* than price, a firm's competitive advantage will come from its ability to provide products or services that are more *attractive* to potential customers, based on customers' differing needs.

This is *differentiation*, in which firms provide products or services that are different from those offered by the competition; different in ways that make them attractively unique in the eyes of customers. Differentiation is accomplished in one of two basic ways: by providing the customer with a feeling of comfort, confidence, security, or convenience (e.g., quality, reputation, service, location); or a valued image (e.g., prestige, exclusiveness, inclusiveness, social status). Whereas differentiation based on comfort, confidence, security, or convenience may satisfy customer *needs*, when it's based on providing a valued image, differentiation may respond more to customer *wants*.

A major advantage of differentiation over low-price leadership is that successful differentiation can enable a firm to sell its products or services for *premium* prices.

Although there are many other competitive strategies, some will be explored later in this chapter, an organization must first determine which of these two fundamental strategies it will pursue, because that decision will have a major influence on how it will have to operate to be competitively successful.

If its fundamental strategy is *low-price leadership*, the organization will have to be structured to achieve efficiency and take advantage of economies of scale. For a manufacturing firm, for example, this would usually involve large capital expenditures in plant and equipment; investments that may not be easy to recoup if the firm should decide to change its basic strategy, or its market, in the future. A major part of the organization's workforce is likely to be unskilled, and production processes divided into activities that are simple and repetitive, resulting in lower wage costs and high-volume production.

But if its fundamental strategy is *differentiation*, the organization will more likely be structured to facilitate research, development, and innovation, and it may invest large sums in advertising, to develop and maintain brand loyalty among customers. Its workforce will include more skilled, professional and technical people, and production processes will likely be more complex. Costs are likely to be considerably higher than if it were trying to be a low-cost leader, but premium pricing will give it the opportunity for higher margins and greater profitability.

Whichever fundamental strategy it chooses, the organization will invest significant amounts of time, money, and effort in establishing a dominant competitive position; investments that should, for all practical purposes, be considered "sunk costs;" non-retrievable if it decides to change fundamental strategies. For these reasons, the choice of fundamental strategy should not be taken lightly.

Which fundamental strategy an organization chooses will depend, to some extent, on the structure of its industry; how many competitors there are and how fiercely they compete. In Chapter 4 we discussed *industry structure*, from the perspective of the number of firms in an industry, and the way that affects how they compete. On a continuum ranging from a monopoly (i.e., one firm) at one extreme to a free market (i.e., hundreds, or thousands of competitors) at the other, most industries are somewhere between "consolidated" and "fragmented," as shown in Figure 8.

In a consolidated industry the majority of the market-share is likely to be controlled by a few large firms, and competition is most likely to be driven by competitors' ability to differentiate their products/services from one another. Competition in a consolidated industry is rarely cut-throat or price-driven, and the overall attitude of the major competitors is likely to be "live and let live" and "don't rock the boat."

In contrast, a fragmented industry is one that has a large number of competitors, none of whom is dominant. Although competition may be based on differentiation, it is more likely to be driven by price. As shown in Figure 8, the more fragmented the industry the lower its overall profitability. Whereas in a consolidated industry there can be significant profit potential, in a fragmented industry only the most efficient firms are likely to be profitable.

With that in mind, the more fragmented an industry, the more likely customers view its products or services as commodities, and that low-price leadership will probably be the fundamental strategy of most competitors.

Another consideration in choosing a fundamental strategy should be the industry life-cycle. As discussed in Chapter 4, every industry evolves through a life-cycle beginning with infancy, followed by a period of growth, then maturity and. ultimately decline (Levitt, 1965). See Figure 9.

Knowing the current life-cycle stage of an industry is essential to designing the most effective competitive strategy, since it will influence the number of competitors, how fiercely they compete, and how profitable the industry as a whole is likely to be.

We won't duplicate the Chapter 4 discussions about how the industry life-cycle affects competitive strategies, except to review how they are likely to affect an organization's choice of fundamental strategy.

In its "Infancy" the dominant functional strategy will likely be differentiation, as innovators are more concerned with developing a market for their products or services, by establishing their individuality, and less concerned with keeping prices low.

Chapter 7—Competitive Strategy

During the "Growth" stage, the number of competitors will increase, as "followers" attempt to gain a piece of the market once its potential has been demonstrated by the first movers. These "imitators" are not willing, or perhaps not financially able, to gamble on an uncertain market but will move quickly to take advantage once its potential has been demonstrated. As long as market growth stays ahead of competitor demands this should be the most profitable stage of the industry life cycle, and the dominant strategies will be those directed at gaining market share, some firms using differentiation and others focusing on low-price leadership.

As an industry reaches "Maturity," which usually means the market is no longer growing, the competitive picture can change considerably. As long as all competitors are content with their current market shares, the industry can remain stable and reasonably profitable, and competitors can stay with their current fundamental strategy, be it low-price leadership or differentiation. But if any firm decides to increase its market share, by taking it away from someone else, the equilibrium will be broken and the industry is likely to see a rapid shift to price-based competition. Firms whose fundamental strategy has been differentiation may have to face the prospect of changing to price-based competition, or getting out of the industry.

When an industry reaches the stage of "Decline", the dominant competitive strategy is survival. By definition, decline means a diminishing market; fewer customers. As the number of customers declines, somebody's market share has to decline, as well, and the more the market declines, the more it is likely to affect all competitors. When that happens, *survival* becomes every competitor's mission, and price-cutting becomes the primary strategy, sometimes to the point where products or services are priced *below* what it costs to produce them. So, in its final stage, the primary goal of everyone in the industry is to hang on until everyone else drops out.

By now it should be clear how important it is for a firm to understand the life-cycle stage of its industry before determining a fundamental competitive strategy.

A final note about fundamental strategy. Whereas a firm's fundamental strategy will be the foundation of its competitive position, a fundamental strategy is not, by itself, sufficient to establish a competitive advantage. The choice of a fundamental strategy is primarily a response to the fundamentals of the competitive arenas, the dynamics of the industry (i.e., how firms compete,) and the needs of the market/customers and how they make buying decisions. It helps define how an organization should be structured. Although I use the word "choice," fundamental strategy isn't always our choice to make. Once we are in an industry, the industry often makes that choice for us, and we have to compete using whichever fundamental strategy happens to drive competition in the industry.

So fundamental strategy doesn't, by itself, determine how the firm will establish and maintain a competitive advantage. That's where *contingent strategies* come in; more specific strategies that are designed to fit a particular organization and its circumstances of the moment.

CONTINGENT STRATEGIES

Although we are limited to just two choices of fundamental strategy—differentiation, or low-price leadership—the possibilities for contingent strategies are almost limitless, and should be tailored to fit the uniqueness of the organization and its competitive environment.

Hambrick and Fredrickson (2001) suggest that, to be effective, a strategy must provide answers to five questions:

1. *Where* will we compete? (What business will we be in?)
2. *How* will we *get there*? (R&D, imitation, acquisitions, etc.?)
3. *How* will we *differentiate* ourselves, to gain a competitive advantage? (What will we do to get the customers to buy our products/services instead of those of our competition?)
4. *How fast* will we move, and in *what sequence*? (What must be done, in what order, and when?)
5. *How* will we make a *profit*? (Lowest prices, premium prices?)

Although some of these questions will have been addressed by our choices of mission (Question 1.), and fundamental strategy (perhaps Questions 3 and 5), all should be given additional consideration as we examine the possibilities for contingent strategies.

Following are brief descriptions of some of the more widely-used contingent strategies, any of which can be used in almost any organization regardless of its fundamental strategy, and may also be used in combination with other contingent strategies.

Focus (Niche) Strategy

A focus strategy is described as "...focusing on a particular buyer group, segment of the product line, or geographic market;..." and "...built around serving a particular target very well,..." (Porter, 1980:38). A focus strategy is a deliberate choice of depth over breadth. The organization's competitive activities can be focused in a variety of ways and for a variety of purposes, but our discussion will concentrate on just two: focusing on specific product lines, and focusing on geographic markets.

When entering a new industry or competitive arena, a sure-fire formula for failure is to compete head-to-head with an established competitor. Even if we begin competing in an area in which customers are not being served well, competitors are likely to respond to our threat by increasing their own efforts. When that happens, we wind up in direct competition with established firms, a situation we would prefer to avoid unless we have a distinctive competence that will give us a competitive advantage. So, generally we will be better off trying to position ourselves where the competition isn't, or where they are weak.

When Canon, for example, first began considering entering the U.S. market for copiers, they knew they couldn't compete with Xerox which, at that time, was the dominant copier company in the world. So, to avoid direct competition with Xerox and the retaliation that might bring, Canon chose to enter with a low-cost personal copier, a market segment that Xerox had ignored. With no direct competition, Canon introduced what ultimately became a very successful product, created a new market segment, and began establishing a reputation for quality and customer service. Once its reputation was assured, Canon was in a position to compete more directly with Xerox, and in subsequent years, did so quite effectively. But the key to Canon's successful entry into this market was choosing a segment in which it would not be opposed. Had Canon attempted to enter through direct competition, Xerox and other powerful competitors could have made entry very difficult, if not impossible.

The principle of focusing on a narrow market segment can also be applied by carefully choosing in which *geographic* areas to compete. Entering a market where a competitor is well entrenched is like starting your boxing career by stepping into the ring with the champion: unless you have a secret weapon your career will probably be over before it has begun. We will usually be better off making our entry in an area where there is little or no competition. This may mean beginning in a sparsely populated area, for instance a large area with low population density, which larger firms have ignored while concentrating on more highly-populated urban areas.

This was Wal-Mart's initial strategy for avoiding direct competition with powerful competitors like Sears, K-Mart, and Penney's. Wal-Mart originally located all of its stores in rural areas, small towns with populations of just a few thousand, completely ignoring the larger urban areas in which established competitors were located. Within a few years Wal-Mart had established such a strong reputation for low prices and customer service that it had created a pent-up demand among potential customers in the more highly-populated urban areas. With that demand and their reputation preceding them, Wal-Mart was able to move into direct competition with its larger rivals, and soon began taking significant market share from them. Had Wal-Mart decided, instead, to enter new markets in direct competition with its well-established competitors, it may have never been able to get off the ground. And Wal-Mart didn't stop there; it reinforced its potential for success by focusing its efforts in two additional ways: 1) concentrating on discount retailing, and 2) completely avoiding vertical integration. Vertical integration (discussed in detail later in this chapter) involves taking on, within the company, additional operations that have been, or could be, done by outside contractors.

In fact, Wal-Mart's strategy seems almost the reverse of vertical integration: they focus on just one piece of the value chain: buying products from manufacturers and distributing them to stores located in areas that are convenient to customers. That's all they do, distribute products from manufacturers to customers, and they do it better than anyone else. And, confident that Wal-Mart will always have what they need at competitive prices, customers do the rest. Why do customers prefer Wal-Mart to other stores? Perhaps because of another Wal-Mart focus: Everyday low prices. Instead of pricing their products in mid-range, augmented by frequent "sales," Wal-Mart prices them as low as possible so that customers can purchase products at low prices *any time*, instead of having to choose between paying a higher price and waiting for a sale.

There are, of course, other ways of focusing our competitive efforts. But however we do it, it is important to remember the primary advantages of this strategy: avoiding direct confrontation with established competitors; focusing our competitive activities until we are in a position to expand; and limiting the exposure of new products or services until they have been proven.

Offensive Strategy

The dictionary defines *offense* as "the act of attacking or assaulting" (American Heritage Dictionary, 1983), and *offensive strategies* are just that: strategies for attacking the market; strategies for positioning the organization in the market; strategies for gaining market share. Offensive strategies can be based on the use of distinctive competencies to offer products or services that are superior to those of competitors, or products/services that are equivalent to those of competitors, but at lower prices. Or they can be directed at exploiting competitors' weaknesses, utilizing quality, service, delivery, and product performance. Whatever approach is used, the principle of offensive strategy is to be the aggressor; to keep advancing; to keep the competition trying to catch up; to keep them on the defensive.

An offensive strategy usually means going after additional market share, even if it has to be taken from competitors.

Defensive Strategy

Defend, of course, means "To protect from danger; guard." *(American Heritage Dictionary,* 1983), so it should be obvious that a *defensive strategy* is intended to protect what the organization already has. In the competitive world, this means protecting an existing market position, or a product's existing market share. Whereas an offensive strategy involves aggressively seeking more customers, defensive strategy is concerned with protecting current market share, just as aggressively. The organization may not be trying to steal customers from its competitors, but will be making it difficult for competitors to steal its customers.

An interesting strategy that is often used for defending market share is *signaling*—sending messages to competitors, through the organization's actions, that it will not stand idly by in the face of competitors' attempts to invade its markets. One way to do this is by making public statements about the organization's strong intention to maintain current market share; in effect warning the competition that the firm will defend its territory against any action that threatens current market share.

First-Mover Strategy

Although every firm strives to be competitively successful, not all of them aspire to be leaders in their markets. Some prefer, instead, to follow the leaders. And largely it's a matter

Chapter 7—Competitive Strategy

of risk; those who try to be the leaders, referred to as *first-movers*, are willing to take on more risk than those who follow, because they know that greater rewards come from being first in the market. First-movers are like pioneers: they move into uncharted territory hoping to lay first claim to the opportunities it presents. In this case, their territories are the markets they enter through the products and services they develop and introduce. The risk they assume is the uncertainty of whether there is, in fact, a market where they thought there should be, and the demand they hoped would be there. By the time they actually have a product/service to offer they may have invested a great deal of money, time and effort in research and development, and if the market doesn't develop as they had planned, their entire investment may be lost.

But when they do succeed and become the leaders in a growing market, the rewards can be immense. A first-mover's competitive advantage includes: a head start moving down the learning curve; an opportunity to set the standard for others; and a chance to build customer loyalty before other competitors get up to speed. First-movers will usually be faced with significant investments in research and development, and their success is likely to be heavily dependent on their ability to attract and retain creative people, original thinkers, and to maintain a culture that supports ongoing innovation.

First-movers are often able to solidify their competitive advantage and extend its duration by protecting their intellectual property rights, through patents, copyrights, or licensing. These are legal rights to the exclusive use of their innovations, inventions, or discoveries. In the case of a patent, this protection can last for 17 years, time enough to build an insurmountable competitive advantage.

Follower/Imitator Strategy

For every firm that decides to pursue a first-mover strategy there are usually several that choose to pursue a *follower*, or *imitator strategy*. Followers are willing to forgo first-mover advantages to avoid the risk and expense associated with such a strategy. Instead, they keep an eye on the first-movers and are quick to respond when a developing market begins to show signs of growth. The success of a follower strategy hinges on how quickly the firm can follow the leading company and introduce a product/service that is sufficiently attractive that customers will choose it instead of those of the first-mover. To follow this strategy successfully requires a technical staff that is not so much innovative as it is flexible and responsive, because the key to a successful follower strategy is the firm's ability to either copy or invent around the first-mover's design. Generally that will entail doing enough reverse-engineering to see how the design works, and then copying it. But if the first mover has a proprietary design, if it is patented or patentable, followers will have to develop designs that serve the same customer needs without violating the patent, not always an easy task. In either case, time is an important factor; the longer it takes followers to come out with comparable designs, the greater the opportunity for the first-mover to build up an insurmountable competitive advantage.

So, where first-movers must have innovative cultures, followers will need to develop cultures that are flexible and responsive; that can move quickly to develop and introduce new products while there is still growth opportunity in the market. In some ways, a follower strategy is more difficult than that of a first mover, but done well it can result in substantial market opportunity with little of the first-mover's risk. There are, in fact, numerous examples of markets in which the dominant design, the product or service that ultimately became the industry standard, was *not* the first product to market, but one of the followers. A notable example is the CAT-scan, for which an EMI scientist was awarded the Nobel Prize, but EMI was ultimately forced to withdraw and surrender the market to GE and other companies. Another is RC Cola, which was the first to market with both soda in cans and diet soda, but was unable to exploit either innovation to achieve or maintain market leadership. So, although a first-mover strategy may lead to an early competitive advantage, it carries no guarantee of maintaining market leadership. A well executed follower strategy may offer just as much, or more opportunity at less risk.

Vertical Integration

Vertical integration means taking on, within the organization, *activities* involved in developing, producing and distributing its products/services that had *previously* been *performed* by *outside* firms. *Backward* integration includes any activities involved in providing organizational inputs, such as parts fabrication, and sub-assembly work, while *forward* integration addresses output activities, such as those involved in sales, service, and distribution.

Vertical integration is generally a strategy for gaining more control over processes, and how, when, and where they are performed, frequently in response to poor, slow, or inadequate service by outside contractors. Although the failure of an outside supplier to meet a company's needs sometimes comes from poor communication, more often it is based on the supplier's ranking of the relative importance of its customers. Every firm knows who are its most important customers and makes them its top priority. Importance, in this sense, is usually measured by the monetary size of a customer's orders; the largest buyers get preferential treatment. Ultimately this determines who gets served first and who must wait, and when a supplier is pressed for time or capacity, the largest customers will always be given first priority on what they need, when they need it, while the smaller customers generally have to settle for what's left over. So the smaller your organization, the less you can depend on getting what you need, when you need it. That's why firms that are frustrated by their inability to get critical inputs when they need them are likely to consider bringing those parts of the process inside the organization, so they *can* be controlled. Although this example discusses backward vertical integration (to control inputs), the same principles apply to forward vertical integration (to control outputs).

Let's consider, for example, an organization that sells its products through independent manufacturer's representatives, as many firms do. Rather than being employed by the companies they represent, these salespeople are self-employed, and their income is based entirely on commissions they receive for the products/services they sell; the more they sell the higher their income, and if they don't sell anything they have no income. To provide some consistency in their income, they often diversify by selling products for more than one company. Like the suppliers previously mentioned, these salespeople are well aware of which products sell for the highest prices (therefore paying the largest commissions), and are likely to put forth more effort to sell them than to sell lower-priced products. In addition, they are likely to concentrate on the products that are *easiest* to sell, and neglect those that require more time and effort. So, if a company's products are being sold through independent manufacturer's representatives, or even distributors for that matter, who are not giving them the time, attention, and effort they deserve, it is likely to seriously consider forward integration, and hiring its own sales force.

Smaller firms are generally more prone to vertically integrate than large ones, because they are much more likely to be shortchanged by independent contractors. But any firm, regardless of size, may at some point face circumstances that make them feel the need to gain greater control over a portion of their transformation process. One form of vertical integration frequently used by large firms is the company-owned franchise.

McDonald's is an example of such a firm. It grows by franchising, which involves licensing independent businesspeople to use the McDonald's name, reputation, products, and processes in their own restaurants. In this sense, McDonald's and other firms that franchise are really in the business of franchising, *not* in the restaurant business. Yet, even though they would prefer to have every outlet owned and operated by an independent contractor, McDonald's actually owns and operates some company outlets, themselves, rather than franchising them to somebody else. In effect, they forward integrate into the restaurant business, to gain direct control over certain outlets. Why do they choose to own some restaurants instead of franchising them?

Most businesses depend on repeat customers for their ongoing success. Restaurants are particularly vulnerable, in the sense that customers who don't have a good experience are not likely to come back. Not only that, they are almost certain to pass their opinions on to others, so restaurant owners take great care to make sure that they do everything they can to meet customers' expectations. But large franchisers know that some of their outlets are likely to "free-ride" on the company's system. Free-riding occurs when one person, or organization, rides along on the efforts of others, without doing a fair share of the work. Large franchisers found that franchises located along busy highways, where a high percentage of customers are transient, just passing through and unlikely to ever come back, were much less likely to measure up to company standards for service, cleanliness, quality, or promptness. Unlike most franchises, which are highly dependent on repeat business, owners of highway franchises quickly realized that people will come in because of the parent company's reputation, but a bad experience won't keep them from coming back; they would probably never be back anyway. So these franchise-owners don't have as much incentive to meet customer expectations. They can do just fine by doing the minimum possible, and riding on the company's reputation.

But the parent companies soon learned that these free-riders were hurting the company's reputation and having a negative affect on the other franchisees, so they began buying back their highway franchises and having them managed by company employees. They do it to control the quality of the customer's experience. So these companies are, in effect, vertically integrating, taking on a part of the value-chain that they would prefer to have done by outside contractors (franchisees).

When/if your firm reaches a point at which you are considering vertical integration, I urge you, before you jump in, to carefully consider three concerns, one a word of caution; the other two significant drawbacks. First, and most important, there's only one reason for vertically integrating that makes good business sense: to gain or enhance a competitive advantage. It is not usually justifiable for any other reason. Consider growth, for example: vertical integration is the wrong way to grow, as the next two points demonstrate.

First, when we vertically integrate, it is usually to solve a *current* problem by gaining greater control. And, on the surface, there's nothing wrong with that; it can seem like a clever strategic decision. But we should never vertically integrate without first looking into the future, because an integration that gives us a competitive advantage *today* can easily become competitive *disadvantage* tomorrow. Vertical integration invariably requires hiring more people, to perform the activities that were formerly done by employees of other firms. Hiring people, unless they are clearly classified as "temporary," should always be considered a one-way process, because in today's legal environment it is much easier to hire employees than it is to "un-hire" them (i.e., fire them, or lay them off). In other words, we should understand that when we hire full-time people they will almost always view their jobs as a permanent. And in vertical integration we will often be adding an entire group of people, perhaps a new department, and that group or department will be seen by employees throughout the organization as a permanent addition to the firm. Once a work group or department has been created it is very difficult to justify ever disbanding it, even if it becomes a competitive disadvantage. Therefore the first serious drawback of vertical integration is that, once it's done organizations seldom have the objectivity to recognize when it becomes a disadvantage or the fortitude to undo it, to vertically de-integrate. But how does vertical integration become a disadvantage? The answer leads us to the second significant drawback.

Once vertical integration has served its initial purpose, and given us the control we need to compete effectively, the integrated process quickly becomes a relatively invisible part of operations, and is likely to remain so until the day somebody in the organization realizes that it has become a disadvantage. How could a competitive advantage suddenly become a disadvantage? Competitors' costs for a particular input or output can often be reduced significantly by purchasing from an outside contractor, one who specializes in that particular process and who, because he supplies several firms, is able to gain the economies of scale that come from producing in large quantities. This specialization can put vertically-integrated firms, which produce only in the quantities necessary to meet their own needs, at a distinct cost disadvantage. So, if you don't notice when vertical integration has become a disadvantage, or if you don't have the fortitude to discontinue it, you may let a competitive advantage erode into a competitive disadvantage. The experience of General Motors is a vivid example of vertical integration becoming a serious disadvantage.

During the early years of the automobile industry there was such a strong trend toward vertical integration that some large auto companies even had their own rubber plantations, iron ore mines, and glass companies. But that began to change during the 1970s and 80s when, faced with serious competition from overseas, manufacturers began looking to outside suppliers as a way of reducing manufacturing costs. By decreasing their dependence on vertically-integrated processes, GM's competitors found that not only could they purchase sub-assemblies at less cost, but also that supplier partnerships brought with them the advantage of supplier involvement in the design process. The result? Not just lower costs, but better designs at lower costs. Meanwhile, GM had resisted contracting out any part of its production process (due, at least in part, to the resistance of its unions), and found itself at an increasing competitive disadvantage, from two aspects: 1) its production costs remained much higher than those of competitors; and 2) in some areas (e.g., brake systems) competitors were able to offer more advanced systems than those produced by GM. Therefore, because of its high degree of vertical integration, coupled with the fact that it couldn't purchase the more advanced systems offered by outside contractors, GM found itself at such a competitive disadvantage that lost significant market share. The company paid a high price in lost market share, for allowing itself to be locked into high-cost production processes and outdated products. (GM has since spun off most of its internal suppliers into a separate organization called Delphi.)

So, before we decide to vertically integrate any process that is currently being done by outside contractors, we should make sure that we have honest answers to four questions:

- *Why* do we want to do it?
- *What kind* of competitive advantage will it provide?
- *How long* is the competitive advantage likely to last? and, most important
- What is our *exit strategy* for when it becomes a disadvantage?

Strategic Alliances

As previously mentioned, *strategic alliances* are a popular way for organizations to join forces in order to reduce the uncertainty of their external environment. Their purpose can be to develop synergies, gain economies of scale, increase their ability to influence the external environment, gain entry into new markets, or simply eliminate one competitor. Strategic alliances include acquisitions, mergers, and joint ventures.

Daft defines mergers and acquisitions this way: "An *acquisition* involves the purchase of one organization by another so that the buyer assumes control. A *merger* is the unification of two or more organizations into a single unit."(1998:100) In both cases a change in ownership is used to gain access to resources that a company needs, usually for competitive reasons.

When an organization wants to start a new business or enter a new industry it has three basic choices: internal start-up, which means building the new business from the ground up (sometimes referred to as "greenfield investment"); acquisition, which involves purchasing another company with cash or stock; or merger, which is a marriage of equals.

For the organization contemplating an internal start-up, all of the principles of strategic management as discussed throughout this book are likely to be involved, and will not be repeated here. This section concentrates, instead, on acquisitions and mergers, and why they might be preferred over starting up a whole new operation. We will also discuss joint ventures and how they differ from mergers and acquisitions.

Acquisition

The primary advantage of acquisition is time; it is usually faster to acquire another company than it is to build one from scratch. While some organizations have the time and expertise to start up a new business, for others acquisition may be a better alternative, although it involves two major risks.

First, when a firm becomes an acquisition target it is likely to hold out for the highest possible price. In fact, the firm's board of directors has a legal responsibility to get the best possible price for its stockholders. In addition, once the acquiring firm has set its collective mind on acquiring a company, it is likely to become so psychologically committed to the purchase that it ends up paying more than it had originally intended. So the first risk of acquiring another firm is overpayment; the acquiring firm invariably pays more than it should.

The second risk is one of culture. Seldom do the two principals in an acquisition have compatible cultures, and any attempt at physical integration risks demoralizing one or both workforces, often resulting in the loss of key employees. To compound matters, acquiring companies often attempt to change the culture of the acquired firm to fit their own cultures, which can easily destroy many of the qualities that made the firm valuable to the acquirer in the first place.

An example of this is what occurred after Tenneco's acquisition of Houston Oil & Minerals Corporation in 1980. Tenneco was one of the largest corporate conglomerates, with a workforce numbering more than 100,000 engaged in shipbuilding, insurance, agriculture, manufacturing, real estate, and energy. The company was highly bureaucratic, budget-driven, and reliant on paperwork; a very "mechanistic" organization.

Houston Oil was much smaller, employing 1200 people, and specialized in just one area: locating oil fields. It was very aggressive for a firm its size, and was more successful in exploratory oil drilling than Tenneco, Standard Oil, Mobil, and Conoco; the giants in the field. The way the company was run, described as "freewheeling and informal," was ideal for attracting the types of geologists who were best at finding oil. And they found lots of it; so much, in fact, that Houston's incentive plan enabled a number of employees to become millionaires. Part of the reason they were so successful was the organizational flexibility that allowed them to do what they thought necessary, make quick decisions, and take risks, all without close supervision or unnecessary bureaucracy.

In an attempt to keep Houston's most valuable people from leaving, Tenneco agreed to let the company continue to operate as an independent subsidiary, but that didn't last long. The restrictive atmosphere and slow decision-making of the parent company ultimately lead many of Houston's top explorers to leave the company. The reasons given were perhaps best summed up by one Houston executive who left to lead a much smaller oil company, saying "It's the ability to generate ideas, move fast and see an almost immediate impact on the bottom line." Ultimately, because of its inability to protect and maintain Houston's culture, Tenneco lost many of the most valuable assets of its acquisition, as well as its economic advantages.

Those same two shortcomings: paying too much, and tampering with the culture, play a major role in the estimated 90% of acquisitions that fail to live up to their original expectations. With that in mind, when considering an acquisition, you should *always* set a limit on how much you will pay for the acquisition, to guard against getting carried away in a bidding contest. Then, once you've made the acquisition, pay careful attention to the value of acquired firm's culture, and to what you might lose by trying to change it to fit the culture of the parent firm.

Merger

For all practical purposes, the only real difference between a *merger* and an acquisition is that a merger is intended as a partnership of equals. I say "intended," because a characteristic of many mergers, perhaps most, is that after the courtship is over, the partnership becomes dominated by one of the partners, a fact that might have been predicted by anyone whose objectivity wasn't clouded by overblown expectations.

Daimler-Chrysler is a good example. It didn't take long after the merger was consummated for the signs of an equal partnership to begin fading, and it soon became obvious that Daimler had, in fact, *acquired* Chrysler; not merged with it. And the way this "merger" turned out is probably more the norm for mergers, than an exception.

The lesson here is that, should your organization ever consider a merger, make sure you understand, in advance, whether your firm will be first, or second, among equals, because if business history is any guide, it isn't likely to remain an equal partnership for long.

And a final note: whereas in acquisitions there may be a choice as to whether or not the corporate entities will be physically integrated, mergers are most often predicated on some form of physical integration, at least at the top levels of the organization. And seldom is the merged firm managed jointly by two CEOs. One or the other invariably assumes full responsibility.

Joint Venture

There are two primary differences between a merger and a joint venture: 1) a joint venture does not involve exchange of ownership; and 2) a joint venture is usually much more limited in scope than a merger, and does not usually involve the entire company.

The GM-Toyota joint venture, NUUMI, in California, is an example. General Motors entered into the alliance to learn Japanese production methods, and Toyota to learn American marketing techniques, and through the relationship both companies were able to improve their competitive positions.

Any discussion of mergers and acquisitions would be incomplete without mentioning that perhaps the most frequent reason given to justify them is *diversification*.

Diversification

Diversifying, defined as "spreading out activities or investments" *(American Heritage Dictionary,* 1983), is usually undertaken to balance an organization's risk or income, or both. Diversification is, in a sense, the opposite of a focus strategy. Instead of depth, diversification seeks breadth; to keep from having the company's risk too concentrated in one area.

A classic example of diversification is the traditional "Ice and Coal" company that was such an important part of the American community in the late 19th and early 20th centuries. Originally, ice companies delivered blocks of ice, several times a week, to cool the "ice boxes" that preceded electric refrigerators in the kitchens of most homes. While business was brisk during the summer, there was little need for ice during the winter. As a result, their workers and equipment were idle during much of the winter. But there were other companies that delivered coal to these same homes, to fuel their stoves and furnaces throughout the winter. These coal companies faced the same problem as ice companies, except in a different season. Although they were busy during the winter, there was little demand for their product during the summer.

At some point somebody recognized that a coal company could, by diversifying into the ice business (or maybe it was an ice company that decided to diversify into the coal business), use the same inputs—the same delivery people and the same horse-drawn wagons (later replaced by trucks)—to achieve multiple outputs. Their drivers could deliver ice in the summer and coal in the winter, both to the same group of customers. Combining these two very cyclical, but seemingly-unrelated businesses created a single business that was not only more stable, but also could gain synergies which made much more efficient use of people, facilities and equipment; an almost ideal marriage, and a good example of economies of scope.

Diversification creates value when an organization acquires poorly-managed company and manages it more effectively; or when it transfers its existing skills or assets to another company to gain synergy, or economies of scope (Hill & Jones,1998). Synergies come from the ability to apply one firm's competencies to another firm, and economies of scope are achieved when it costs less to operate the combined organizations than it does to operate them independently. A well-known example is Philip Morris's purchases of Miller Brewing and

Kraft Foods. While, on the surface it wasn't obvious how a tobacco company could add value to either a brewer or a food company, in reality, Philip Morris's consumer-marketing ability and its expertise in brand-positioning and promotion were directly applicable to the products of both Miller and Kraft.

There are generally two classifications of diversification: related and unrelated.

Related Diversification

Related diversification is diversification into related businesses or industries, where such things as existing technologies, production processes, or brand names can be shared for competitive advantage, or to gain synergies or economies of scope.

A colorful example is J.M. Smucker's acquisition of Jif peanut butter from Procter and Gamble, an agreement in which Smucker, a leader in jams and jellies for more than a century, also became the leader in peanut butter, and doubled its sales volume in the process. As pointed out by a *Fortune* magazine article, "...what could be better than peanut butter marrying jelly!" (Oct. 29, 2001: 192)

Unrelated Diversification

Unrelated diversification occurs when one company buys another with no intention of gaining either economies of scope or operational synergies. An example is when a company sees an opportunity to take over a poorly-performing firm and manage it more effectively. Although the acquired firm may have nothing in common with its acquirer, it may be viewed as a good investment of cash reserves, but only if the acquisition adds more value than the cost of the acquisition.

Unfortunately, too often companies acquire other companies in the name of "growth," forgetting that, unless the acquisition adds value to one or both firms, it is a waste of investors' money and is likely to *reduce* the value of one or both companies.

For that reason it is wise, when considering diversification, to question our logic; to ask ourselves *why* we're doing it. We should never diversify without clearly understanding our *reasons*, and the value it will add for our company's owners.

And we should *never* acquire another company solely for the purpose of diversifying stockholders' risk. Management's job is to increase the value of stockholders' investments in this company, *not to make additional investments for them*. Stockholders can do that themselves; probably more effectively.

Divestiture

Whereas strategies to merge, acquire, or diversify generally increase the size of a company, it is sometimes necessary to do the opposite: divest parts of the company. Although the purpose of divestiture may not be to make a company smaller, that is usually its effect. Divestiture is usually a consideration when a piece of the company no longer seems to work, or fit, is no longer valuable, or when it would be more valuable as a separate entity, but it may also be done simply to raise cash or reduce debt.

Divestiture often occurs shortly after a merger or acquisition, when the combined company seeks to get rid of unrelated or unnecessary operations. It may also become necessary when an alliance fails. When that happens, it's difficult to admit that it didn't work, and that divestiture may be the best strategy. But it's always to a company's advantage when its executives have the objectivity and foresight to recognize such failures and make the hard decision, before the decision is forced on them.

PORTFOLIO STRATEGY

It is important to understand that an organization doesn't have to use the same contingent strategy for *all* of its competitive activities. A particular strategy can be applied to some products, or businesses, and not to others. In small companies with a single product line or only a few products or services, one contingent strategy may work very well across the board, but the more products a company has and the more markets it serves the more likely it is to need more than one strategy. The use of more than one strategy is sometimes referred to as a portfolio of strategies, or simply portfolio strategy.

Portfolio strategy most often applies to companies that are in multiple businesses, are in more than one market, or have a broad range of products. Portfolio strategy isn't, in itself, a competitive strategy, and won't prescribe *how* any individual business or product competes in

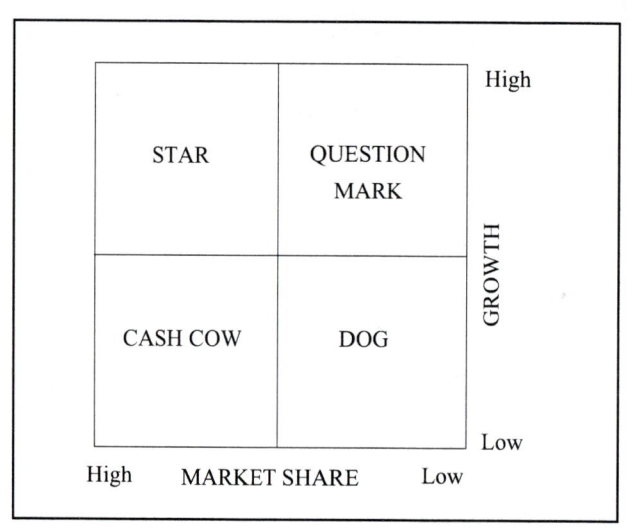

STAR	QUESTION MARK	High
CASH COW	DOG	Low
High	MARKET SHARE Low	GROWTH

Adapted from *Long Range Planning*, 1977, "strategy and the Business Portfolio," Hedley, Copyright © 1977, with permission from Elsevier Science.

Figure 11. Growth/Share Matrix

its market. It is more a corporate-level risk-management and cash-flow strategy, used to determine how to balance the company's competitive strategies (to keep from having all of its eggs in one competitive basket), and to smooth out, as much as possible, the volatility and cyclical nature of cash flow.

The Boston Consulting Group (BCG) developed what they called the Growth/Share Matrix, shown in Figure 11, which categorizes each product or service into one of four categories: *Dog*, *Question Mark*, *Star*, or *Cash Cow* (Hedley, 1977:12).

A Dog is a weak product that either loses money or is not very profitable. A Question Mark is a high-potential product that hasn't yet proven itself. A Question Mark that succeeds becomes a Star: a market leader in a high-growth market. A Question Mark that *doesn't* succeed becomes a Dog. And when a Star's market-growth slows down the Star becomes a Cash Cow: market share may no longer be increasing, but the product is still producing cash for the firm.

The BCG category definitions can be useful in determining which type of strategy is likely to be most effective for a particular product or service.

For example, any product classified as a *Dog* may not be worth the time and effort to support it and we should consider dropping it unless we feel it is necessary to round out a product portfolio, or to serve as a loss-leader. Portfolio-rounders are useful when customers prefer to buy from a competitor who has a full line of products/services, or when a product fills a gap that might serve as a point of entry for a new competitor. Loss-leaders are products or services that are priced to attract customers, with the intention that those customers will also buy other products. If we decide to keep the product alive we would likely employ a defensive strategy to protect its existing market position.

If a product is a *Question Mark* and appears to have a good chance of succeeding, we should consider promoting it aggressively, probably using some type of offensive strategy.

Stars are, by definition, market leaders in high-growth markets, and to keep them there we would probably also use an offensive strategy.

Defensive strategies, on the other hand, are likely to be most appropriate for *Cash Cows*. Even in markets that offer no opportunity for growth, Cash Cows can be milked to supply the money necessary to support the development of Question Marks and Stars. Therefore, we will generally want to protect their cash flow as long as we can. Appropriate defensive strategies might include: controlling costs through long-term contracts with suppliers; guaranteeing sales through long-term contracts with customers; or maintaining a high degree of customer loyalty through superior quality, customer service, or on-time delivery.

By managing our product or business portfolio in this manner we can maintain a continuing flow of new products/services that can, if done effectively, keep our organization in the growth stage of its life-cycle indefinitely.

CUSTOMER SERVICE

Though seldom discussed as a separate strategy, and often taken for granted, customer service can be one of the most effective, and sustainable of all competitive strategies. Research has consistently shown that companies with high customer-satisfaction consistently outperform the S&P 500, in return on investment, stock value, and consistency of cash flow. What is customer satisfaction and how is it related to customer service?

An important element of customer satisfaction is the customer's *expectations*: how well is the company meeting them, in terms of price, quality, delivery, service? Another key is how the customer feels about her *relationship* with the company: how is the company treating her? do they really care about *her*, or is she just a number?

When a customer buys a product or service, he expects to receive what he paid for, in terms of price, quality, delivery, and service, and he expects *everything* that was promised, *every* time. Unfortunately, no company has ever been able to deliver a defect-free product or service 100% of the time. That's perfection, which no company is ever likely to achieve. A very good company may come close; 99% of its products or services may completely meet customer expectations, but that still leaves 1 dissatisfied customer out of every 100. While most of us would consider 1 dissatisfied customer out of 100 pretty good, our opinion would be different if we were the one who was dissatisfied.

Now we all know what happens when a customer isn't satisfied: she tells at least a dozen other people how she feels, and some of those people are sure to pass it on to others. The satisfied customers, on the other hand, may say good things about the company, but they won't be nearly as adamant about spreading the word because, after all, the product they received was what they had *expected*, and the expected isn't really news; we're a lot more likely to talk about the unexpected—the thing that happens only one time out of 100. But there is a way to get more customers to spread *good* news about the company.

We can turn customers with problems into some of our strongest supporters, by the way we solve their problems. In fact, a company can build stronger customer loyalty by quickly and caringly solving their problems, than it could if its products never had problems. Solving customer problems is one of the best ways of building customer relationships. It is an opportunity to show them that they're not just a number, and that you care about them.

The first step in building relationships with frustrated customers is to *accept blame*. Many companies try to side-step customer problems, either by trying to convince the customer there *isn't* a problem, or by trying to make it the *customer's* problem. Companies with high customer-satisfaction have learned to accept the blame, even when it isn't the company's fault.

The second step is to *apologize*, even if you don't think it's the company's fault. Once you've done that, you have taken responsibility for the problem, which usually removes most, if not all, of the customer's frustration and antagonism.

Step three is to ask the customer *"what can we do to solve the problem?"* And then *do it*.

These three steps will almost always turn a dissatisfied customer into a strong supporter, and this customer will spread the *good news*, because being treated this way by a company is a rare exception to the norm.

But there is one element that's absolutely essential to developing an effective customer service organization, and a reputation for exceptional customer service. That's a high level of employee satisfaction, and an organizational culture that nurtures employee satisfaction. Because customer satisfaction isn't developed between a group of customers and an organization; it comes from one-on-one relationships between two individuals—one customer and one employee—and it's developed through hundreds, or thousands, of such relationships, one transaction at a time.

Great customer service comes from high levels of customer satisfaction, but high levels of customer satisfaction are only developed through relationships with satisfied employees; there is a direct, and measurable link between the two: increased employee satisfaction will invariably lead to higher customer satisfaction.

So the key to customer service, and customer satisfaction, is an organizational culture built around employee satisfaction, respect for customers, solving customers' problems, and constantly seeking answers to the question, "What can we do to keep the customers coming to us, rather than going to our competitors?"

SUMMARY

Once we have finished selecting our strategies—fundamental (i.e., low-price leadership or differentiation), contingent (e.g., focus, offensive vs. defensive, first-mover vs. follower), and, if necessary, portfolio—we have completed the *planning* part of the strategic management process. We have now determined our *mission* (purpose), what *goals* (outcomes) we need to achieve in pursuit of that mission, and what *strategies* (actions) we will take to leverage our distinctive competencies (expertise) into a sustainable *competitive advantage*. The next step is strategy *implementation*: doing what it takes to put our plan into action.

Implementation requires determining what types of resources (e.g., people, skills, capabilities, information, money, equipment) will be needed, how to organize them most effectively, and what activities, at all levels of the organization, will be required to achieve the organization's goals. So the first requirement in implementing the strategic plan is another level of planning: translating the strategy into organizational actions. The translation process involves setting goals and developing strategies for achieving them, at every level of the organization, down to and including the most important level: the individuals who will make the decisions, carry out the activities, and achieve the goals. They are the ones who will make it all happen.

The second part is making it happen. When it all comes together and works the way it should, strategic planning and strategy implementation will lead to the achievement of individual goals, which will lead to the achievement of group and department goals, and so on, until the combined efforts of everyone in the organization achieve the major organization-level goals.

It is important to understand that, in this process, the sustainable competitive advantage we are seeking will *not* come from *technology*; it will come from *people.* Although technology can be a temporary advantage, unless it is proprietary the competition will soon be utilizing the same technology, and it will no longer be an advantage for anybody. It will, instead, have become a *necessity* for everybody. Sustainable competitive advantage will more often come from the *human* side of the organization: from *innovation*, from *service*, from *leadership*, and from organizational *culture*.

Southwest Airlines is an excellent example of the advantages of a strong culture. Frequently asked why Southwest has been, for more than 20 years, the most profitable airline in the world, Herb Kelleher invariably credits its success to culture. Although other airlines can copy everything that Southwest does, none has been able to successfully duplicate its most distinctive feature: its culture.

One final, but important, comment: the strategic plan should be considered a *starting point*, rather than an end in itself. Since it is impossible, during the planning process, to anticipate every conceivable circumstance that may influence our actions, we can be sure that elements of the plan will have to change soon after we begin implementation. A large part of our experience, as individuals and organizations, comes from trial and error. We think we know how something will work, but invariably things don't happen the way we had planned. When they don't, we must quickly analyze what didn't go according to plan and revise it accordingly. Therefore, we should never consider the original plan inviolable. Instead, we should always be ready to change it, not arbitrarily, but as circumstances justify change.

Chapter 8

GLOBAL STRATEGIES

*"If we could read the secret history of our enemies,
we should find, in each man's life,
sorrow and suffering enough to disarm all hostility"*
(Henry Wadsworth Longfellow)

Firms expand into other countries for a variety of reasons, with three of the most common being: to enter new markets; to achieve lower costs; or to access natural resources.

Companies search for *new markets* when their current markets become saturated; when increased competition begins reducing revenues and profits; when domestic markets do not offer enough sales volume for economies of scale, or when they limit future growth. As long as there are untapped domestic markets, global expansion may not be necessary, but when domestic markets are exhausted, or have been exploited to the degree that future expansion is not likely to be profitable, global markets become more attractive.

The ongoing search for lower costs sometimes leads companies to manufacture in other countries, where labor costs are lower, and material and technology may also be less expensive. Sales in those same countries can also help, by increasing a company's economies of scale.

Some firms depend on other countries for access to *natural resources* that are not available domestically, not available in sufficient quantities, or not available at favorable costs. Examples are oil, gas, rubber, bauxite.

Whatever the reason for expanding globally, it is important for companies to understand that competing in other countries can be significantly different than domestic competition, and that will require a good understanding of *international market differences,* and a firm grasp of *international strategies.*

INTERNATIONAL MARKET DIFFERENCES

Basic markets differ from country to country in a number of ways, including:
- buyer needs/habits
- distribution channels
- driving forces

- competitive pressures
- environmental issues
- economic development
- political environment

Of particular importance are *exchange-rate* fluctuations, host-government *trade policies*, and manufacturing *cost variations*.

Exchange Rates

The stability of a country's currency is an important consideration in deciding which countries to enter. For U.S. companies the advantages or disadvantages of operating in another country depend on how much the value of that country's currency fluctuates with respect with the U.S. dollar. When the dollar is strong, U.S. companies can have a cost advantage, but that advantage can quickly erode when the dollar falls. In addition, the currency of some countries is much more volatile than that of others.

To hedge against exchange-rate variations, many companies actively buy and sell the currency of the countries in which they do business. Other firms prefer to accept payment only in U.S. dollars. Some countries, usually those that do not want what little currency they have taken out of the country, choose to make barter-type arrangements, and pay for goods with commodities instead of money.

However a company chooses to do business in a foreign country, it is important to realize that it is not uncommon for some currencies to fluctuate more than 20% per year which, without proper arrangements, can more than wipe out the advantages of doing business in that country.

Trade Policies

Most countries have trade policies, some of which can make doing business much more difficult for foreign firms than for its own companies. Some of the more common include: *tariffs/quotas*, *local-content* requirements, *price-regulation*, limits on *fund-withdrawal*, *local-ownership* requirements, and *capital-spending* approval.

Tariffs/Quotas

Tariffs are, in effect, taxes on imported goods, usually designed to protect local business organizations from being undercut by lower-cost foreign products or services. Tariffs are a way of raising prices on imported goods, to make them less attractive to local buyers, thus giving local suppliers a competitive advantage.

Quotas limit the quantities of foreign goods that can be imported into a country. The intent is the same as that of tariffs, but instead of raising prices of the imports, quotas limit the quantities a foreign competitor can import.

Local-Content Requirements

Countries with local-content requirements are attempting to help their local economies in two ways: by providing jobs, and by making sure that some of the money earned by foreign firms stays in the country. These policies, usually found in less-developed countries that are trying to build their economies, require foreign firms to do some of their value-adding processes within the host-country, rather than simply shipping in finished products. Some companies meet this requirement by shipping in sub-assemblies and setting up a final-assembly facility in the host-country.

Price Regulation

Regulating prices of imports is another way of accomplishing the same thing as tariffs: protecting local companies by making sure imported goods are priced high enough that they can't undercut local producers.

Withdrawal of Funds

In an effort to ensure that foreign companies don't just come in, sell products, and take money out of the country, some countries limit the amount of money that a foreign firm can take out of the country.

Local Ownership

In some countries foreign firms are prohibited from competing unless some part of the company, sometimes as much as 50%, is owned by local interests. While the intent is probably to keep opportunistic companies from preying on local patrons and businesses, many companies aren't willing to give up that much control so, in most cases, such policies severely limit the number of companies who are willing to enter the country.

Capital Spending

Some countries restrict capital-spending by foreign firms, and may have complicated approval processes that those companies must go through to obtain approval to build new facilities, or expand existing facilities.

From the foregoing examples it should be apparent that any company considering doing business in another country should give careful consideration to the many ways in which the country is likely to control or limit what foreign competitors can do.

Cost-Variations

When doing business in another country primarily to achieve lower costs, companies should be aware of some disadvantages that may offset those perceived advantages, things like *productivity*, *quality*, *inflation* rates, *energy*-availability/cost, and *taxes*.

Productivity/Quality

When entering another country for its lower labor-rates, it is important to consider not just wages, but also quality and productivity. While we are all aware that different countries have different customs and different cultures, we don't always consider how those may affect the overall cost of doing business.

Many U.S. firms, for example, set up manufacturing facilities in Mexico to take advantage of significantly lower labor rates in that country. But they soon learned that in some countries, particularly those in warmer areas, the pace of life, and work, is slower, which is often reflected in greatly-reduced productivity. In addition, quality was sometimes an issue, particularly during what often turned into a long learning-curve.

Inflation

While the economies of some countries have fairly stable inflation-rates, others are much more volatile. A high rate of inflation can quickly deplete any perceived economic advantages of doing business in such a country.

Energy-Availability

In the United States we take for granted unlimited access to low-cost energy, but in other countries access may be limited, costs significantly higher, and reliability of service erratic. Therefore, if the availability of energy is essential to a company's operation, that should be a primary consideration in its choice of overseas markets.

Taxes

Another consideration in choosing international markets should be the host-country's tax policy, particularly on foreign firms, or on imported products. The rate at which a company's products are taxed can easily make the difference between profit and loss.

INTERNATIONAL STRATEGIES

Although there are many possible ways of competing globally, most of them fall in one of five categories: *licensing, export, multi-national, global,* and *strategic alliances.*

Licensing

A low-risk strategy for a company entering a foreign market is to license a host-country firm to use its processes or technology, produce its products, or offer its services. The key to licensing is a proprietary product, process, technology, or service, to which other firms have no access except through the firm that owns it. Typically, the foreign company will pay the entering firm for the licensing right, and may additionally pay a royalty on each product produced or on each use of the process, technology, or service.

Licensing may be a good strategy when a firm has either valuable technical know-how or a patent-protected product or service, but does not have the capability, resources, or desire to compete in other countries.

Some advantages of licensing are additional income, access to new markets without significant investment, and/or broader exposure, which may lead to additional opportunities.

Export

Export, in which a firm manufactures in its home country and exports its products to foreign markets, is perhaps the most widely-used international strategy. It requires little or no capital investment, only moderate risk, and offers the opportunity to increase a company's economies of scale.

The most common approaches to export are through:

- foreign distributors, who buy (take title to) the product,
- then re-sell it to end-users;
- foreign sales firms, which sell the product for the manufacturer;
- company-owned sales offices in foreign countries.

Export is a low-risk strategy for testing foreign markets, or for growing international sales. However, a company should be aware that domestic products may have to be adapted to suit local market differences. Differences may require only simple accommodations, like providing instruction manuals in different languages, but they may be as complex as re-designing products or services to suit different needs or uses.

Another consideration, should a firm choose to open company-owned facilities in foreign countries, should be those countries' labor laws. For example, whereas your company's vacation policy may be two weeks vacation after two years of service, three weeks after ten years, and so on, some European countries require a brand-new hire be allowed five weeks of vacation from his/her first day of employment. Needless to say, such policies can dramatically increase a company's cost of sales.

Multi-National

Sometimes called "multi-country," a multi-national strategy is a portfolio of strategies, in which a firm's international strategy is a collection of strategies; possibly a different strategy for each country. A firm may choose to license in some countries, export to others, and manufacture in others. And its fundamental and contingent strategies may be different in different countries (e.g., differentiation in some and low-cost leadership in others.)

Essentially, a multi-national strategy is developed on a country-by-country basis, to respond to host-country trade policies, market differences, buyer needs, and competitive conditions. A company's strategic moves in one country are independent of its strategies in other countries. Multi-national strategy is often used when diverse national markets do not allow the economies of scale that might be available if the same product was appropriate for every country.

Multi-national strategy's primary disadvantage is that with little coordination or commonality across markets, it gives a company little or no *global* advantage. However it may be seen as a necessary step toward a global strategy.

Global

When a company's strategy is essentially the same for all countries it is a global strategy. It requires integrating and coordinating the company's strategic moves on a world-wide basis, and is generally based on selling only in countries that have significant markets and buyer demand.

Unlike a multi-national strategy, a true global strategy allows a firm's competitive position in one country to strongly affect (and be affected by) its position in other countries. This helps it gain a sustainable competitive advantage over its rivals - both international and domestic.

There are three primary ways of gaining competitive advantage through a global strategy:

- *location* of activities
- *coordination* of activities
- *cross-subsidization*

Location

A company gains competitive advantage from locating various activities (e.g., R&D, manufacturing, assembly, distribution, sales) in the countries where they can be done most

Chapter 8—Global Strategies

efficiently or effectively. Before deciding on locations, the company should answer two important questions for each activity:

- Should it be located in just *one* country, or in several?
- In *which country* or countries, should it be located?

The choice of one or more locations will be influenced by the answers to three additional questions:

- How critical are *economies of scale?*
- How steep is the *learning curve?*
- How significant is the *cost advantage* to being in just one location?

Dispersing an activity to several countries may be more advantageous:

- For buyer-related activities (e.g., sales, advertising, service).
- When transportation costs are high.
- When trade barriers are high.
- To hedge against exchange-rate fluctuations.
- To avoid supply interruptions.
- To protect against adverse political developments.

Except for those reasons, most operations can be de-coupled from buyer locations, and performed wherever the best cost advantage lies.

Co-ordination

A sustainable competitive advantage can sometimes be gained by coordinating activities across different countries:

- The know-how gained in one country can often be transferred to other countries.
- Brand-recognition can be enhanced.
- The firm can choose where and how to challenge competitors.
- Production can be shifted from country to country:
  o To take advantage of exchange-rate fluctuations,
  o To leverage host-country governments,
  o To respond to changing wage rates, energy costs, trade restrictions.

Cross-Subsidization

One advantage of cross-subsidization is to use profits from other markets:

- To support a competitive offensive against key rivals.
- To gain penetration in a critical market.

A global competitor who is able to cross-subsidize can also gain market share from domestic competitors, by:

- Underpricing the competition.
- Building market strength.
- Covering losses with profits from other markets.

For these reasons, domestic-only companies in global industries may be living on borrowed time, and their only defense may be:

- Government protection, in the short term,
- Strategic alliances or global strategies in the long term.

Strategic Alliances

A strategic alliance is a cooperative agreement between two firms, for:

- Joint research.
- Technology-sharing.
- Joint use of production facilities.
- Cross-marketing of products.

Strategic alliances are a way for firms in different countries to compete globally, while remaining independent which, in many cases, is preferable to mergers or acquisitions.

It is a good strategy for:

- Gaining economies of scale, in manufacturing or marketing.
- Filling gaps in technology, manufacturing, expertise, products, know-how.
- Gaining access to new markets.

The primary advantages of strategic alliances are:

- Economies of scale from combined volumes, which reduces costs.
- The opportunity to learn.
- Reduced competition between rivals.

Their major disadvantages are:

- Cultural barriers.
- Language barriers.
- Suspicion/mistrust – among managers
- Difficulty coordinating:
  - Different companies.
  - Different motives.
  - Different objectives.
- Danger of becoming dependent on another company's expertise/capabilities.

Strategic alliances may be best utilized as a transitional strategy, to offset temporary competitive disadvantages in international markets. Ultimately, every firm must either:

- Develop its own capabilities, or
- Merge with another firm that has those capabilities, or
- Not attempt to compete in international markets.

SUMMARY

Companies consider global expansion for a variety of reasons, and their decisions about why, when, where, and how can have major impacts on their future success. Therefore each of those four questions—Why? When? Where? and How?—must be given careful and thoughtful consideration before taking the first step.

Tempting as the potential of operating globally may be, it is important to understand that expansion into other countries will always be more complex and difficult than expanding domestically, and the grass on the other side of the fence will seldom be as green or lush as it looks from this side.

While there's no reason a company can't be a global player, it's important to be realistic about what it hopes to accomplish, and even more so about the tradeoffs it will have to make to get there. So make sure you question your own motives, by first understanding *why* you want to do it, and making sure there's a good, solid *business* reason.

PART II
PEOPLE

People are the most important consideration in strategic management. Understanding how they think, what they desire, what they fear, what inspires them, and how they are different is essential to the success of any organization. Without that understanding, we will never be able to attract, retain and inspire those who have the knowledge, skills, and abilities that any organization must have for sustainable success.

The chapters in this section focus on how *people,* and the way they are treated and managed, affect the success or failure of the strategic *implementation* process—the process of converting the strategic plan into action.

Chapter 9

Organizational Culture

*"... a strong culture has almost always been the driving force
behind continuing success in American business."*
(Deal & Kennedy, 1982:5)

People are an organization's most valuable resource, so they should be its primary consideration. Organizations are created *by* people and *for* people, and people will determine the success or failure of their organizations. Which people are most important, employees or customers, has been an ongoing discussion in organizations for years. Salespeople, on one hand, argue that without customers there would be no revenue from which to pay employees, or to reward investors. On the other hand, human resources people insist that without the capabilities and efforts of its employees, the organization will have no customers. Of course both views are right; both customers and employees are absolutely essential to the organization. In fact, Peter Drucker declares that people, not money, raw materials, or technology, are the key to developing the entire economy. But we will focus primarily on the people who are *inside* the organization, the employees, and the role they fulfill in making the organization successful.

Employees make up the culture of an organization, and the culture, in turn, plays a major role in what the organization does and how it does it. Culture is defined as "The arts, beliefs, customs, institutions, and all other products of human work and thought created by a people or group at a particular time." *(American Heritage Dictionary,* 1983) Although that definition is precise and specific, for our purposes culture can be defined more simply, as a set of shared values that influences behavior within the organization. This is more in line with descriptions of culture like "The way we do things around here." (Bower,1996:41), and "What people do when no one is telling them what to do." (Colvin,1997:300). No matter how we define it, culture can have a powerful influence on the decisions and actions of an organization.

An organization's culture is usually developed in one of two ways: the firm can deliberately develop a particular culture, or it can do nothing, and let the culture develop on its own. When an organization has no preference for a particular culture it may be because management doesn't feel that culture is important and, if that's the case, it's likely because management doesn't understand how much its culture can influence the organization. Whatever the reason, when there is no conscious effort to develop a culture one will evolve on its own, and when it does it will usually grow following the path of least resistance; going in whichever direction is easiest; doing whatever is most popular. And when a culture develops on its own, without strong guiding principles, the organization's decisions will more likely be based on doing things the easiest way (i.e., "going with the flow"), rather than the "right" way. Unfortunately, making the "right" (i.e., morally right) decisions quite often requires taking the more difficult path, so a "default" culture (i.e., one that developed on its own) is much less likely to make the hard decisions; much more likely to take the easy way out.

For example, in some competitive arenas paying bribes to influence customers is an accepted, even expected, practice. Despite the fact that it is illegal for members of U.S.-based firms to engage in such activities, the unwritten, but clearly understood, philosophy of many competitors is "do whatever we have to (i.e., do what everyone else does) or we'll be at a competitive disadvantage." Perhaps this is because that approach seems quicker and easier than trying to develop a competitive advantage based on significantly better products or services. This type of philosophy is much more likely to prevail in a weak, or undefined, culture than in one that has been deliberately developed and nurtured.

SOCIAL RESPONSIBILITY

Every organization should let a fundamental philosophy of social responsibility guide its decisions and actions. Social responsibility can be defined as the responsibility of an organization (including its leaders and members) to everyone who is, or will be affected by its decisions and actions. This means a responsibility to all of the organization's stakeholders to assure that the decisions and actions of the organization are guided by *moral* principles and actions; *not* by convenience, opportunism, or self-interest.

It should go without saying that every *individual*, whether within or outside an organization, also has a responsibility to those affected by his or her individual decisions and actions. This responsibility is generally referred to as *ethics*, defined as "... rules or standards governing the conduct of...members..." *(The American Heritage Dictionary*, 1983). The cornerstones of individual ethics and organizational social responsibility are essentially the same: recognizing and respecting the rights of others, and accepting responsibility and accountability for our own actions. It sounds so simple and, in principle, it is. But not so simple in practice. Why? It has to do with values.

VALUES

One of our definitions of culture referred to "shared values," a concept that is central to the importance of culture. Value is defined as "A principle, standard, or quality considered inherently worthwhile or desirable." *(American Heritage Dictionary,* 1983), or "...an enduring belief that a specific mode of conduct ... is preferable to an opposite... mode of conduct ...." (Rokeach, 1973:5) We, as individuals, have different sets of values that influence our behaviors. Some of us have very intensely-held values that strongly influence our decisions and actions, while others are less firmly committed to any particular ideas or principles and may be influenced more by circumstances than by any guiding values of their own. Those with strong values know who they are, what they believe in, and where they're going, while those without a clear sense of values tend to be influenced by the philosophies of those around them, philosophies like the popular "if it feels good, do it". Stated another way, those with strong values have internal direction, while those without them tend to be more influenced by external sources. This distinction is similar to the concept of *locus of control*, which suggests that people who feel they can influence outcomes by their own efforts have an *internal* locus of control, while those who feel outcomes are outside of their control have an *external* locus of control.

We will find, in every organization, people of both types. And if the organization makes no attempt to define, develop, or nurture any particular culture, it is likely that the evolving culture will be dominated by those with the most strongly-held values, those with the strongest drive to achieve their individual goals, those who are strongest-willed, or simply those who are the most vocal. In this type of culture, those without firm convictions or values are likely to follow whoever is best able to influence them, and the values of those with the strongest convictions become the organization's "shared values." Unfortunately, the culture that results may misappropriate significant organizational resources trying to achieve its own objectives, which may not be in the best interests of the organization as a whole.

But the organization that decides to develop the type of culture that will best serve its mission will begin by clearly defining the guiding values that will shape that culture. Whatever those values are, they will become the principles that govern behavior throughout the organization; the values that will be shared by all organizational members. It helps if values are reinforced with incentives that reward people who support the values and culture that the organization is trying to establish and maintain. For those employees *without* a strong sense of their own values, the organizational values will offer clear guidance for their individual behavior, and they will be less likely to be influenced by any values, decisions, or actions that are not consistent with those of the organization. On the other hand, those employees who *have* a strong sense of values will need to come to terms with the organizational values. If some organizational values are in conflict with their own individual values, they will have to decide if they can live within the organizational value system while at work. If not, they may have to leave the organization. In any case, a strong set of organizational values will send the message "here's the behavior we expect of everyone, and if you can't or won't play according to these rules, there's no place for you in this culture."

Values give *meaning* to what we do, influence our attitudes, shape our behavior, and have an important role in an organization's strategy. Just how important? Charles Handy says, "...what enables a corporation to succeed in the longer term is a wish for immortality, or at least a long life; a consistent set of values based on an awareness of the organization's own identity; a willingness to change; and a passionate concern for developing the capacity and self-confidence of its core inhabitants, whom the company values more than its physical assets." (1997:8) This is a good description of how a company becomes an institution; something that only happens through the kind of visionary leadership that understands the value and strengths of a positive culture.

Values, along with the organization's history and experience, define the organization's culture. Culture, in turn, generates a commitment among the organization's members to beliefs and values that are larger than their own. Culture influences how organizational members operate: how they process information, make decisions, and interpret and manage the organization's external environment.

A primary consideration in determining the right culture for an organization is that the culture must support the strategy. Let's use, for example, an electric utility company that has, throughout its entire history, operated under government regulation but which is now facing de-regulation. In its regulated environment the company has been able to operate as a monopoly, providing electricity for a defined group of customers for whom there are no other providers; no other companies offering a competitive service. Now the company faces a de-regulated market, in which other companies will be competing in its market; competing for the same customers. With this scenario as a background, let's try to picture the company culture, as it is now, and as it will need to be in the future.

As it stands, the company operates in a *protected* environment; an environment in which it is insulated from the outside world. Although it faces many of the uncertainties presented by the external environment, a major force is absent: competition. Using the 5 Forces framework as a guide, let's examine what it means to "compete" when there is no competition.

The most powerful of the five forces is *rivalry* but, in a monopoly there is no rivalry, so there is no concern about market share; the monopolistic firm has it all. With its market share guaranteed, the company has no need to develop or maintain a distinctive competence, because its customers have no other choice; they either buy from this company or do without.

Next is *entry threat*. As in rivalry, there is no threat of entry, since a regulated industry prohibits other firms from enter its territory.

Then there's *buyer power*. Since the company is the only source of supply for customers in its territory, those customers who want electricity have no choice but to buy it here, so they have no buyer power.

So only two of the five forces are likely to be of concern to a monopolist: *supplier power* and *substitutes*. But the absence of rivalry, entry threat, and buyer power means the company can operate pretty much the same way year after year. It doesn't have to concern itself with cutting costs or with providing better products or customer service. Perhaps most important, this company doesn't have to worry about profits. The law allows it to set its prices based largely on maintaining a set margin of profit over and above its operating costs.

So, in its current situation, this company has little incentive to improve its products, services, or processes. Therefore, its culture is likely to be passive, set in its ways ("if it ain't broke, don't fix it"), complacent, not very innovative, and not very concerned about what other companies in its industry are doing. That's in a non-competitive industry; but it doesn't take much foresight to see that a company with this culture couldn't be successful in a *competitive* environment.

It would require an entirely *different* culture for the firm to survive in competition, because the current culture would make it easy prey for aggressive competitors. In a competitive environment the company *must* have a competitive strategy, and it will have to be based either on being able to price its products/services lower than the competition, or on differentiating itself by offering higher quality, increased reliability, improved service, or something else that the customer will prefer over the offerings of the competition. Either of those strategies will require some combination of increased innovation, lower costs, better customer service, better equipment, and a greater concern for public relations. In short, this company must have a more dynamic culture to survive; one that complements its competitive strategies.

Developing the right culture takes a concentrated effort, and maintaining it requires a long-term commitment. Nurturing culture involves, first, an employee-selection process that assures that new employees have not only the skills and capabilities needed, but also personal values that are not in conflict with those of the organization. Proper selection helps assure that the organization's values will be shared and actively supported by all members of the organization. Once employees have been selected, gaining their commitment to the organization, its mission, and its goals becomes paramount. But the payoff can be what Thompson and Strickland call "a spirit of high performance":

"Companies with a spirit of high performance typically are intensely people-oriented, and they reinforce their concern for individual employees on every conceivable occasion in every conceivable way. They treat employees with dignity and respect, train each employee thoroughly, encourage employees to use their own initiative and creativity in performing their work, set reasonable and clear performance expectations, use the full range of rewards and punishment to enforce high-performance standards, hold managers at every level responsible for developing the people who report to them, and grant employees enough autonomy to stand out, excel, and contribute. To create a results-oriented culture, a company must make champions out of the people who turn in winning performances." (1998:346)

SUMMARY

An organization's culture has great potential to influence its success or failure. A culture *will* develop whether or not the organization wants one but any culture that is allowed to evolve on its own is much less likely to be an asset to the organization than one that has been consciously developed. In fact, a self-evolving culture is more likely to be a liability than an asset.

Our organization's culture should be based on the set of values that we feel will best guide the kind of behavior we want in the organization. When developed in this manner, the culture can have a powerful influence on desirable behavior and be a strong deterrent to improper or unacceptable behavior. Our culture, in effect, defines our attitude, and it constantly reminds each of us of the organization's values, beliefs and responsibilities, as well as our own.

We build positive cultures on values such as honesty, integrity, loyalty and trust, to name just a few. We nurture and maintain culture through our hiring practices, reward and incentive programs, day-to-day communication, and ongoing orientation and training. But perhaps the most powerful influence on an organization's culture is the example set by the top management team. In this sense, what they *do* and *how* they do it send a much clearer message of their values and beliefs than anything they could possibly say. Or, as Emerson put it, "What you *are* stands over you the while, and thunders so that I cannot hear what you *say* to the contrary." [italics added]

As our organizations become more dependent on knowledge and less on manual labor, the people we hire will expect more flexibility in how, where, and when they do their jobs. That will mean they will not be easily monitored or controlled. These will be much more "organic" organizations, in which outcomes will be predictable, but the processes through which they are achieved may not be. When we can't directly control people, or what they're doing, we have to depend on other ways of making sure they don't go beyond certain boundaries. A strong culture provides well-defined boundaries for even the most chaotic process. And there are no better boundaries than the values, beliefs, and understood practices of a strong culture.

In their book *Organizing Genius: The Secrets of Creative Collaboration* (1997) Bennis and Biederman analyze seven organizations, which they call "great groups," that provide vivid examples of the power of culture. They suggest that the successes of Walt Disney Studio, Xerox Palo Alto Research Center (PARC), Apple Computer, the 1992 Clinton Presidential Campaign, Lockheed's Skunkworks, Black Mountain College, and the Manhattan Project, were based, at least in part, on common characteristics, including:

- they were filled with gifted people—people who *wanted* to be working on the project (more than anything else in the world)
- they were made up of sometimes delusional optimists
- they believed their group was in a mortal struggle with a powerful enemy
- they believed their group was on a mission from God

In introducing the book, Charles Handy declares "There are groups, and there are Great Groups. To turn the first into the second must be every leader's dream." (1997:xi)

The type of culture that makes a group a Great Group is unlikely to evolve on its own. Every Great Group was the result of a visionary leader—someone who knew exactly what he wanted to accomplish, then created the team and the culture that would make it happen.

Chapter 10

INCENTIVES AND REWARDS

*"Good and evil, reward and punishment,
are the only motives to a rational creature;
these are the spur and reins
whereby all mankind are set on work, and guided."*
(John Locke)

*"The only happy people I know
are the ones who are working well
at something they consider important."*
(Abraham Maslow, 1998:9)

Incentives and rewards are the keys to gaining commitment from employees at all levels. The most effective incentives are those that offer each of us the opportunity to meet our most important needs, or to achieve our greatest desires. So when we are able to show people how, by achieving the organization's goals, they can achieve their own goals, their work takes on greater meaning and they become more committed to their work. But before we can design effective incentive and reward systems we must first understand the relationship between incentives and rewards.

An incentive is defined as "Something inciting.... action or effort." *(American Heritage Dictionary,* 1983). In other words, an incentive is something that *motivates*; makes us *want* to do something. Of course, there are many ways to incent someone, but most generally we think in terms of *positive* and *negative* incentives, or *reward* and *punishment*. A reward is defined as "Something, such as money, that is given... for some special service,..."; and punishment as "A penalty imposed for wrongdoing." *(American Heritage Dictionary,* 1983). Our incentive becomes obtaining the reward, which must therefore be something desirable, or avoiding the punishment, which must be something threatening enough to make us want to avoid it at all costs. Although *rewards* have proven both effective and appropriate for honoring individual performance, *punishment* is *not* always the most effective way to deal with underperformance.

It is true for most of us that, when we under-perform in our jobs, we do not do so deliberately nor willfully, but for any of a number of reasons, many of which may be beyond our control. For example, we may fail because we lack the proper training, or do not have the right equipment, or because the outcomes that were expected of us were not clearly explained, or because we did not have enough time, or because we were held accountable for something over which we did not have control, or because we were expected to do a job for which we were either not suited or not qualified, or for any of a variety of personal reasons. But, whatever the reason for below-par performance, we must remember that most people *want* to do a good job; they *want* to succeed and when they don't it may not be *their* fault. And when it isn't their fault, *punishment* is *not* the right response.

Although we *should* reward those who accomplish objectives, we should *not* punish those who fail. Instead, we should *withhold* rewards from underperformers until we can find the cause of their failure and remedy it, and put them on the path to success. So we should structure our reward programs to do two things: 1) reward *only* those who *achieve* their *objectives*; and 2) *withhold* rewards from those who *don't* achieve their objectives, but help them improve their performance so they *can* be rewarded. In this way, those who perform well are rewarded accordingly, and those who fail are but given assistance in finding the reasons for their failure and correcting them.

It is also important to know that reward programs that work well are always those that make sure that rewards are given only *after* objectives have been achieved; not before or during the process. Otherwise the reward has little value as an incentive

INCENTIVES

While any discussion of rewards is likely to be centered on monetary rewards, many of the most powerful incentives are *non-monetary*. For that reason, providing effective incentives requires an understanding of what motivates people; what makes us *want* to do something. For the most part, motivation is self-induced. Whereas we may be able to *force* someone to do something, we can't necessarily force them to *want* to do it. In other words, *we can't motivate someone else*; they have to motivate themselves. *Wanting* to do something is internal; it comes from our own desire to do it, either because it allows us to gain something of value or because it helps us avoid something undesirable. So, although we can't force someone else to do something, we can offer an incentive that will make them *want* to do it; something that will make them motivate themselves. The key to effective incentives is knowing *what* will be desirable (i.e., be an incentive) to a particular person. But how can we know what another person *needs* or *wants*? How can we learn the desires of someone else? One way is to use Maslow's well-known Hierarchy of Needs (1998:xx).

Araham Maslow, a pioneering researcher in human behavior, identified 5 sets of basic needs that motivate the behavior of individuals. Shown in Figure 12, they are, in ascending order: physiological, safety, love, esteem, and self-actualization.

Needs are hierarchical in the sense that our most basic needs will monopolize our thoughts and actions until they have been satisfied and, until they are, we will concentrate on those needs, and only those. Once those needs have been satisfied our primary needs become those on the next higher level, and so on.

Chapter 10—Incentives and Rewards

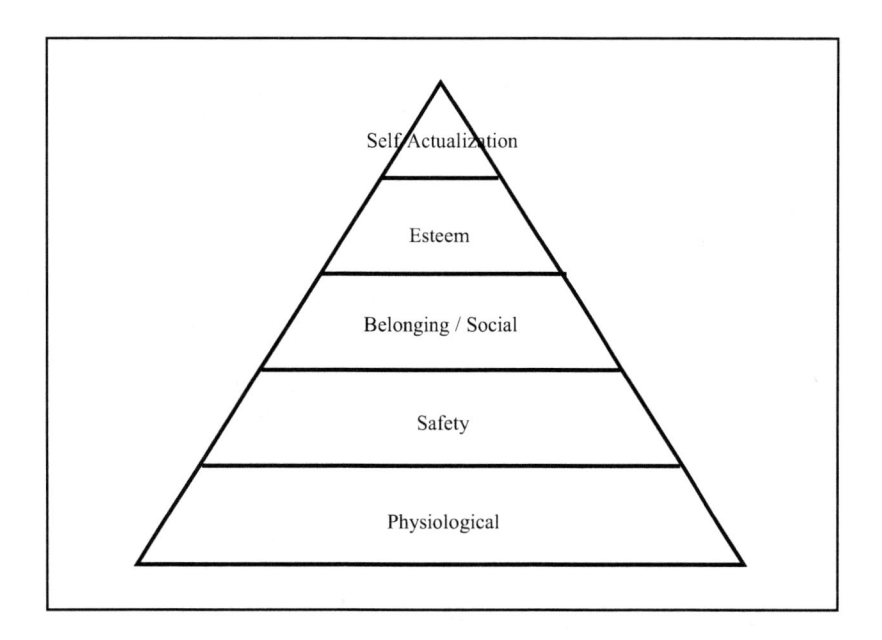

```
              /\
             /  \
            / Self \
           /Actualiz.\
          /-----------\
         /   Esteem    \
        /---------------\
       / Belonging/Social \
      /-------------------\
     /       Safety         \
    /-----------------------\
   /      Physiological       \
  /_____\
```

Adapted from *Maslow on Management*, Maslow, Copyright © 1998 by Ann R Kaplan. Reprinted by permission of John Wiley & Sons, Inc.

Figure 12. Maslow's Hierarchy of Needs

Physiological needs include our needs for food, water, and procreation, and until they have been met, they will be just about all we think about and work toward. But once they have been satisfied a new set of needs takes precedence, our safety needs.

Safety needs include, for example, protection from the elements, from our enemies, and from illness, accidents, and disease, and as long as we have concerns about our safety or that of our family we are unlikely to be motivated by anything else. However, once our safety needs have been satisfied, the next level beckons: love.

Love needs include love, affection, and the need to belong. Until these needs have been met, we are likely to be obsessed with finding a mate, having children, and establishing friendships, but once they have been satisfied our greatest need is likely to be for self-esteem.

Esteem needs include feeling good about ourselves, having self-respect and self-esteem, and being respected and appreciated by others. Once esteem needs have been satisfied there is our highest-level need: self-actualization.

Self-actualization is our need for self-fulfillment, to realize our potential, to make a contribution to the greater good, to make a difference, to have made a difference with our lives. As you might imagine, this is the most individual of all needs, and often the most powerful.

Whatever the level, needs vary significantly from one person to another and this is a key to effective incentive programs; they recognize the *differences* in individual needs. They recognize that motivates one person will not necessarily inspire another.

Most organizations are made up of people from all walks of life: people of different ages, backgrounds, experiences, interests, and capabilities. As a result, the people in any organization have a broad range of needs. There may be some who are still at the *physiological* level, struggling just to survive and keep food on the table. Others, just starting out on their own, may be at the *safety* level of Maslow's hierarchy, with primary needs including a home, job security, and insurance to protect them in case of illness, death, accident, or fire. Some will be at the *love* level, depending on the social aspect of organizational life to help them make friends and perhaps even meet a future mate. In many organizations a majority of people are likely to be at the *esteem* level, where the most important needs they have are for recognition, appreciation, and to feel as though they are valuable to the organization. Finally, there will be, in any organization, at least a few who are seeking *self-actualization*, the opportunity to feel as though they've accomplished something worthwhile with their lives. So, what does all of this mean to us, as far as rewards and incentives are concerned? Can we possibly satisfy so many different sets of needs?

Yes we can, but first we must *understand* the current needs and wants of everyone in the organization; not just as groups but as individuals. Then we must determine how we can offer each person the opportunity to meet his or her particular needs; achieve his/her individual goals. It should be apparent from looking at Maslow's hierarchy that only the first two levels of needs are likely to be satisfied by *monetary* rewards: physiological, and safety needs.

This means that, for those whose needs are on one of the top three levels (which is likely to include the majority of employees,) other types of rewards are likely to provide more powerful incentives than money. For those people, recognition and appreciation for their efforts, and feeling important to the success of the organization, will be some of the most effective incentives, a fact reinforced by periodic surveys asking workers what factors are most important to their job satisfaction.

Year after year three factors consistently rank among the top five responses: recognition, appreciation, and feeling important to the organization. In these same surveys, money seldom ranks higher than 5th, clearly demonstrating that the most powerful incentives don't have to cost a lot of money. Something as simple as a brief, hand-written note of appreciation from the boss can have a surprising effect on the morale, commitment, and loyalty of an employee.

REWARDS

Incentives and rewards should be highly visible. The more visible they are, the more effective they are, which means that every time we reward a person it should be done in a manner that catches the attention of as many co-workers as possible. When we praise or recognize someone, we should always do it as publicly as possible. Promotions and bonuses are opportunities to publicize the fact that superior performance is rewarded. And most important, we must make it clear and visible to everyone that different levels of performance bring different levels of rewards, beginning with wages. To make this happen, we must have clear performance standards for every job in the organization, and make sure that the superior performers

Chapter 10—Incentives and Rewards

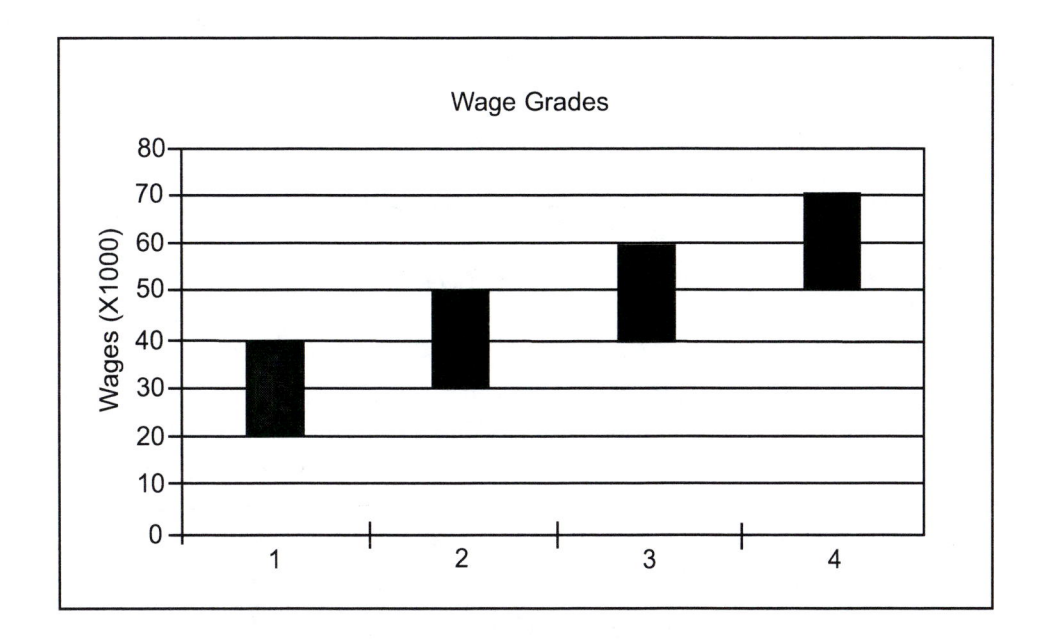

Figure 13. Wages

in every job are paid more than the average performers, and that below-average performers are paid less. These wage differences should be substantial, so that differences in performance *mean* something and the incentive for improved performance is appealing.

We can begin by making sure that wages, for every job in the organization, are competitive with those of other organizations who hire people with similar skills. That requires knowing the market value of every job in the organization, then basing our wage scales on those market values. Every job can then be placed into the appropriate wage grade based on its value relative to other jobs in the organization. Each wage grade can then be assigned a *range* of wages, to allow for differences in performance among different people within the range. See Figure 13.

In a wage program that is administered effectively (i.e., fairly and objectively), the wages of the below-average performers in any wage grade should be in the lower portion of the grade (e.g., the bottom quarter), the good performers in the middle half, and only superior performers would earn wages in the upper 1/4 of the range. In this type of program only two factors determine a person's wage: the market value of his/her skills, and how effectively he/she performs with those skills. For example, in Figure 13, those in Wage Grade 1 whose performance is below average would be paid between $20,000 and $25,000, but could never earn more than $25,000 until their performance improved. Good performers would earn between $25,000 and $35,000, but only superior performers would earn more than $35,000, and could go as high as $40,000.

So when we consider only market value and individual performance, cost-of-living allowances become unnecessary, as any increase in the cost of living will be reflected in the changing market value of a job. Also unnecessary will be increases for seniority or length of service. A person's length of service adds value to the organization's productivity only as long as his/her performance is improving (i.e., as long as a person is on the learning curve, or is finding more effective ways of doing the job), and will be rewarded by performance-based wage increases.

A final note regarding wages: in the most effective pay-for-performance wage programs, individual wages are *not* kept secret; every person's wage is published, so everyone knows what everyone else makes. This openness has several advantages. First, it eliminates salary speculation from the organization's rumor mill. This is important because such speculation is often totally off-base and inaccurate. Second, it forces managers to be fair in giving wage increases, because with differences in wages visible to everyone, every manager must have a sound, logically-justifiable reason for each wage increase. Third, seeing the higher wages of superior performers can be an incentive for lower performers; an example of the rewards for improved performance. Finally, having their wages visible to everyone else serves as another form of reward for the superior performers; public recognition of their excellence.

Although pay for performance is an individual incentive, and an important one, it should *not* be a person's *only* incentive. In fact, individual incentives can be counter-productive to the organization, particularly if they are administered in a way that promotes competition among employees. Such competition can be avoided by doing two very important things:

1. measuring individual performance by comparing it against *performance standards*, *not* by comparing one person's performance with another's.
2. providing *group* or *organizational incentives*, in addition to pay-for-performance incentives.

When individual performance is gauged by measuring one person's performance against his co-workers, the workplace can become a competitive arena in which the primary objective of every person is to out-shine everyone else. In such an environment, cooperation becomes a rarity. After all, why should I help someone else improve their performance? The worse their performance, the better mine looks by comparison. In fact, some companies have taken this kind of competition to the extreme of requiring managers to force-rank their employees then, in some cases, go so far as laying off the bottom-performing 10%.

The effect of this type of incentive is similar to the plight of two men hiking in the woods who are surprised by a bear. One quickly stops and puts on his running shoes. When his partner asks, "Why are you doing that? You know you can't outrun a bear," the other responds, "I don't have to. I only have to outrun you."

In a forced-ranking performance system, it is likely that most people are concentrating less on working toward the company's goals than they are on out-running their fellow employees. And, some may even go so far as to undercut their peers, to keep them performing at a lower level. What can we do to avoid this kind of counter-productive performance-measurement?

An effective way is to focus on measuring each person's performance against pre-set standards, rather than against co-workers. This type of measuring system not only avoids pitting one person against another, but gives everyone the opportunity to be a top level performer, and encourages them to do so. In fact, coupled with organization-level incentives that encourage people to work more productively, this method can encourage people to *help* one another achieve higher level individual performance. For these reasons, we should design both individual and organizational incentives so they work together to encourage the kind of performance and cooperation that leads to success for both the individual and the organization.

EMPLOYEE SATISFACTION

Maslow's final research on self-actualization gives us another perspective on non-monetary incentives, when he tells us, "In general, we may say that management theory can stress roughly two products, two consequences: one is the economic productivity, the quality of products, profit making, etc.; the other is the human products, that is, the psychological health of the workers, their movement toward self-actualization, their increase in safety, belongingness, loyalty, ability to love, self-respect, etc." (1998:98)

This, of course, reinforces the idea that an organization does more than just produce products or provide services. It also plays a major part in the overall satisfaction (or dissatisfaction) of its employees, not only at work but also outside the workplace. And paying attention to the well-being of its employees is not inconsistent with an organization's "economic" side, but actually enhances it. Research has shown a strong positive correlation between employee satisfaction and customer satisfaction, and a similar correlation between customer satisfaction and corporate sales. In other words, employee satisfaction has a direct bearing on the overall success of the organization.

Since employee satisfaction is so important, organizations need to understand where it comes from, and how to develop it; they need to know the most effective drivers of employee satisfaction.

At one time money was the most frequent reason given when a person left one company for another, but that's no longer the case. Today, the leading reason is for better career opportunities. That means that, although recognition, appreciation, and feeling important to the organization are still highly prized by people in organizations, for today's knowledge workers, career opportunities, personal growth, and challenging work are even more important.

Mihaly Csikszentmihalyi, a professor at the University of Chicago has done extensive research on what he calls the "optimal experience", which he describes this way: "we have all experienced times when... we ... feel in control of our actions, masters of our own fate. On the rare occasions that happens, we feel a sense of exhilaration, a deep sense of enjoyment...that comes as close to what is usually meant by happiness as anything we can conceivably imagine." (1990:4)

Csikszentmihalyi calls this optimal experience "flow": "the state in which people are so involved in an activity that nothing else seems to matter; the experience itself is so enjoyable that people will do it even at great cost, for the sheer sake of doing it." (1990:4) He goes on to suggest that any job could be made more enjoyable by designing it in accordance with the principles of flow, and that employee surveys show that "When challenges and skills were both high they felt happier, more cheerful, stronger, more active; they concentrated more; they felt more creative and satisfied." (1990:159)

Csikszentmihalyi's research is particularly relevant if we think about how people's skills and capabilities are utilized in organizations. It is a fact that organizations do not utilize their people nearly as effectively as they could. Most people in organizations spend a significant percentage of their time doing routine tasks; tasks that are well below their capabilities; tasks that could, and should, be done by less qualified people. Yet these organizations pay those people their *full* wages; they do not pro-rate them based on the value of the work they are doing. Let's consider the cost of the under-utilization of just one employee.

We hire an engineer to design products for our company, at, let's say, a salary of $80,000 per year, the current market value of that set of skills. Now let's he spends 50% of his time doing the level of engineering work he is capable of (in most organizations, 50% is probably an optimistic estimate), and the other 50% doing routine work, like running copies, answering the phone, reading email, writing reports, attending meetings, etc. If we ask ourselves just how many of these routine tasks require his level of expertise, the answer would probably be "very few." And if we estimate how much it might cost to have those tasks done by people at lower levels of pay, we would undoubtedly find potential for significant cost savings.

Let's say, for example, that the average annual wage of the people who could take over those tasks is as high as $50,000 per year. That would result in a minimum savings of $15,000 per year, for each engineer at that level; or looking at it another way, a need for only half as many engineers. And that's just the cost savings; think about the increased personal satisfaction of those engineers who are now being utilized at their highest and best levels, and their satisfaction will ultimately lead to decreased turnover among engineers, and increased customer satisfaction.

SUMMARY

Successful incentive and reward systems do not happen by accident. They must be thoughtfully designed and carefully maintained. Thompson and Strickland (1998) offer the following guidelines:

- Monetary *rewards* must be a *major* part of total compensation—at least 10% of base wages
- The *incentive plan* should include *everyone* in the organization—managers and workers alike
- The plan must be *administered* carefully and *fairly*

Chapter 10—Incentives and Rewards

- *Rewards* must *only* be given for achieving the *objectives defined by the strategic plan*
- *Individual objectives* should include *only* outcomes the *individual can affect*
- Keep the *time* between the performance and reward *short*
- Make liberal use of *non-monetary* rewards—don't rely solely on money
- Do *not*, under any circumstances, *reward non-performers*.

In 1998, a Gallup survey of 55,000 workers found four worker attitudes that correlate strongly with higher profits for their organizations:

- Workers feel they are given the opportunity to do what they do best, every day.
- Workers believe their opinions count.
- Workers sense that their fellow workers are committed to quality.
- Workers have made a direct connection between their work and the company's mission.

Note that none of these attitudes mentions "money." All are associated with Maslow's higher order needs.

Chapter 11

CONFLICT, POWER AND POLITICS

"...we have this consolation with us, that the harder the conflict the more glorious the triumph."

(Thomas Paine)

CONFLICT

Conflict is an inevitable part of organizational life, and generally the more diverse an organization's workforce the more conflict it is likely to have; conflict that will have an influence on organizational activities, especially decision-making. Defined as "A clash of opposing ideas or interests; disagreement; to be in opposition;..." *(American Heritage Dictionary,* 1983), conflict is largely an issue of perception: if just one person senses conflict, it exists, at least in the mind of that person. Conflict usually occurs when we believe that someone else may be preventing us from achieving our objectives.

Many of us seem to have an aversion to conflict, and do whatever we can to reduce it, eliminate it, or to avoid it entirely. And most managers and executives are little different; they attempt to eliminate conflict in any way they can, and some go out of their way to avoid any possibility of conflict.

While conflict can sometimes be counterproductive, we should recognize that it isn't *always* bad. It can certainly upset the status quo, which may be one reason it's seen as the enemy by those who feel that the key to organizational efficiency is maintaining harmony. They focus on keeping things moving at a constant rate, without interruption, and to them conflict is interruptive. But should harmony be our primary objective?

The answer is "no; our objective should be to make the organization *effective,*" and effectiveness is measured by how well the organization achieves its our major goals. This means we should be less obsessed with *harmony,* and eliminating conflict, and more concerned with *effectiveness,* and doing whatever it takes to achieve our goals. Working toward organizational goals may sometimes require reducing or eliminating conflict, but at other times we might benefit from *increased* conflict. Therefore, our job as managers is *not* to *eliminate* conflict, but to *manage* it; to make sure we have the *right* amount; to right-size conflict. Doing that requires understanding conflict and its sources; what causes it, and how to manage it.

Frequent sources of conflict in organizations include:

the external environment	technology	organization structure
goal incompatibility	task interdependence	distribution of power
participative management	low formalization	decentralized decision-making
resource allocation/scarcity	poor communication	change/uncertainty
heterogeneity	incentive/reward system	lack of information

Knowing the source of a particular conflict is one of the keys to managing it; knowing allows us to determine whether we should reduce or eliminate the conflict, or just let it be. While there may be cases in which we see a need to *increase* the conflict, for those situations in which we need to reduce conflict, a number of conflict-resolution techniques are available for our use.

Resolving Conflict

One of the most common conflict resolution techniques is *formal authority*. When parties in disagreement reach an impasse the next higher level of authority frequently becomes a "court of last resort". A judgment from somebody in higher authority is generally considered acceptable by all concerned, even if the participants don't particularly agree with the decision. Although this method reduces the conflict, at least on the surface, unless it resolves the basic issues that are causing it the conflict will probably bubble up again sometime in the future.

Or we can also call in *third-party consultants* to mediate or arbitrate the conflict. We assume that they can remain detached from the emotions involved and bring an objective perspective to the discussion. A possible side benefit of this approach is that, in addition to a resolution the management team may be able to learn from the consultants and be able to do it themselves the next time. But even if participants learn *how* to do it, they may not be able to do it with the same degree of detachment and objectivity as outsiders.

When the conflict is caused, as many are, by competition for scarce resources (e.g., money, equipment, space), the simplest solution may appear to be to *expand* those *resources*, and provide more of everything so that everyone gets what they want. This way everybody wins except, of course, the organization. It is a fact of life that few, if any, organizations have enough resources to be able to give everybody everything they want. In fact, having limited resources can be an advantage, because it forces people to prioritize and can, as a result, make the organization more efficient and more effective.

Mutual problem-solving requires the parties who are in conflict to work together to identify the underlying problems, then jointly look for solutions. The way this technique seems to work best is when participants focus on analyzing their differences, with the intention of arriving at a solution that is satisfactory to both (i.e., "win-win"), rather than pointing to one party as "right" and the other as "wrong." When done right, this method can strengthen understanding and improve communication across the organization.

Another way of resolving conflict is to *reduce interdependence* between the conflicting parties. For example, if one department is dependent upon another for its ultimate success, and a conflict arises between them that they cannot resolve, they may attempt to erect some form of buffer between them that will reduce their interdependence. A common example is when one department's output is another department's input, which makes the second department dependent on the first. If the first department gets behind schedule, it slows down the second, making the second look bad. This problem can, of course, be resolved by creating a larger inventory of the first department's output. But, although this reduces the interdependence between the two, it does nothing to get to the root of why the first department is behind schedule. And, although this form of conflict resolution reduces the conflict between the departments, it does so at a cost: the cost of carrying excess inventory, which reduces the profitability of the entire organization. And imagine the inventory costs if this method was adopted by every department; if every department developed an inventory buffer.

Although there are other ways of reducing conflict, perhaps the most effective technique, from the perspective of the organization as a whole, is getting everyone to focus on *super-ordinate goals*; the organization's major goals. Getting everyone in the organization committed to and focused on the same set of goals can reduce conflict dramatically, because any conflict that looks like it might slow down progress toward those goals will be seen as a common enemy, and *joint problem-solving* will become the preferred means of resolving the conflict. This method removes much of the emotion from the process.

Among the methods of conflict resolution that we have discussed, it should be apparent that some will work to benefit the entire organization, while others may benefit only a part of it, often at the expense of the organization as a whole. From an organizational standpoint, those methods in which conflict is resolved by those who are involved in it are usually most effective because they are more likely to lead to long-term solutions rather than temporary fixes. But conflict resolution is only part of conflict management. What about the other part, conflict stimulation?

Stimulating Conflict

An organization that is completely free of conflict is liable to become stagnant, complacent, and resistant to change (change is one of the biggest sources of conflict). This suggests there *should be* some degree of conflict in organizations; at least enough to encourage change, innovation, creativity, and diversity of thought. How do we know when more conflict is needed in an organization? Robbins (1990:416) offers a set of questions for us to ask ourselves:

1. Are you surrounded by "yes" people?
2. Are subordinates afraid to admit ignorance and uncertainties to you?
3. Is there so much concentration by decision makers on reaching a compromise that they may lose sight of values, long-term objectives, or the organization's welfare?

4. Do managers believe that it is in their best interest to maintain the impression of peace and cooperation in their unit, regardless of the price?
5. Is there an excessive concern by decision makers for not hurting the feelings of others?
6. Do managers believe that popularity is more important for obtaining rewards than competence and high performance?
7. Are managers unduly enamored of obtaining consensus in their decisions?
8. Do employees show unusually high resistance to change?
9. Is there a lack of new ideas?
10. Is there an unusually low level of employee turnover?

Once we've determined the need to increase conflict in the organization, how can we do it? First, it might be useful to think of it in terms of *change*; stimulating *change*, rather than conflict. For some, it may be easier to understand the need for change than it is to understand the need for conflict.

Robbins (1990) suggests three possibilities for stimulating conflict (change): heterogeneity, competition, and communication.

Selecting people with *heterogeneity* in mind ensures that the organization will enjoy a wide range of viewpoints, which almost guarantees differences of opinion and a certain degree of conflict. The last thing we should want in an organization is a homogeneous culture: one in which everyone thinks alike, and in which decisions tend to be by acclamation. Any homogeneous organization may, from time to time, need to introduce pockets of heterogeneity to deliberately disrupt the status quo. This disruption can be done by introducing a few people with diverse backgrounds, experience, and views. Sometimes it just takes one person who is willing to question and challenge the traditional perspective.

Introducing competition between individuals and departments is a sure-fire way of stimulating conflict. Decentralized organizations, in which different business units are given the autonomy to pursue their own markets in their own ways, depend on the competition among business units to produce superior performance for the organization as a whole. Recognizing that competition of this type can be counter-productive to the organization, policies that control *how* units may compete are essential. One sure means of control is a reward system in which a significant part of the payout is based on achieving organizational objectives, rather than just business-unit objectives.

Competition between individuals can also stimulate productive conflict. For example, competition is inherent in many college classes, in which every student is a grade-seeker. A grading system that is designed as a "zero-sum" game—only a certain percentage of students can be awarded "As", so every one who gets an "A" assures that somebody else won't get one—introduces the maximum conflict. It pits the students against one another, and assures "dog-eat-dog" competition, with every student for him/her self. Changing to an absolute grading system, in which grades depend on pre-defined standards (e.g., 90-100 = A; 80-90 = B, etc.), reduces the conflict, since nobody's grade is dependent upon how well another students does. Although, in this system there may still be some conflict, it will primarily be between the student and his/her own performance; an internal conflict.

We see the same competitive dynamic at work in the promotion processes of most organizations; several people competing for every empty box on the organization chart, or for a limited number of partnerships in a law firm.

Another method of stimulating conflict is through communication, using ambiguous or threatening messages (Robbins' 1990). It is probably obvious to most of us how a *threatening* message can create or stimulate conflict. An announcement that the survival of the organization is in doubt can be a powerful attention-getter, particularly if management truly believes its message and doesn't try to minimize the risk. On the other hand, deliberately overstating the risk is a ploy that will only work one time with most people. After that they will no longer believe what they hear from that source; those managers will no longer be trusted, and their word will always be suspect. So threatening messages can be effective conflict-stimulators, but only when they are credible; only when there really *is* a threat. On the other hand, misleading people, whether through deliberate deception or through *ambiguous* communication, is more likely to have negative consequences, and to reduce or destroy trust between the organization's members and its managers.

Overall, the best way of ensuring constructive conflict may be to make sure the organization's culture is heterogeneous, which can be done by hiring people with diverse backgrounds, experience and ideas. This diversity will require *conscious* effort, since our natural tendency is to hire *homogeneous* candidates; those people who are most like us, or like other people in the organization. There will also be occasions when we can influence conflict by creating or managing competition in ways that will make the organization more effective. But, if we always communicate openly and sincerely, and if we endeavor to tell everyone in the organization as much as we can about everything that's going on, we may not need to deliberately stimulate conflict. Most people are perceptive enough to know the value in different points of view, and will be happy to give theirs if they believe managers sincerely want it.

POWER

The distribution of power within an organization can be a major source of conflict. The design of an organization; the way it is structured; is influenced by a number of factors, including its size (i.e., the number of employees), dominant technology, external environment, industry, and competitive strategy. In an ideal world the design of an organization would be based primarily on those elements, and other *logical* considerations. But in reality, organization design is based only *partially* on common sense; much of the rest is determined by power and organizational politics.

Power is defined as authority, or the ability or capacity to exercise control *(American Heritage Dictionary,* 1983). In other words, power is the ability to influence others—their decisions and actions. Some positions carry with them a certain amount of authorized power, called *authority*, which gives the person in that position the right to command, and judge, those individuals who report to the position. Commanding, of course, means directing others to act, while judging involves evaluating how well those actions were carried out, and then rewarding or punishing people accordingly. Although those with authority do have power, theirs is *not* the *only* source of power. Others in the organization are sometimes able to create power bases that give them as much, or sometimes even more, influence than those who have formal authority. Power of this sort is often a structural issue, created by the fact that some tasks are more important than others, or that some people have greater ability, or more opportunity, to exert influence than others. And when these types of power exist, they are sometimes used to influence decisions that are different than those intended by the organization. Among these *informal* sources of power are: expertise, control of information, control of resources, network centrality, and persuasion. Each will be briefly discussed in the following paragraphs.

Expertise comes from capabilities or knowledge that are valuable to the organization, and therefore make a person's opinion more influential, regarding his/her area of expertise. This form of power is based, not on the person's position in the organization, but on respect for what he or she knows, has experienced, or is able to do.

The power associated with c*ontrol of information* comes from *information asymmetry*, in which an individual needs or desires information that is not easily available, or which can only be obtained from a limited number of sources. A familiar example is the used-car market. When we are considering buying a used car we would like to know if there is anything wrong with it, and the seller is the only one who has that information. So the seller has the power of control of information; only he has information the seller wants. If there *is* something wrong the seller may not be willing to say so, for fear it will lower the price or kill the sale. As potential buyers, we aren't sure whether or not there is anything wrong with the car, and we're not sure that the seller would tell us if there were. The seller has the upper hand and the only way we can get the information we want is to pay for it, by: paying the seller's price and taking the risk of having to pay additional for repairs; hiring a mechanic to check the car; or buying a maintenance contract to cover the cost of repairs.

The power associated with *control of resources* is similar to control of information (information *is* a resource). Power comes from controlling a resource that is scarce, such as money, raw material, property, knowledge or any of a number of other items. If it's scarce and in demand, and if we control it, we have power. On the other hand if it isn't scarce, or isn't in demand, or if we don't control it, we have no power. Harley-Davidson is a good example of the power associated with control of resources. With the demand for its motorcycles far exceeding its ability to manufacture them, most of Harley's dealers have been in the enviable position of having a waiting list of buyers for every motorcycle they can get their hands on. They have been able to take cash deposits for motorcycles months (even years) in advance of when they will be able to deliver them, and have been able to charge a much higher price than they normally would. Some of their customers have also realized the power of control of resources, by *selling* their places on the dealer's delivery list, in some cases for

Chapter 11—Conflict, Power and Politics

several thousand dollars. Mind you, they are making a profit, not for selling a motorcycle, but for selling their *place on a waiting list*. That is control of a resource!

Network centrality exists when a person occupies a position through which others must go to get what they want. Within organizations, this generally includes positions that integrate other functions, or those that can reduce organizational dependence, or are part of the organization's distinctive competencies. Executive secretaries, for example, often have an inordinate amount of power because of their ability to make access to their boss easy or difficult. Many support functions within an organization have some degree of power because of their network centrality; their ability to provide, or withhold, critical types of support. Examples are plant maintenance, payroll, technical support, and human resources. In manufacturing companies where the incentives are based on productivity, those who maintain production machinery are held in high esteem by those who operate the machines, because their bonuses depend on having machines that don't break down. This is an important, but often overlooked, form of network centrality.

Although respect is an important element in all forms of power, it is absolutely essential to those whose power is based on *persuasion*. Some people, like traveling "hucksters," are able to persuade people by deceit, since they are continually on the move and may never encounter the same person twice. But any member of an organization can only remain persuasive by maintaining the respect of those he/she hopes to influence; a respect based principally on trust. Trust can only be developed and maintained by meeting commitments and keeping promises, so those who desire the power of persuasion would do well to make sure they never promise more than they know they can deliver, and then do everything they can to assure delivery.

POLITICS

The dictionary defines *politics* as "intrigue or maneuvering within a group." It should be understood that politics is *not* an inherent part of power. Power becomes politics when it is used to bypass an organization's *authorized* decision-making process. This bypassing is often done by someone who is trying to achieve *different* objectives that those desired by the organization, and is a misuse of power, usually benefiting one person or group of people at the expense of the organization as a whole. When politics are allowed to play a role in an organization, the structure of the organization, and the way people communicate and cooperate, share information, responsibility, and authority, may be designed to serve the self-interest of a few rather than the best interests of the majority. For these organizational "politicians," maintaining or increasing their control becomes more important than the success and effectiveness of the organization. For that reason, we should always be alert for signs of organizational politics, and do everything we can to stamp them out before they can misappropriate organizational resources. We should focus on *what* is right., rather than *who* is right.

We should also understand that true authority cannot exist by edict, alone. What William Henry Harrison said in his inaugural address about governing applies to authority, as well,

"We admit of no government by divine right...the only legitimate right to govern is an express *grant of power from the governed*" (italics added). Authority, like government, only exists when granted by subordinates. Our power does not come from our position but from the respect we earn.

SUMMARY

Conflict is an important part of life, both as individuals and in organizations. Rather than giving in to our natural tendency to eliminate it, we should see and appreciate it for what it is: differences in the way we see things; different perspectives; different points of view. Differences of opinion are a valuable part of organizational problem-solving and decision-making. The more different opinions we have, the more alternatives we are able to consider, and the more effective our ultimate decisions become. So we should pity, not envy, the organization without conflict. And we should nurture organizational environments in which different views are welcome, because in our differences lie our strengths.

It is important to understand the difference between personal conflict and conflict of ideas. Personal conflict is almost always counterproductive, and should not be allowed to affect the organization or anyone in it. Conflict of ideas, on the other hand, is the kind of conflict that can add great value to the organization.

Power is also an important part of organizational life, but it must be balanced in a way that guarantees that organizational resources will be utilized in ways that best serve the interests of the organization and its stakeholders. One way to ensure an effective balance of power is to make sure it is shared as widely as possible, something often referred to as *empowerment*. Empowerment involves granting as much power as possible to organization members, so everybody can have more latitude in accomplishing their jobs. Empowerment includes providing more information about the organization and its performance; encouraging and assisting workers in increasing their knowledge and skills; delegating more decision-making authority; and broader use of performance-based rewards and incentives. In short, empowerment means recognizing that people at all levels of the organization would like as much responsibility as they can handle, and then trusting them with the authority necessary to be more self-sufficient. In other words, give them plenty of responsibility and enough authority to make sure they can make the necessary decisions. Peter Block calls this stewardship, and he defines it as "The willingness to be accountable for the well-being of the larger organization by operating in service, rather than in control, of those around us." (1993:xx) Block offers nine principles of stewardship, which can be paraphrased as:

1. Let workers determine how their jobs can best be done.
2. Give workers maximum opportunity to manage themselves.
3. Let performance measures be determined by those being measured.
4. Let the decisions be made where the work is being done.

5. Make service, to customers, subordinates, and associates, your primary responsibility.
6. Minimize the number of management and staff jobs; let workers decide what services they need.
7. Give out as much information as possible, and tell the truth all the time.
8. Demand a commitment from each employee to act in the best interests of the organization.
9. Tie everybody's fortune to the success of the larger organization. Make all employees owners and managers.

A final note about politics in organizations—although politics can have either a positive or negative influence on an organization, all too often they are utilized for self-serving purposes. Ideally, we would like to have problem-solving and decision-making done in a rational (i.e., logical) manner, in which reasonable alternatives are considered and the best possible decision made, but it doesn't always work that way. And when it doesn't, negotiation becomes part of the decision-making process, and negotiation doesn't always result in outcomes that are best for the organization. Although it isn't always possible to eliminate politics from the process of reaching agreement, we should always be alert to when politics are playing a role, and do everything we can to make sure it is a productive rather than a subversive role.

Chapter 12

TIME MANAGEMENT

"Time is the most valuable thing a man can spend."
(Theophrastus, d.278 B.C.)

Time is one of our most limited resources—we have only 24 hours of it each day, and nobody knows for how many days. Despite its scarcity, many organizations consistently waste much of the time that's available to them.

"… because we can't do everything that we'd like to do, and we can't have everything we'd like to have, we have to make choices, and we have to give up things. For every thing we choose to do or have, there will be something else that we can't do or can't have." (O'Neal, 2006:54) And the use of time is this kind of zero-sum game—what we use for one purpose isn't available for anything else. As a result, the tradeoffs we make, in how we use our time and other resources can be the difference between success and failure, for individuals as well as organizations.

TIME-WASTERS

Many of us manage our time very effectively, either because we've read how to do it (many books have been written on the subject) or because we've learned from our own experience. But what happens to our use of time when we work in organizations? Unfortunately, no matter how effectively we may utilize our own time, the organizations for which we work aren't likely to use it nearly as well. Although this was discussed in an earlier chapter, it was primarily from an organizational viewpoint. Here, we will look at it from an individual perspective. Consider yourself, for example. How much of your time at work do you spend working at your highest capability?

Wasted Talents/Abilities

Real estate assessors consider the "highest and best use" of a property when they estimate its worth. In other words, the property isn't valued based on its current use or its actual use, but on its most valuable potential use. When organizations hire people, they have to do it according to the same principle. To get the people they want, they have to pay competitive wages, market value, which are based on a person's highest and best use: his/her most valuable potential. In other words, organizations have to pay employees based on what they are capable of doing, not on what they actually have them do, so it only makes sense they should utilize those employees at their highest possible levels all of the time, not just some of the time.

Bear in mind, I'm not suggesting that organizations work people harder; I'm suggesting that they utilize people more effectively; make sure they are making full use of the knowledge, skills, and abilities for which those people were hired, and for which they're being paid. Now, let's go back to the question, "How much of your time at work do you spend working at your highest capability?" If you're like the majority of employees in most companies, your answer is probably "Not nearly enough!" which means you're just one the multitudes who are being under-utilized.

Routine Tasks

Part of our under-utilization is the result of the hours we spend doing things that could be done by someone at a lower pay level. I've wasted countless hours in that way, hours that could have been used to much greater advantage by my company. I didn't do that by choice, but because that's the way some organizations cut costs: they eliminate support people. Then, with a shortage of support people, professional, technical, and knowledge workers have to take time away from their primary (and most valuable) responsibilities to do routine things (e.g., run copies, type memos, make phone calls), which could have been done more efficiently, and at less cost, by a lower-paid person.

While eliminating support people may bring short-term savings, the opportunity cost of key people wasting valuable time on routine tasks can significantly reduce the company's long-term potential, costing it much more in the long term.

Meetings

How many times have you come away from a meeting resenting how little was accomplished for the time you spent? Unnecessary or inefficiently-run meetings are the bane of people in most organizations.

TIME-SAVERS

Highest and Best Use

High performing organizations know that an important element in attracting and retaining key people is the company's ability to challenge them; to keep them thinking; to allow them to stretch and grow. And they succeed at this by proactively working to ensure that each em-

Chapter 12—Time Management

ployee is working at his/her highest and best use a high percentage of the time. How can they do that? By applying the advice of a long-ago management consultant.

Charles Schwab, an early president of Bethlehem Steel, hired a consultant to show him how to manage his time more effectively. The consultant gave Schwab the following note, and told him to follow its advice every day:

> "Write down the six most important tasks that you have to do tomorrow and number them in the order of their importance. Now put this paper in your pocket and the first thing tomorrow morning look at item one and start working on it until you finish it. Then do item two, and so on. Do this until quitting time and don't be concerned if you have finished only one or two."

After trying his advice for several days, Schwab was so impressed with the results that he paid the consultant $25,000 for his one-paragraph note. To put that into context, it's important to note that this was during the time when the average American worker made less than $2000 per year. (Bluedorn, 2002)

It seems to me that consultant's advice could serve as a guideline for every manager in every company: help your employees set goals, significant goals, then allow them to concentrate on achieving those goals without wasting time on menial tasks.

Routine Tasks

Hire people to do routine tasks, or contract those types of activities to outside firms who specialize in them. However you do it, make sure you don't allow people hired for higher capabilities waste their time on tasks that are below their capabilities.

Effective Meetings

To maximize the effectiveness of meetings, and minimize wasting participants' time, meetings should be short, to the point, and well organized. Following are some guidelines for effective meetings

- Purpose—let everyone know the purpose, in advance, so they'll be prepared.
- Goals—set practical goals, so participants know what they'll take away.
- Agenda—make it short—1 topic is ideal, but no more than 3 or 4.
    - send it out in advance, so participants come prepared.
- Attendance—invite only those who need to be there, make attendance required, and require anyone who can't be there to send an alternate.
- Take control—set definite start and finish times,
    - start on time,
    - set ground rules, including inputs expected from participants,
    - meeting should be to solve problems, not just give information
    - focus on one issue at a time,
    - results should be decisions, not just discussion,

- should be about the future, not the past,
- recap at the end of the meeting,
- keep it short – no more than 1 hour,
- end it on time (or sooner.)
- Minutes—distributed to participants, showing what was accomplished.

SUMMARY

Time is one of our scarcest and most valuable resources. Every person should be taught how to manage his/her own time, and those who supervise others should be trained in how to maximize the capabilities of those who report to them.

Effective management of time can pay enormous benefits, in at least two ways: 1) increasing the company's capabilities and potential to better serve its customers; and 2) improved employee morale, from the satisfaction people get from realizing their own potential. And with increased employee morale comes lower turnover, and increased employee satisfaction, which invariably leads to increased customer satisfaction.

PART III
ORGANIZATION

The purpose of an organization is to bring people together to accomplish a specific objective. No matter what an organization is trying to accomplish, the primary role of the organization itself is to support that cooperative effort. And it does this by allocating responsibility, authority, and resources, and by assuring good communication, cooperation, and a continuous flow of information.

The chapters in this section discuss the second part of strategy *implementation*—how to develop, structure and equip the *organization* so that it can most effectively support the efforts of the people who are working to implement the strategic plan.

Chapter 13

DESIGNING THE ORGANIZATION

"Water answers to gravity, to downhill, to the call of the ocean. The forms change, but the mission remains clear. Structures emerge, but only as temporary solutions that facilitate rather than interfere. There is none of the rigid reliance on single forms, on true answers, on past practices..."

(Wheatley, 1992:16)

Understanding why organization design is important to strategic management requires knowing the answers to two questions: "What *is* an organization?" and "What does an organization *do*?"

One definition of an organization is "... a consciously coordinated social entity, with a relatively identifiable boundary, that functions on a relatively continuous basis to achieve a common goal or set of goals." (Robbins, 1990:4) Although a bit academic, that definition includes all of the important elements of an organization, and can be usefully paraphrased as "a managed group of carefully selected people who work together on an ongoing basis to achieve what they would not be able to achieve as individuals."

No matter how we define it, in its most basic sense an organization *is* "a group of people working together to accomplish something," and the most important thing to remember about that definition is the part about *people working together*. When we design the structure of an organization our objective should be to *help people work together*. More specifically, we want to structure the organization in a way that will help people work together *to achieve the goals of the organization*. And therein lies the answer to the second question, "What does an organization *do*?"

An organization brings people together to achieve goals. So an organization *is* people working together, and what it *does* is achieve goals, and the organization's performance is measured by how well it achieves those goals. So we can conclude that the effectiveness of an organization, how well it achieves its objectives, will be based on how well people work together. And just how does an organization help people work together effectively?

By *organizing* work; dividing it up so that it can be done in the most effective way. This requires structuring the organization to allow for the most efficient division of *responsibilities*, clear lines of *authority*, effective *communication* and *information flow*, and careful *coordination* of the interaction among activities.

Clear allocation of *responsibility* assures that each of us knows exactly what we are expected to accomplish, and minimizes confusion among employees about who is responsible for what. It also ensures that everything that needs to be done gets done (that nothing "falls between the cracks") and that there is no duplication of effort. The organization's incentive and reward system should be designed to reward those employees who meet their responsibilities and to withhold rewards from those who don't. Individual performance should be evaluated, and rewarded based on how well each of us fulfills our responsibilities.

Authority defines reporting relationships within the organization—who reports to whom. Authority is important because, as previously discussed, it defines both our decision-making jurisdiction and the degree to which we are allowed to direct others. It is important that each of us understands not only the extent of our authority, but also to whom we report, and all other lines of authority that affect us.

Working together requires effective *communication,* which is only possible when *open* communication is encouraged and assured. Open communication means people at all levels *willingly* sharing information, not just when specifically asked, but whenever we feel that somebody else would benefit, even if they haven't asked. This degree of communication is possible only when there is a high degree of trust among all levels of the organization, and a clear sense among everyone that cooperation is the surest way to achieve both our objectives and those of the organization. An important part of effective communication is making sure that the necessary *information* is available to whomever needs it, wherever they need it, and whenever they need it. This requires a clear understanding that the more we share information the better we can all make the decisions necessary to perform at our best. In fact, Wheatley (1992) suggests that information is what brings novelty and order to the organization and should, therefore, be created and shared freely and transmitted in all directions.

If we address the issues of responsibility, authority, communication, and information flow effectively, *coordination* and *integration* of activities will be assured. When we are well aware of who has what responsibilities and what are the proper lines of authority, and when we have easy access to the appropriate knowledge and information when and where we need it, we will be better able to coordinate and integrate our activities with those of our associates.

In deciding how best to divide up the work of the organization, it is useful to refer again to the organization as a transformation process: one that transforms inputs into outputs (Figure 10, Chapter 6). We accomplish the process of transformation through a series of coordinated activities. In this process, the *organization structure* we have designed coordinates our activities, *resources* are what we transform and what we use to do the transformation, and *technology* is *how* we do what we do. (*Technology* and *resources* will be covered in later chapters.) Although there are many ways to organize the work in any organization, most are based on three fundamental types of organization structure: *functional, decentralized,* and *matrix.*

FUNCTIONAL STRUCTURE

A functional structure is one in which jobs are grouped by the type of work they involve. For example, all jobs that involve engineering are in the engineering department, and report to the head engineer, and all jobs associated with marketing are in the marketing department; as shown in Figure 14.

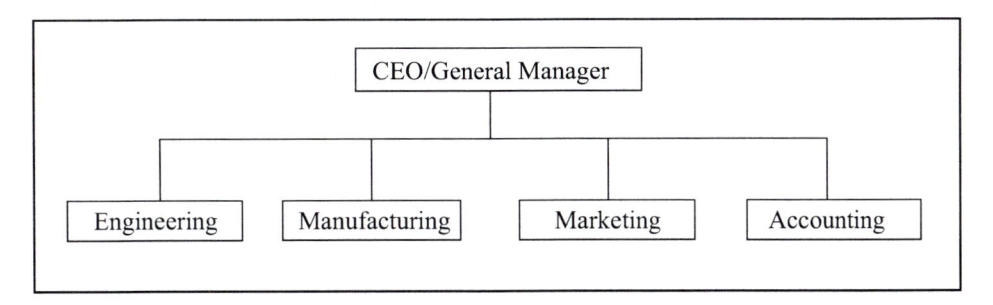

Figure 14. Functional Structure

Every form of organization has both advantages and disadvantages, and this one is no exception.

Its primary advantage is efficiency; grouping people who are doing similar work makes it easy to shift work among them as necessary, thus making the most efficient use of their time and effort and maximizing their output. A functional organization also facilitates on-the-job training and learning, as new members in a discipline have the opportunity to understudy and be mentored by their more experienced colleagues. This degree of specialization can be instrumental in developing core competencies, both individual and organizational. With these considerations in mind, an organization that seeks maximum efficiency in utilizing its resources should seriously consider a functional structure, but only after gaining a clear understanding of its shortcomings.

The weaknesses of this form of organization include: difficulty coordinating *across* functions, strong *departmental* loyalties and agendas, and a tendency to be *rigid* and *inflexible*. Although individual departments may see these characteristics as advantages, from the perspective of the overall organization they are more often weaknesses and are responsible for the reputation this type of organization has earned for its "silos" or "chimneys." The parochialism that exists in this type of organization often results in functional departments acting more like they are in competition with one another than in cooperation. When allowed to persist, this attitude stifles open communication and free sharing of information across functions, making the overall organization *less* efficient, rather than more. That's the reason for the references to silos and chimneys—functional departments are seen as only communicating upward and downward, with nothing passing through the walls to other functional areas. And when individual departments that are supposed to be working together to satisfy customers are allowed to operate in their own interests rather than in the interests of the organization, the organization will not be as customer-sensitive as it could be, thus weakening its competitive advantage.

DECENTRALIZED STRUCTURE

The decentralized structure also has both advantages and disadvantages. Its primary advantages address the major *disadvantages* of a functional structure: increased flexibility and responsiveness to customers, improved communication and information flow across functions, and more effective coordination of activities across functions. While these advantages tend to be more obvious, a hidden advantage is that the overall performance of the entire organization can also be better. Also referred to as "divisional," a decentralized organization structure is organized according to geographic regions, products, or markets, rather than by functional expertise.

Geographically Decentralized

Let's begin our discussion with a *geographically*-decentralized organization, as shown in Figure 15.

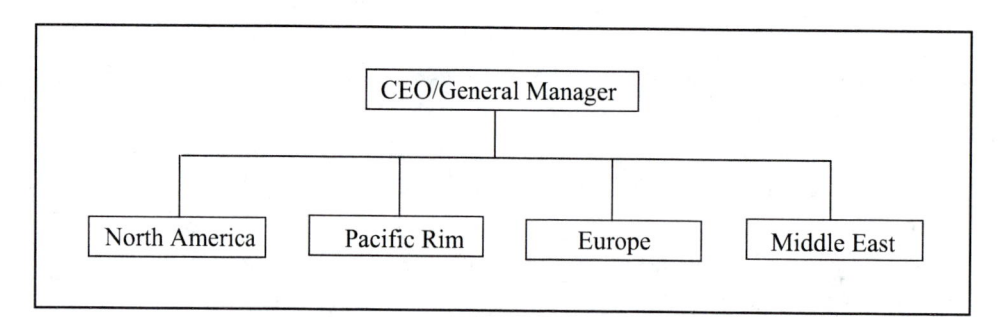

Figure 15. Geographically Decentralized Structure

In Figure 15, the boxes on the chart represent different geographic areas. The person responsible for each of those geographic areas is responsible for everything that effects the organization's customers in that entire area, including, for example, product development, manufacturing, marketing, sales, and service. With that responsibility comes the authority (to make decisions) and autonomy (to do things independently) necessary to be competitively successful in that market area. As a result, each area manager (or director, or vice president) is, in effect, running his/her own company, and is rewarded (or punished) based on the results it achieves. This degree of autonomy tends to inspire those involved and, coupled with the excitement generated by competition with other geographic areas, serves as a major incentive for outstanding performance.

Although each geographic manager's organization may be, in effect, a miniature version of a functional organization, in this context it is easier to control the cooperation and communication among functional departments, and easier for functional managers at this level to see the value of working together rather than in competition. And that is what enables this type of organization to be more responsive to its customers and markets. The entire effort of each geographic organization is directed at understanding the needs of its customers and developing the products and services that will serve them best. Normally the reasoning for a geographically-decentralized organization is that customer needs differ significantly from one area to another. This organization form allows for more flexibility and responsiveness in meeting those needs.

A further advantage, and an important one, is that implied by the name of this organization form—decentralized. In business terms this means that top-level executives have delegated some of their decision-making authority to lower-level managers. Giving up some of their decision-making allows top- level executives more time to do what they *should* be doing in the first place: envisioning the organization's future and developing their successors—the next generation of organizational leaders.

The negative side of a decentralized structure is its relative inefficiency. Compared to the functional structure, in which all similar functions are grouped in the same part of the organization, this form breaks each function into pieces and distributes them to different geographic areas. Although they may have similar functional interests, workers in one geographic area will not be physically available to assist their colleagues in other areas. As a result, there may be times when, for example, engineers in one area will be so busy they have to hire additional help, while those in other areas have excess time on their hands.

Another inefficiency of this type of structure is the additional layer of management that is often created above functional-level management, and the staff functions, such as personnel, accounting, and computer services, that are likely to be duplicated in each geographic area. Since these additional positions are all pure "overhead" because they represent additional fixed costs that do not directly add value to the product or service, so they make the organization more expensive to operate.

Although some see, as an additional limitation, the top executives further removed from what is going on in the organization, that can be an opportunity for them to concentrate on what they *should* be doing, rather than spending valuable time micro-managing the operations of the organization.

Product/Market Decentralized

Before we go on to other organizational forms, it is important to briefly discuss another way that we can decentralize an organization, by organizing around products or markets, rather than geographic differences. This form is almost identical to its geographic counterpart, except for the responsibilities of those who manage the decentralized units. In this configuration shown in Figure 16, each manager is responsible for a particular line of products or a particular market, rather than a geographic area.

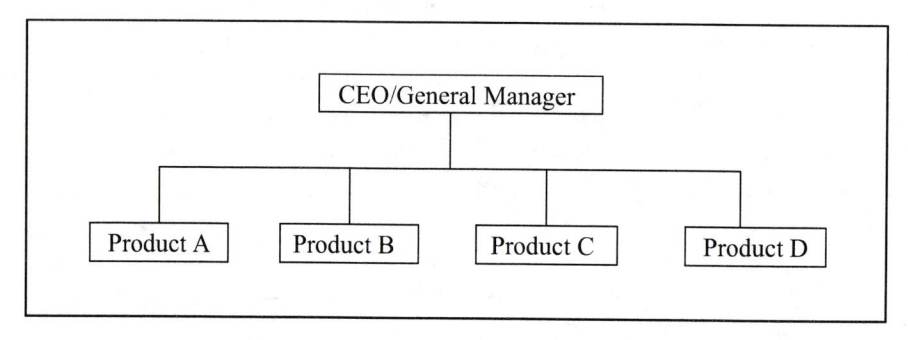

Figure 16. Product/Market Decentralized Structure

In most other respects they are alike, having the same advantages and disadvantages, but with two additional disadvantages: the potential for detrimental competition among business units, and for duplication of services.

Whereas geographically-decentralized business units have little or no opportunity to steal business from each other (due to their physical separation), those that are product or market oriented may very well be operating in the same geographic areas, thus having the opportunity, and perhaps an incentive, to compete against each other. This competition can result in one business unit growing at the expense of another, with no net gain, or even a loss, for the parent organization.

The risk of duplication of services occurs when several business units are operating in the same area, each with its own sales organization and, perhaps, its own service organization. When that happens it is possible to have several sales people traveling the same area at the same time, calling on different or sometimes even the same customers. This overlap is less of a problem in a densely-populated market in which the distance between customers is small, but in markets where customers are far apart, duplication of travel expenses can be a significant drain on profits. So it is important for managers in this type of organization to make sure that their autonomy does not lead to excessive duplication of efforts or expenses.

Overall, if efficiency is what is most important to the organization, a functional organization may be preferable but, if flexibility and responsiveness are necessary, a decentralized structure will likely be more effective.

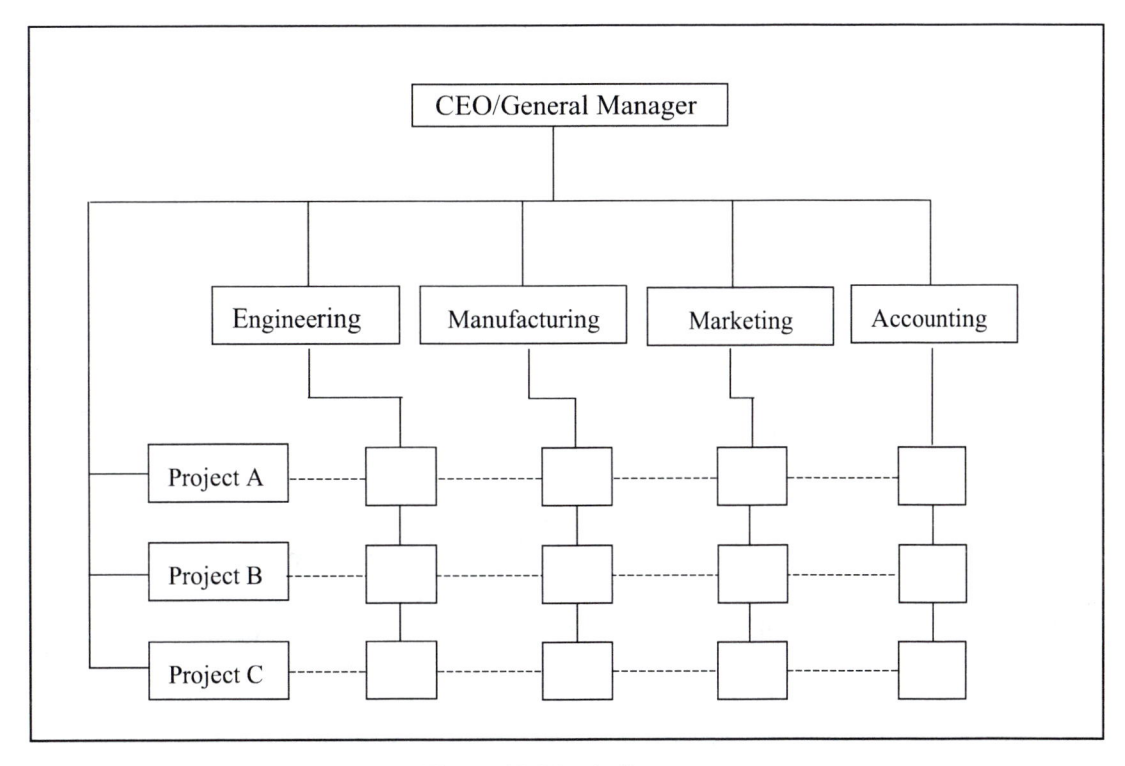

Figure 17. Matrix Structure

MATRIX STRUCTURE

The matrix organization combines elements of the functional and decentralized structures. It is, in effect, a decentralized structure laid horizontally over a functional structure. See Figure 17.

Beginning with a functional organization, in which similar skills are grouped together, the matrix adds a horizontal level across those functions. In our diagram, instead of four management boxes reporting to the CEO, there are eight: four along the top and four more down the left-hand side. The top four represent the engineering, production, sales, and accounting departments, while the four on the side represent projects A, B, C, and D. All people in the organization report to one of the functional departments, each of which is headed by a manager.

Note that the project boxes also represent managers, but these managers have no people, that is no permanently-assigned people. Here it is useful to think of each functional department as a bundle of resources (e.g., people, equipment, knowledge, information, and raw materials), and the projects as opportunities for those resources to be applied in the manner that is of greatest benefit to the organization. Remember we said earlier that, in the organizational transformation process, resources are *what* we transform, technology is *how* we transform them, and the structure of the organization is how we *coordinate* the transformation *activities*. In a matrix organization, the functional departments provide the resources and the technology (the "how to"), and the project teams use those resources and technology to create outputs. Notice the term project "teams." But how can we have teams if there are no people in the project boxes?

Therein lies the key to the matrix organization: a single set of resources serving the needs of two sets of managers. First are the functional managers, whose responsibilities are quite similar to those of managers in a functional organization. But we also have project managers, whose responsibilities are similar to those of the managers in a product-decentralized organization, except that they have no people reporting to them. The functional managers are responsible for hiring, training, developing, evaluating, and rewarding the people in their functional areas. In this sense, the role of each functional department is similar to that of a staffing service: hiring people and having them available for others to utilize. Each project manager, on the other hand, has responsibility for a project, such as developing a new product, for which he/she will need people with the appropriate knowledge and skills. Since projects generally have a finite life and a project team is finished when its project has been completed, these managers don't hire permanent people; they borrow them from the appropriate functional managers.

In this system, although all employees report permanently to functional managers, they may spend most of their time under the direction of project managers, sometimes under more than one manager at the same time, on temporary assignments. They will apply their expertise when needed and as long as needed, often jumping back and forth between assignments from one day, or week, to the next.

The key to the success of a matrix organization is super-ordinate goals; everyone in the organization, particularly the functional and project managers, must clearly understand what are the organization's major goals, then be willing to work together to achieve them. This cooperation is, of course, important in every type of organization structure, but more so in a matrix organization, which *will not work* without this clarity and commonality of purpose. And therein is the primary weakness of a matrix system. Unless all of the top-level managers (there are 7 in our example) agree on and work toward the same objectives, the people who report to them will constantly be torn between the needs of their functional manager and those of their project manager. In that sense, this type of organization is complex to manage. Managers must be constantly aware of the risk of placing their people in conflict, and willing to do whatever is necessary to present a united front to their shared employees. This coordination requires excellent communication among all of the managers.

Another difficulty in managing in a matrix organization is the negotiation that managers must go through to agree on the makeup of the project teams. Let's use project manager A as an example. She has just been assigned responsibility for developing a line of products for a new market and needs to put together a cross-functional team to get the job done. She determines that she will initially need a marketing representative to help assess the needs of the market and, when that is done, an electronic engineer and a software specialist to do the ini-

Chapter 13—Designing the Organization

tial product design, an industrial engineer to assist in determining the most efficient methods for manufacturing the products and modeling the prototypes, and a cost accountant to make sure the product can be manufactured and sold within its pricing targets. So, the project manager needs one team member now and four others within the next few weeks. With this knowledge she will go, first, to the marketing manager and request a marketing specialist, and here the negotiating will begin, because she will probably not ask for just *a* marketing specialist, but for a *particular* marketing specialist by name. And this will be typical of all requests by all project managers: they don't want just any functional specialist, they want the *best*; the one who has proven to be most creative, or most experienced, or most productive; because the project manager's performance will be evaluated by the effectiveness of her project. In other words, if the success of my career hinges on the success of my project, I don't want just anybody on my project team; I want the best. But so do all of the other project managers, so they will all be asking for the same people for their teams.

And that's why the keys to the success of a matrix organization are the functional managers. They are the ones who have to convince the project managers, "you don't need my most experienced person for this phase of your project; so-and-so will do fine. Then, when you get to the next phase, we will let you use him" Or, "She is now working on project C, which has a higher priority than yours, so she won't be available until...." Or, "Yes, you can have him now, but only until next Wednesday, when he has to be on project B." This means the functional managers will have to be constantly negotiating with the project managers, trying to be realistic in assigning resources in the manner that best achieves the organization's most important objectives. Doing this effectively requires not only a clear understanding of organizational goals and priorities, but also in-depth knowledge of every project and a good grasp of negotiating skills. For it is the functional manager who assures that every project is provided the resources necessary for its success, and does it with a limited pool of resources and in a manner that assures that the organization's most important objectives are achieved.

When this system works, it works because of excellent communication and cooperation among the functional and project managers. And when it works, it does two things better than almost any other organization form: 1) it makes the most efficient use of resources; and 2) it focuses those resources more effectively to achieve only those objectives that have been agreed on as most important to the organization. In short, when it works it resolves conflict, builds consensus, improves communication, and helps people at all levels more clearly understand things from an organizational perspective. And when it doesn't work it can be one of the most ineffective kinds of organization structure, and certainly among the most demoralizing for those involved in it.

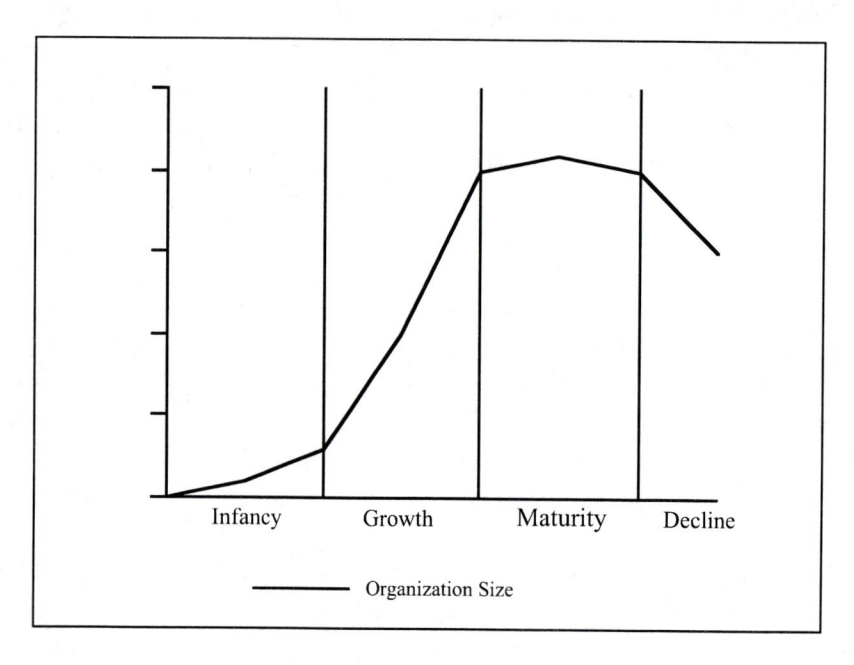

Figure 18. Organizational Life Cycle

WHICH ORGANIZATION FORM IS BEST?

First, it is important to understand that there is no perfect or ideal organization structure. Although the most widely-used is the functional structure, that may be happening for the wrong reasons. For many years the only objective of organization design was *efficiency*, and because it was the most efficient, the functional structure became the standard. And of all of the possible structures, functional is among the easiest to manage and control, so it is a favorite among those who want to closely monitor and control their people, whether for efficiency reasons or simply to maintain their power. But the functional structure may be dominant for a more innocent reason: because it's the most natural way for organizations to grow.

To see how, let's apply the concept of the industry life-cycle (Figure 6, Chapter 4) to the growth of an organization, as shown in Figure 18.

The same cycle applies to organizations: they are born, and if they survive their infancy they go through a period of growth, finally reaching maturity, and then often through a period of decline and ultimately death. Now, let's follow an organization from its inception through its life-cycle.

Every organization begins as an idea in somebody's mind, and many never go any further. But once in a while one of those ideas becomes an infant organization, perhaps for a while just a one-person organization. But if the idea seems to work the firm may eventually grow into a small organization, employing several additional people. At this point, the orga-

Chapter 13—Designing the Organization

nization, with its handful of people, probably looks much like one of the project teams that are part of a matrix organization. To provide the balance of skills necessary to move the organization forward, the first few people are usually from a variety of disciplines: perhaps an engineer, a marketing person, an accountant, and a production specialist. So this first group of people is quite diversified in their skills, expertise, and experience. But as the organization progresses through its infancy and starts into the growth stage additional employees will be added, and the natural tendency is to assign each of them to work under one of the original members, typically the one whose skills are most similar to those of the new person. So if we hire another engineer, we are liable to have him report to the engineer who was on the original team, and we will do the same with additional marketing, production and accounting employees, having them report to their functional predecessors. Now if we keep following this tendency we will perhaps unconsciously build a functional organization; not necessarily because we intended to, but perhaps due more to our inexperience and lack of familiarity with other organization forms and their advantages and disadvantages. And so it goes; the organization grows until it reaches the point at which it becomes difficult to remain effective with a functional structure. And how do we know when we've reached that point?

Generally it begins with the realization that we are losing our competitive edge to companies that are more flexible, more responsive to customers' needs. Inflexibility is a symptom of centralized decision making, which occurs when most decisions are made by those at the top of the organization. The time it takes for a request to go from the lower levels of the organization to the top, and for the decision to be made and then transmitted back through the organizational hierarchy to the lower levels, gets longer as the organization gets bigger. And as decision-making time gets longer, the organization becomes less able to respond to the needs of its customers quickly enough to demonstrate its interest or concern for them. That's how a functional structure outgrows its usefulness: since it is inherently a centralized decision-making organization, as the organization gets bigger that process becomes a competitive disadvantage. So now that we know *why* a functional structure outgrows its usefulness, what can we do about it?

If *centralized* decision-making is making the organization *less* responsive when it needs to be *more* responsive, the most logical thing to do is *decentralize* decision-making. Organizations learned that the hard way, many years ago, and developed what was originally called the M-Form (for multi-divisional) organization, the same thing we are discussing here as the *decentralized* organization. (Personally, I like *decentralized* better, because it is more descriptive of *why* this organization form is most often used: to decentralize decision-making.) So when the functional structure no longer meets its needs, when it doesn't allow the organization the flexibility and responsiveness necessary to be remain competitive, organizations have traditionally decentralized decision-making by delegating some of it to lower levels of the organization. And since this happens when organizations get big, we can logically assume that, whereas the functional structure is dominant in the early stages of growth, continued growth may ultimately force an organization to change to a decentralized structure.

Following this train of thought, it is logical that unless organization design is part of an organization's strategic planning process, its structure is likely to evolve through the different stages of its life-cycle by default, by *reacting* to significant decreases in the organization's effectiveness, rather than by design, in *anticipation* of its future needs. The difference, of course, is acting according to a deliberate plan to gain and maintain competitive advantage *before* the organization is threatened, versus reacting *after* circumstances have placed the organization at a disadvantage. This suggests that a forward-looking organization will *deliberately* design its structure to meet its future needs rather than allowing it to evolve in its own way, or worse, allowing it to be designed by those who have private agendas, to serve their own needs. Without the intervention of either strategic planning or self-serving interests, we can predict that, in its infancy an organization is likely to resemble a matrix structure; as it grows it will become more functional; and, if it gets big enough, it will likely become decentralized. That said, how can we determine what is the best organization structure for us?

As stated earlier, there is no magic structure and no easy formula or recipe that will guide us in designing an organization. But there are several thoughts to keep in mind. First, the best structure is the one that best fits the situation at the moment. Next, since change is inevitable, the organization should be thought of as dynamic rather than static; a work in process. Third, the best structure is the simplest one that will do the job. And, finally, we should never think that we have to choose a single organization structure for the entire organization. A more useful perspective is to view the different forms of organization structure that we have discussed as a set of tools that can be used in any combination to meet the circumstances of the moment.

If, for example, our organization needs to have these features: ongoing product development to maintain its market leadership, an efficient manufacturing process to keep costs and prices low, and a customer-sensitive sales and service organization, we should consider combining three different organization structures. A matrix structure might be best for product development, while low-cost manufacturing would require the efficiency of a functional structure, and a decentralized structure is likely to provide the flexibility and responsiveness needed by sales and service. So we design a hybrid organization, using the features we need, where we need them, and when we need them.

Summary

Whichever forms are selected, we should never think in terms of *permanence* where organization structure is concerned. We should keep it as temporary and flexible as possible, so that everyone will understand that organizational success and permanence do *not* come from the structure of the organization, but from its versatility and flexibility in allowing people to work together in the most effective way. In support of this philosophy, some organizations discourage, or even forbid, the creation of organization charts because of the tendency many of us have of, once having seen our names in a box, assigning that arrangement a permanence that was never intended. In addition, many organizations and organization theorists today are leaning more toward the belief that everybody, regardless of their job or level in the organization, should be given as much responsibility and decision-making authority as they are comfortable with; in effect encouraging organizations to operate much more *organically* than before.

In mechanistic (i.e., functional) organizations, jobs are usually divided into their most basic functions and performance is measured by the quantity and quality of output. As a result, mechanistic organizations tend to hire people more for their physical capabilities than for any intelligence, creativity, or knowledge they may have. Employees in these organizations have essentially been hired to be automons—to produce and not think. And these employees have lived up to their end of the bargain. By day they have faithfully performed their repetitive, often mind-numbing work, frequently enduring the monotony by dreaming of the interests they pursue at night and on weekends; activities like raising orchids, rebuilding cars, running for political office, or running their own sideline businesses. But some organizations realize that these people have good minds; minds full of ideas for improving the organization, if only someone would give them the opportunity. And the organizations that tap into this long-ignored source of ideas are benefiting from unprecedented innovation and productivity.

To provide the type of atmosphere that nurtures individual creativity, we will have to allow, even *encourage*, our organizations to be more organic, more chaotic. Perhaps more like that envisioned by Cohen, March, and Olsen, "An organization is a collection of choices looking for problems, issues and feelings looking for decision situations in which they might be aired, solutions looking for issues to which they might be the answer, and decision makers looking for work" (1972: 2). This suggests an organization structured around its distinctive competencies and how they are being used at any particular time—a fluid, continually-changing structure. This is in sharp contrast with the natural desire of most managers to maintain equilibrium and control. In this new type of organization, where performance is measured by *outcomes* rather than processes or methods, people will do their work in their own way, rather than by some specified procedure. This will bring a high degree of uncertainty and unpredictability to *how* people do their jobs and, although work processes may look absolutely chaotic, what people will ultimately be able to accomplish is likely to astonish traditional thinkers. Wheatley emphasizes that chaos does not mean a lack of order; that, in fact, all seemingly chaotic systems have boundaries that they never exceed, and offers this advice:

> "We need to be able to trust that something as simple as a clear core of values and vision, kept in motion through continuing dialogue, can lead to order." (1992:147)

Chapter 14

INNOVATION AND TECHNOLOGY

"The prime driver of economic progress is technological innovation."
(Joseph Schumpeter)

Innovation can be defined as *beginning, or introducing something new*, or *being creative*, or *a new product or method*. But fundamentally, innovation simply means *the first time something is done or is done in a different way*.

Technology is defines as *methods and materials used to apply science*, although Daft's description is closer to our purposes, "Technology is the tools, techniques, machines, and actions used to transform organizational inputs into outputs." (1998:119) The word *technology*, Drucker (1993) suggests, is a derivation of *techne*, the mastery of a craft skill, and *logy*, organized, systematic, purposeful knowledge, which we can interpret to mean technology is a combination of *knowledge* and *capability*. Combining these definitions can lead us to conclude that technology means both *things* (i.e., equipment) and *processes* (i.e., methods), but in its most basic sense, technology simply means *how we do something*.

If innovation means *creating new things*, and technology means *how we do things*, what is the relationship between innovation and technology? It seems there are at least two relationships: one in which innovation leads to, or creates, a new technology, and one in which technology leads to, or creates, innovation. In either case, innovation and technology work hand in hand. New technology comes from innovation, and innovation can come from unique applications of the technology it has created. Now that we have a better idea of what innovation and technology are and what they do, let's examine their roles in strategic management.

TECHNOLOGY

Looking at the organization as a transformation process, technology is the *how*: *how* we transform the organization's inputs into outputs. Transformation processes may involve a broad range of technologies, from those that are extremely sophisticated, involving complex software or digitally-controlled robotics, to those that are quite simple, like tightening bolts by hand. Regardless of the technology we use, it is strategically important to determine in advance, what will be our organization's dominant technology, because the technology we choose can have a major influence on how we structure the organization.

Product Technology

The organization's strategic plan should be a primary factor in determining which technology will be most appropriate. Let's use a manufacturing company as an example. Before we can determine what processes, methods, and equipment will best support our competitive strategy, we need to know what types of products we will manufacture, in what quantities, and in what price ranges they will be offered. A major factor in pricing will be production quantities. Figure 19 shows a model developed by Woodward (1965) to show the relationship between technical complexity and production quantities.

If, for example, we decide to lower costs by producing large quantities, we will need to reduce the complexity of each job in the production process by breaking down each phase of the process into a series of small steps that are easy to learn and quick to perform. This will allow us to get volume discounts on the raw material and parts we purchase, keep wages low by hiring unskilled workers and reduce set-up costs by scheduling long production runs.

At the other extreme, if we decide to build products one at a time to individual customers' specifications, we will not be able to set up for long production runs or buy raw materials in discounted quantities. And, since custom-built products generally require greater skills, knowledge and individual initiative, we will have to pay higher wages to hire the people we need. This means that our production costs will be higher and we will have to charge higher prices for our products. With this in mind, we had better confirm in advance that our customers will be willing to pay a premium price for their customized products.

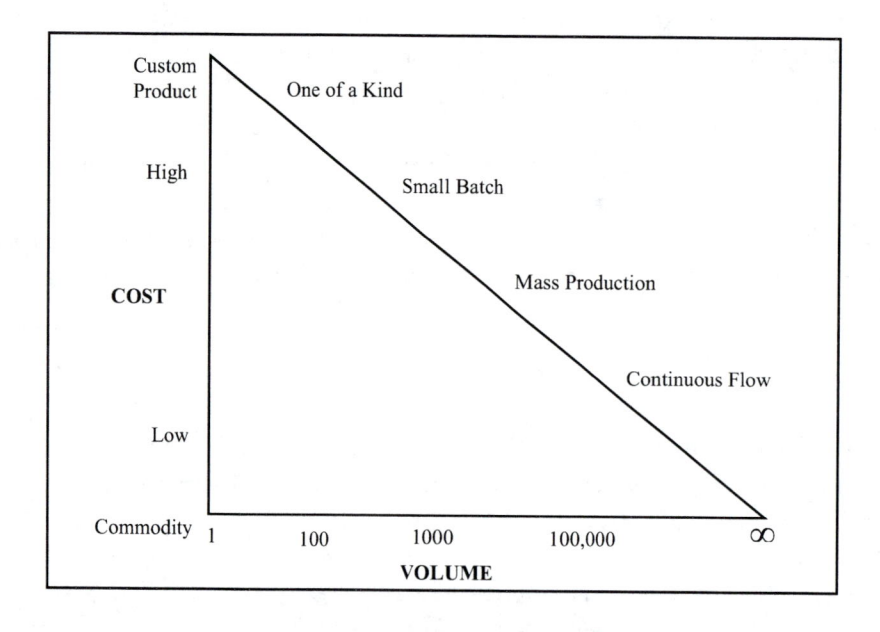

Figure 19. Production Technologies

When we compare these two situations we should be able to see that the technology we use will be quite different in one case than in the other, and the way we staff and structure the organization will be different as well. In the first case, with a focus on high volume and low costs, we will need to structure for mass production, and make significant investments in plant space and high-volume production machinery. We will purchase inputs in large quantities, have either large inventories or just-in-time delivery, and hire primarily non-skilled workers. Since we will need to standardize our production processes to assure consistency and quality of output, this will be a tightly-controlled operation, with highly-centralized decision-making (leaving few, if any, decisions to be made by production workers.) All of this points to a functional organization; one capable of producing large quantities of products at low cost, but requiring little innovation, except possibly in the development of production processes.

The second organization will look quite different. Since we will not be making large production runs there will be less need for either a large plant or high-volume production equipment. Inputs will be purchased in smaller quantities and there will be a greater need for people who have specific skills, and who will earn significantly higher wages. Although quality will be just as important, or perhaps more important, we won't require the same level of consistency, so this organization won't have to be as tightly controlled. It will be more organic, with workers expected to know how to do their jobs and to be able to make their own decisions. This organization is likely to be more decentralized, possibly with elements of a matrix structure. Innovation is likely to be more important, and certain to be more prevalent, than in a functional structure.

These examples are, of course, taken from opposite ends of the spectrum of production processes: at one extreme are products that are mass produced, in quantities of thousands, hundreds of thousands, or millions; and at the other, those that are custom-made, one at a time, to meet the demands of individual customers. Between those extremes are production quantities in batches of a few products at a time, a few dozen at a time, or a few hundred at a time, requiring organization structures that vary accordingly. But *production quantities* are not the only way that technology affects organization design.

The types of people we hire are affected not only by our production quantities but also by the *complexity* of our production processes. The kinds of technology we use will affect the knowledge, skills, abilities, and decision-making that are required of the people we hire, in a more complex way. The amount of knowledge and experience required to make decisions depends on how *routine* those decisions are.

Routineness is determined by how predictable a process is. A process that is *routine* is predictable, in that things always happen in the same way. *Exceptions* are *rare*. Seldom does anything happen that hasn't happened before.

A *non-routine* process is *un*predictable, because things *don't* happen the same way every time. *Exceptions* are likely to be *frequent*. Workers can expect to face situations that they have never before encountered.

In the first example, workers will seldom need to make decisions, and when they do the situations will usually be similar to those they have previously experienced. But the second example will require frequent decision-making, sometimes in entirely new situations, since things don't happen the same way every time. From this comparison it should be apparent that a worker in a non-routine process will encounter more exceptions and will have to make more decisions, which will require more knowledge and experience than a worker in a routine process. He or she is, in effect, facing a more complex set of circumstances. But *how often* decisions have to be made isn't our only concern. *We* must also consider what the decision-maker has to do when an *exception*, a new situation, *does* occur.

Every time an exception is spotted, the decision-maker must *analyze* the situation to determine what to do, what is the most appropriate action. This analysis requires considering different ways of responding to the situation and determining which is the *best* way. This introduces a new perspective to the discussion of routineness: *analyzability*, which means how easy or difficult it is to analyze a particular situation. If the technology is one in which exceptions are relatively easy to analyze the decision-maker will require less knowledge and experience than for a technology in which exceptions are more difficult to analyze.

So the *routineness* of a technology affects decision-making in two ways: how often exceptions are likely to occur, and how difficult the exceptions are to analyze when they do occur. It follows from these discussions that non-routine production processes will require decision-makers with higher degrees of knowledge, experience, intuition, and judgment than production processes that are more routine and, thus, less complex.

So far we have discussed production processes primarily from the perspective of manufacturing technology, but what about service technology?

Service Technology

Technology involved in developing and delivering services can differ significantly from that associated with products. Examples of service companies include restaurants, hotels, all types of healthcare organizations, most participants in the travel industry, banks, schools and universities, social service agencies, and most governmental organizations.

The *output* of a service organization is generally less tangible than that of a product-based organization; it *does something* for the customers, rather than *providing a product* for them. Since the output is a service rather than a product, the *transformation* process will generally be much different than that of a manufacturing company. If a service organization manufactures anything at all it will usually only be those things necessary to support the services it provides. In fact, most of the transformation process takes place directly between a representative of the organization and the customer. Services tend to be customized for each customer and consumed at the same time they are produced, with the customer participating in the transformation process. The fact that the output is usually intangible makes the assessment of quality highly subjective and difficult to measure. Being able to respond to customer needs on short notice is often essential, which also makes the location of the facility an important issue; it may need to be close to the customer. So when the output is a service, and transformation takes place at the time of delivery, can we assume that the inputs are different, too?

Since service is more knowledge-intensive than manufacturing, the production processes of service organizations are more likely to be based on specialized people and the equipment they need to deliver the services. But these firms may not have to invest in the capital-intensive production equipment of a manufacturing company, in large, specialized physical facilities. On the other hand, since services are produced at the same time they are delivered, the output of a service organization can't be inventoried. This means that any cyclicality in the business of a service company can make it difficult to balance staffing needs.

Another important difference between products and services is the proximity of the organization and its customers. The production of products does not have to be near the customer, but delivery or services *does* require the customer to be near or more specifically, requires the organization to be near the customer.

Although it is a fact that a higher percentage of U.S. workers are employed in service than in manufacturing (and the percentage in service is growing, while manufacturing is shrinking), some organizations are neither purely manufacturing nor service, but a combination of both.

We have seen how manufacturing processes can influence the design of an organization, now how about service companies?

Since service organizations provide customized outputs that are consumed at the same time they are delivered, they must be knowledge-intensive and responsive to customers, as well as close to them. From this it should be apparent that a mechanistic organization, with its centralized decision-making and tightly-controlled processes, is not likely to be as effective. Referring again to the manufacturing technology model (Figure 19), we are reminded that customized products require more complex processes than those that are mass-produced, and there is no reason to assume that customized services will be any different. The fact that services are customized means that the jobs of employees in service organizations are likely to be similar to those manufacturing employees who are involved with customized products. With that in mind, we can assume that service employees are likely to encounter a higher number of exceptions in their decision-making processes and, in many situations, greater difficulty in analyzing what decisions to make. Thus, service organizations are likely to require a higher percentage of specialized employees, more knowledgeable and experienced, than manufacturing companies. These kinds of skills will be utilized more effectively through an organic structure, in which employees are encouraged to tailor their transformation processes to the situations they encounter, and to make the decisions necessary to be responsive to customer needs. This suggests an organization form that is more decentralized, or matrix, than functional.

From the preceding discussions it should be apparent that technology, defined here as how we do things, should be a major factor in determining what type of organization structure will be most effective in helping an organization's strategy achieve its goals, and in determining what types of people will be needed to make the organization effective. Now what about innovation? Where does it fit? What role does it play?

INNOVATION

Schumpeter's views (see quotation at the beginning of this chapter) may be even more relevant today than they were when he voiced them. In fact, many economists believe the economic growth of any society is strongly influenced by its rate of innovation (Tushman and Anderson,1997). If innovation is that powerful, and there's a lot of evidence to suggest that it is, think of the role it can play in competitive strategy. It can influence new products, processes, markets, organization forms, even new sources of raw materials. If we believe, as Tushman and Anderson (1997) suggest, that technological change is a major determinant of which organizations will succeed and which will fail, organizations should actively manage innovation to make sure they have a strong voice in our own future. The way we structure our organization, along with the type of culture we develop and maintain, will play a major role in how innovative the organization is. This is further support for the idea that we should organize *consciously* rather than letting organization structure evolve on its own.

The people we hire, and how we organize and manage them are keys to effective innovation. When every activity and every decision is dictated by top executives there is little opportunity for individual initiative, and the only innovation we are sure to have is either that coming from the top down, or from outside the organization. When that is the case, those within the organization will either save their innovations for their outside interests, projects, and organizations, or they will leave the organization to join one that will allow them to *use* their initiative and creativity. That's why so many entrepreneurial companies are started by those kinds of people; people who feel that they have not had, or will not have, the opportunity to develop their ideas in a larger organization. What, then, is the secret to stimulating innovation, and to keeping the most innovative people from leaving?

Much of the impetus for innovation comes from the attitude of the organization's leaders, and the atmosphere they create and maintain in the organization. The more organic the organization, the more freedom employees are given to pursue their own interests, in their own ways. The more encouragement people are given to come up with new ideas, the more nurturing the environment becomes for creative thinkers. Often, the most creative people in an organization are seen as "oddballs" or "troublemakers," because they think differently than most of us, and because they prefer to do things their own way, which is often quite different from what is considered "normal" behavior. To keep these potential innovators content, and to keep them from pursuing their interests in other companies, we need to have the foresight and tolerance to create a nurturing environment for them: one that feeds their creativity, rather than stifling it. If we do that, these people will be more likely to stay with the organization.

SUMMARY

Overall, the keys to developing and maintaining an innovation-driven organization are to staff it with a diverse collection of individual thinkers; organize it to so they can make maximum use of their individuality, initiative, and creativity; and give them the opportunity to develop to their full potential. And this shouldn't apply only to those who design products and services; it should apply to everyone, because we never know who will be the source of tomorrow's innovation.

Brown (1991) suggests that an organization has a responsibility to do more with innovation than just develop products; it should work to make the entire organization innovative. He says that, given the opportunity, people prefer not to follow policies and procedures but use them to understand the organization's goals, and then invent their own work activities in a way that lets them be responsive to changing circumstances. The importance of this perspective shouldn't be overlooked; we should visualize innovation in a much broader context, recognizing that it doesn't just apply to products and services, but can be equally valuable in making an organization's internal processes more effective.

Prahalad (1993) provides a concluding perspective on the role of technology, declaring that competitive advantage doesn't come from technology. Management provides competitive advantage by focusing the attention of organization members on strategic intent, their capabilities on distinctive competencies, and their efforts on organizational objectives and the strategies for achieving them. Technology serves as an enabler in the process.

So the important thing to remember about innovation and technology: innovation is about *thinking*, *imagining*, *experimenting*, and *creating*, while technology is about *doing*. Innovation helps determine the most effective ways to utilize the organization's resources, including technology, and is critical to developing a sustainable competitive advantage.

Technology, on the other hand, is simply a tool—a tool that can give a false sense of security. Unlike innovation, technology by itself is unlikely to be a competitive advantage, at least not for long because, in most cases any competitor will, sooner or later, have access to the same technology, making any advantage temporary.

Innovation is the key to competitive success or failure. In our rapidly-changing globe-spanning competitive environment, innovation is becoming the primary difference between success and failure for an increasing number of organizations. And the interesting thing about innovation is that the potential for it resides in every employee at every level of every organization. So make sure you create an atmosphere in your organization that gives innovation the maximum opportunity to flourish.

Chapter 15

KNOWLEDGE AND LEARNING

"There is only one good, knowledge, and one evil, ignorance."
(Socrates)
"Those who cannot remember the past are condemned to repeat it"
(George Santayana)

Knowledge is defined as "The state or fact of knowing. Familiarity, awareness, or understanding gained through experience or study." *(American Heritage Dictionary,* 1983) *Learning* is "Gaining knowledge through experience or study." (Ibid)

So, basically, *knowledge* is about knowing and understanding, and *learning* is how we acquire knowledge, but how are they important to strategic management?

KNOWLEDGE

Throughout history, people have sought knowledge for two purposes: 1) for self-knowledge, to grow morally, spiritually, and intellectually; or 2) to become more effective, by knowing how to read, write, calculate, and do things.

For most of human history only a very small percentage of people were educated: primarily the privileged few, who needed wisdom to fulfill their role of governing the masses, and religious leaders, who needed it to provide spiritual guidance. Knowledge was essential, to give them a sense of who they were, what they should believe in, and what they should stand for. So, for many centuries, self-knowledge was the dominant form of knowledge; but only available to a select few. The ruling classes needed knowledge but their subjects didn't; they could be told what to do, and could learn how to do it from their fellow workers.

But during the 18th century, practical knowledge gained importance, as the need to become effective became more urgent, driven by a patent system, introduced in Great Britain, that allowed inventors to "own" their inventions and to keep the profits from marketing them. The patent system inspired a dramatic increase in creativity and new inventions and made personal initiative and effectiveness valuable commodities. Suddenly there was an incentive for individuals from all classes of society to develop their individual capabilities: to learn to read, write, calculate, and *do* things more effectively.

The wave of innovation that followed included the development of the steam engine, which probably had more to do with the industrial revolution than any other invention. The steam engine gave us *moveable power*, something not available before. Prior to steam, any process that needed large amounts of power had to be located near the source of that power: most often rivers, or areas that had dependable sources of wind power. But now it was possible to locate production wherever it would be most effective, in terms of the availability of raw material, labor, and customers. As a result large factories began to replace the cottage industries that had previously been the backbone of manufacturing, and the factories' need for workers provided new opportunities for people to move from low-paying farm work to higher paying manufacturing jobs. In these new jobs, individual know-how became more important.

But it wasn't until the 1880s, when Frederick W. Taylor first applied knowledge to analyze how work could be done more effectively, that knowledge was applied to work on a larger scale. Taylor's objective was "to try to develop every workman in our employ, so as to bring out his best faculties and to train him to do a higher, more interesting and more profitable class of work than he has done in the past." (Taylor's presentation at the First Conference on Scientific Management, The Amos Tuck School, Dartmouth College, October, 1911). His experiments offered the first concrete examples of just how much individual productivity could be increased, simply by applying knowledge to the way work was done. Taylor's concept is so important that the relationship in Figure 20 should be permanently etched in our minds.

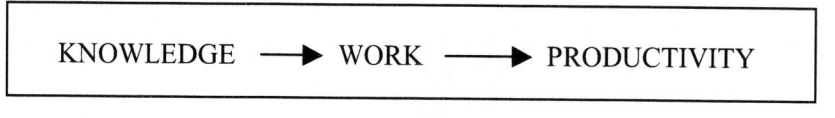

$$\boxed{\text{KNOWLEDGE} \longrightarrow \text{WORK} \longrightarrow \text{PRODUCTIVITY}}$$

Figure 20

Largely overlooked by history is Taylor's intent to teach workers "...to do a higher, more interesting, and more profitable class of work." Although he intended to improve workers' *job satisfaction* and *earning potential*, rather than just increasing their productivity, he is best remembered for increasing individual productivity. Since the introduction of Taylor's scientific management, productivity has increased to such an extent that today a worker can produce more than 50 times as much as in the 1880s. The key lesson in this is that applying knowledge to how we work can result in a continuous process of productivity improvement and can continually elevate the quality of our work life (e.g., greater job satisfaction, less physical strain, less monotony). Just how important is knowledge in organizations? It is the key to continuously improving not only what we do but how we do it, and both are absolutely essential to staying in the competitive race. Notice that I said "staying in the ...race", rather than winning it. This is because, although knowledge is critical to keep from falling behind, it doesn't guarantee a competitive advantage. And knowledge, by itself, doesn't do anything; it's what we *do* with it that matters. That's where learning comes in, especially organizational learning.

LEARNING

Peter Senge describes a *learning organization* as "...an organization that is continually expanding its capacity to create its future."(1990:14). Garvin puts it a bit differently, but in a way that begins to define the role played by knowledge in a learning organization: "A learning organization is an organization skilled at creating, acquiring, and transferring knowledge, and at modifying its behavior to reflect new knowledge and insights." (1993:80) Both definitions emphasize that it isn't just that knowledge needs to be *available* in an organization; it must be *activated*: put into practice by the people of the organization, because an organization isn't *learning* until its people are learning. How can we make sure that happens? How can we assure that people have the opportunity to learn, and that they are encouraged to learn?

We can begin by recognizing that learning is always about answering a question, or solving a problem. There is a cycle we go through in this process, described as a "wheel" of learning (Kolb, et al., 1984). See Figure 21.

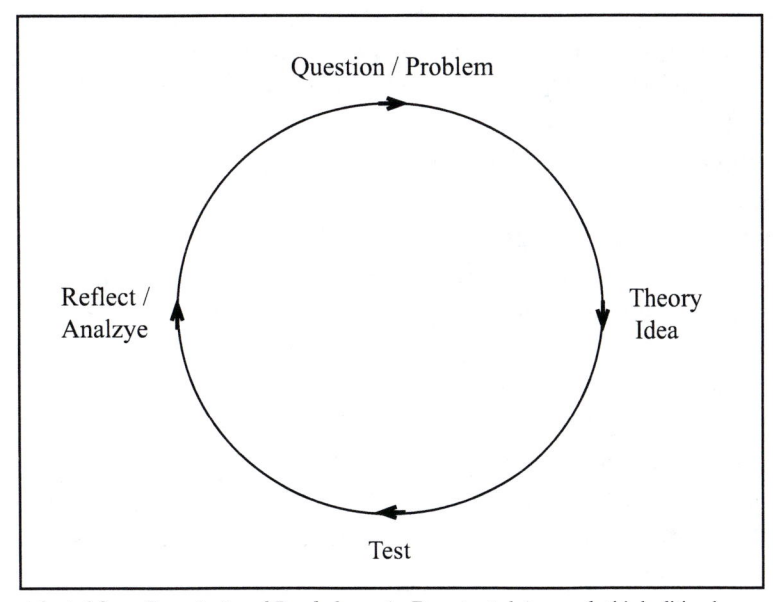

Adapted from *Organizational Psychology: An Experiential Approach,* third edition by Kolb/Rubin/McKinyre, copyright © 1984. Reprinted by permission of Pearson Education, Inc., Upper Saddle River, N.J.

Figure 21. Wheel of Learning

Learning always begins with a question or problem. As we address the problem we consider different ways it might be solved, then decide on a method we think will work. We test our theory by actually trying it, and then we reflect (i.e., think about) on how the test went; we analyze the results. What went as expected, what didn't, and what happened when it didn't? Then we restate the problem and start working on a revised theory. This process continues until we have a satisfactory result. Thinking back on how we learned to walk, or ride a bicycle, or drive a car, or drive a golf ball, we can see this learning process in action. Although we can also learn by listening or by watching, it is by *attempting* to do something that we learn best. And perhaps the most valuable part of learning-by-doing is the experience we gain that makes us better problem solvers. If we truly want our organization to be one in which people feel encouraged to learn, we will have to do at least one thing much different than the majority of organizations do it today, evaluate individual performance.

In most organizations performance evaluation still focuses first on criticizing past performance and then urging us to correct what we have been doing wrong and encouraging us to do it better the next time. It's important to remember that when we are penalized for our mistakes as though we made them *deliberately*, we have a strong tendency to do whatever we can to make sure we don't make any more mistakes. Now let's go back to the wheel of learning and see how this plays out.

If, in fact, all learning comes from trying things until we can do them right, any time we attempt to learn we are destined to make some "mistakes," and the more we try to learn the more "mistakes" we will make. But if we are penalized for those mistakes we will be much less likely to do anything unless we are *sure* we can do it successfully. And since the only things we can be *sure* will work are the things we've done successfully before, we will stop trying new things and stay with the things we've always done, and the ways we've always done them. "If it ain't broke, don't fix it," right? But when that happens, learning will be stifled and innovation will come to a halt, and the most creative people will soon leave for other organizations; organizations with atmospheres that nurture creativity and innovation; organizations that encourage people to try things and make "mistakes". Remember 3M's Post-it Notes? They were based on a "mistake;" an adhesive that didn't work the way it was supposed to. So it's important to remember that we won't have a learning organization unless our performance evaluation process is designed to *support* and *improve* performance rather than just criticize it. In the words of Charles Handy, "The learning organization can mean two things, it can mean an organization which learns and/or an organization which encourages learning in its people. It should mean both." (1990:225)

It is important to remember what learning *is* and what it *isn't*. Learning *is* about questioning, thinking, testing, evaluating, and improving. It *is* about attempting and failing. It *is* about persistence and commitment. Learning *should be* a way of life.

Learning *isn't* memorizing, or knowing the answers, and it *isn't* only about learning from others. Some things we need to learn for ourselves, and those often provide our most valuable experiences.

The importance of learning, however we choose to do it, is reinforced Arie De Geus, former strategic planner for Shell Oil Company, "The ability to learn faster than your competitors may be the only sustainable competitive advantage." (1988:70-74). This may be just as applicable to each of us, as individuals, as it is to our organizations.

INFORMATION

A critical element of both knowledge and learning is *information. Information* is defined as "Knowledge derived from study, experience, or instruction; facts." *(American Heritage Dictionary,* 1983).

Figure 22 shows how information is related to learning and knowledge.

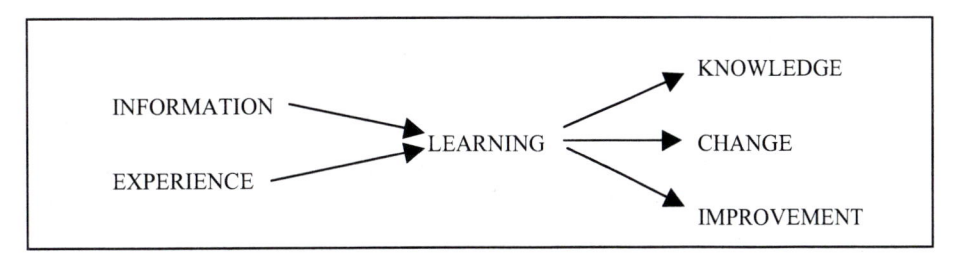

Figure 22.

Advances in information technology, particularly how information is gathered, stored, and shared, have given all of us access to more information. For many years organizations were able to gain competitive advantage through proprietary information; information to which only they had access. In addition, customers weren't able to get much information about a company's products, or about how they compared with those of the competition, so they didn't have much leverage to negotiate prices between competitors. Both of those situations have changed dramatically. In today's competitive environment we should assume that everyone will have access to the same information at the same time, so competitive advantage is much less likely to come from information asymmetry.

Having the information we need, in useful forms, is absolutely essential to keeping up with the competition, but it will only be a competitive advantage for the short time that we have it before everyone else gets it. Increased availability of information is forcing organizations to become smaller, more specialized, and more decentralized, so they can be more flexible and more responsive than their competitors. This has increased the tempo of competition and made information essential to reducing uncertainty in the rapidly-evolving competitive environment. Uncertainty, itself, has been defined as "...the absence of information" (Daft, 1998:332).

Translating information into knowledge requires that we digest it and then put to use. New information will not be the only basis of our knowledge, but will be compared and/or combined with existing information, then considered in the context of our experience, intuition, and perspective. In this sense, understanding the difference between *explicit* and *tacit* (*implicit*) knowledge is important.

Explicit knowledge is knowledge that can be captured, recorded, and passed on to others in documents, or in some other form. It is largely factual and relatively easy to understand. This is the type of knowledge that is most adaptable to non-human decision making. *Tacit* knowledge on the other hand is based on our personal experience, intuition, judgment, and rules of thumb generated by our experience and that of others. Tacit knowledge often includes creative ideas and solutions that we may not even understand ourselves, let alone be able to explain to others.

Organizational learning is based on both explicit and tacit knowledge, which makes it difficult to maintain an "organizational memory." Because it can be documented, explicit knowledge is fairly easy to retain within an organization, but tacit knowledge exists only in the memories of organization members. As people leave the organization, which everybody inevitably will, pieces of the organization's memory go with them. This is a problem many organizations make even worse when they attempt to downsize by offering early retirement programs. Early retirement offers are invariably accepted by those we can least afford to lose; those with the very knowledge and experience that is most valuable to the organization and most irreplaceable. This type of program, in effect, *encourages* tacit knowledge, including important parts of the organizational memory, to go away.

We should, instead, do everything we can to retain that knowledge, by encouraging our more experienced people to *stay*, and by providing incentives for those who have valuable knowledge to share it with those others who are most likely to remain in the organization for years to come. Our organizations are, of necessity, becoming more knowledge-driven, and as they do encouraging loyalty among employees becomes more essential to remaining competitive because, in a very real sense, the organization's competitive advantage increasingly resides in the knowledge of its employees. When they go, it goes.

SUMMARY

Past organizational configurations, which were ordinarily designed to manage machine-based technology and to utilize physical resources efficiently, are being replaced by those designed to manage knowledge-based resources, to utilize ideas and information, and to promote continuous learning, both individual and organizational. The most effective learning organizations will have deliberately-developed cultures that are driven by empowered people who willingly share knowledge and information, are encouraged to learn continuously, and are supported by understanding and nurturing leadership.

Three of the most challenging issues for knowledge-based learning organizations are:

1. finding the *information* they *need*,
2. maintaining a *learning atmosphere*,
3. *retaining* critical *knowledge* (within the organization.)

Finding *information* isn't difficult at all. In fact, our problem is the opposite: there is *too much* information. The problem is finding the *right* information; the information we *need*. It is important to know that there are many programs and technologies available to do this, and we should make good use of them to help us select *only* the information we *need*, rather than allowing people to become bogged down with information that isn't relevant to our objectives.

Maintaining a learning atmosphere is critical to encouraging innovation, and is a key to our competitive success. We must clearly understand that encouraging people to try new things means encouraging them to try many things that won't work. This means allowing time, effort, and money to be spent on some things that will never pay off; something that has traditionally been *discouraged*. So it requires changing our organizational cultures and mindsets, which will require diligence and patience.

Keeping critical *knowledge* within the organization is also largely a cultural issue—creating an atmosphere in which people can do the kind of work they enjoy and enjoy the work that they do. It requires recognizing that people are the key to our success, and that their knowledge is our competitive advantage. Keeping their knowledge in the organization requires creating a desirable environment; one that makes people *want* to be there. The key of course, is how we treat people and how we make them feel about themselves and the organization. People are critical to any organization's success, and should be treated as such., something that doesn't happen in often enough.

Addressing those three issues isn't easy; but the organizations that do it, and do it effectively, will be well on the road to competitive success.

Chapter 16

BOARDS OF DIRECTORS

The board of directors has, as its primary responsibility, providing oversight for the organization in the sense that it provides governance over the firm's management. What do we mean by governance? In its simplest sense governance means watching over the firm's top executives to make sure they manage the company in a way that serves the best interests of its owners, rather serving the executives' personal interests.

BOARD RESPONSIBILITIES

Fulfilling its primary purpose usually requires the board to be involved in at least three roles:
- Control—selecting the president,
    - asking discerning questions,
    - replacing the president (if/when necessary)
- Advise/Counsel—advising the president and the top management team
- Strategy—helping develop the organization's mission/purpose, and policies ratifying corporate strategies

As a general rule, closely-held companies are not required to have boards of directors, because their owners are usually closer to the operation and better able to watch over and control how their companies are run. Nevertheless, most privately-held companies do have boards, but they usually serve primarily to advise and counsel top management. As such, they are generally seen as advisory boards, rather than governing boards.

But any company whose stock is widely-traded (generally this means at least 300 shareholders) is required by law to have a board of directors. The reason? With that many owners (stockholders), most are not likely to be close enough to the company to oversee their own investments (not to mention the chaos that would result if hundreds of different voices tried to tell its managers how the company should be run.)

So, as public-ownership became more popular, laws were passed to provide oversight for those absentee owners; laws that require a company's board of directors to watch over the company's executives; to keep them honest; to ensure they remember they are hired by the stockholders, to protect stockholders' investments.

BOARD COMPOSITION

Most corporate boards are comprised of inside directors, who are full-time employees (usually corporate officers), outside directors, who are non-employees, and a chairperson, selected from and by the board members. While there is no legal requirement for the ratio of inside and outside directors, rules enacted by the Securities and Exchange Commission and New York Stock Exchange require a board's Audit Committee be made up entirely of outside directors.

There is, however, a trend toward limiting the inside directors to the company's president, and perhaps one other officer.

The size of corporate boards vary considerably, from a legal minimum of three directors for publicly-traded companies, to as many as the company desires. The average number of directors on Fortune 500 company boards is generally somewhere around 11 or 12.

Another element of composition, minority board members, is an ongoing challenge. Although there has been some progress, many boards, particularly large-company boards, still fit the popular perception of "good-old-boy clubs," dominated by white males. Despite efforts to change that, many large companies still have no more than token representation: typically one female member and one who is an ethnic minority.

A major challenge to board effectiveness, in this author's opinion, is the practice of many boards to allow (even encourage) directors to succeed themselves, term after term. In fact many boards have no requirement for directors to ever step down, unless they retire or leave the corporate position (usually as CEO of another firm) that made them attractive as a potential board member.

BOARD EFFECTIVENESS

How effective are boards in carrying out their corporate governance responsibilities?

There is a perception, particularly in the business press, that many boards are not effective at all, a view supported by the number of high-profile cases in which major companies found themselves in dire straights before their boards belatedly took appropriate action (which usually included firing the CEO). Notable examples include Enron, Worldcom, Arthur Anderson, and Tyco.

But it's important to put that into perspective by recognizing that those cases represent only a small fraction of the total number of publicly-traded companies, which means there are probably thousands of other companies whose boards are doing their jobs quite effectively. Nevertheless, it is important to examine why boards fail to execute their responsibilities effectively.

Governance failure may be attributed to one or more of the following causes: CEO-duality; stockholder apathy; the proxy system. Let's examine each of them.

CEO-Duality

While the chairperson of the board is selected by and from its directors, the vast majority of boards select the company's chief executive to fill that position. This is called CEO-duality, because the chief executive serves dual roles: chief executive of the company, and chairman of its board. Why is CEO-duality a factor in governance failure?

Because the primary responsibility of the board is to select the company's chief executive and monitor his/her performance. But when the chief executive also becomes board chair he is chairing the group to whom he is responsible. This makes him, in effect, his own boss; an executive responsible for the governance of himself. It's no wonder this is seen by many as analogous to giving a mouse responsibility for guarding the cheese.

The prevalence of CEO-duality has led to the perception that it is a form of role-reversal, in which the board moves from being the body that monitors and controls the chief executive, to a body that serves at the discretion of the chief executive. This perception is reinforced by the fact that most CEOs select the members of their boards, which risks having board members who are beholden to the CEO and perhaps reluctant to "bite the hand that feeds them."

Stockholder Apathy

Corporate governance began as a simple system in which:

- Owners and workers provided inputs (i.e., money and labor),
- Owners hired managers to organize the processes that created outputs,
- Workers received wages, managers received salaries, and owners got what was left (profits).

But as companies began issuing their stock to be bought and sold on the open market, the meaning of ownership began to change. At first, stockholders viewed their stocks as long-term investments, and themselves as minority owners of the companies whose stock they owned.

But in recent years fewer and fewer stockholders see stock-ownership as a long-term investment, or view themselves as owning companies. They have changed from investing to speculating, and now see a share of stock as little more than a "betting slip." So today's owners no longer act like owners.

This means that, although the board of directors is supposed to be retained by the owners to oversee their interests, owners are no longer interested in selecting, evaluating, or replacing directors. This may be understandable considering that ownership of any company is dispersed so widely, among thousands of stockholders, that their powers of ownership are minimal; almost non-existent.

As stockholders lost interest in selecting directors, CEOs and their boards began to assume and exercise this power themselves, determining who would serve on boards, what they would do, and evaluating (or not) how well they were doing it. This may have been a major influence in transferring the governance of management into the hands of the executives, themselves. And as executives took over their own governance, serving the interests of a company's owners often became secondary to corporate growth, because with growth came more compensation, greater promotional opportunity, and more job security, all serving the interests of management.

The Proxy System

The proxy system was developed to allow a company's owners (shareholders) to control the board of directors and, through it, the firm's management. It was designed to allow widely-dispersed shareholders, whose attendance at shareholder meetings is limited by travel requirements, to exercise their right to vote on important corporate issues.

Before the annual stockholders meeting, each shareholder is furnished with a proxy statement that explains important actions (e.g., re-election/replacement of directors, mergers, acquisitions, divestments,) and a "ballot" on which his/her shares can be either voted, or "proxied" to another individual to allow that person to cast the shareholder's vote.

For most shareholders, the proxy system is their only means of controlling the board and, indirectly, corporate management. In other words, it's their only way to influence or change corporate governance but, unfortunately, it has been almost totally ineffective in serving that purpose. Why? Primarily because the way proxies are solicited makes it almost impossible for outside shareholders to nominate candidates for board seats, or to propose issues to be voted on.

Soliciting proxies is generally done by one or more agents, who try to convince absentee stockholders to transfer (proxy) their votes to an agent, who accumulates votes to cast at the stockholder meeting. Agents then have the ability to cast large blocks of votes, giving them more leverage in selecting directors, or in passing or defeating major proposals.

The way proxy laws are written gives incumbent directors a significant advantage in solicitation, allowing them to maintain and control shareholder lists, manage ongoing shareholder relationships, and utilizing corporate funds to do their soliciting.

This means that outsiders (e.g., a shareholder who wants to initiate a proxy contest, either to run for a board seat, or to propose something to be voted on) have to mount such a campaign on their own, without the help of the firm's resources (either human or financial), and without its shareholder list. As a result, proxy contests are few and far between, and successful ones are rare.

As a result, directors who are up for re-election invariably run unopposed and are assured of retaining their board seats as long as they choose; giving them something akin to life-time tenure.

GOVERNANCE FAILURE

What happens when corporate governance doesn't work the way it should; when boards fail in their responsibilities?

Beginning in the 1980s, hostile takeovers drew increasing attention to corporate governance. They spotlighted boards of directors, particularly those that were not sufficiently diligent in overseeing shareholder interests. With management having to answer only to themselves, who was left to look out for the owners?

The takeover wave in the 1980s was viewed by many as the re-emergence of "active investors;" investors whose interests were similar to those who owned and were actively involved in overseeing their own companies prior to the 1940s. These "active investors," more frequently called "corporate raiders," sought out firms whose market values (stock prices) were significantly below what they should/could be if properly managed (i.e., significantly below their intrinsic values.)

They would typically offer to buy outstanding stock of a company, offering more than the current stock price, but substantially less than it would be worth under new management. When they succeeded in obtaining enough stock to have a voice at the board level, their first move was to do exactly what the owners of a firm would have done (and what it's board should have done)—replace top management.

Those takeovers, coupled with the threat of additional takeovers, probably performed a valuable service to many other firms, forcing them to operate more efficiently and effectively. Hostile takeovers became, in effect, a default form of corporate governance—when boards failed in their governance role, the market did their jobs for them.

NOT-FOR-PROFIT BOARDS

Boards of non-profit organizations are considerably different from corporate boards, particularly in size, composition, and operation.

Size

Although some are small, not-for-profit (NFP) boards tend to be larger than their corporate counterparts, and it isn't uncommon for them to have 30 or 40 member boards. The reason for the large number of directors is that non-profit organizations depend heavily on support from corporations and influential individuals, and offering board seats to representatives of those entities is a good way of ensuring their ongoing support for the organization, both financially and socially.

Composition

In stark contrast with corporate boards, NFP boards are generally made up entirely of outside directors. Although the organization's chief executive officer may be present at board meetings, he/she is seldom a member of the board.

Another contrast is the minority makeup of NFP boards, which usually include a significant percentage of ethnic minorities, and almost always (except in men-only or women-only organizations) nearly equal numbers of women and men.

Finally, board members are elected for specified terms, generally three years, and most NFP boards limit their directors to two consecutive terms, which keeps new blood and new ideas rotating through the board.

Operation

Because the size of the board makes it difficult to discuss issues and decisions in a timely manner, NFP boards tend to get things done through standing sub-committees and ad-hoc committees. This has the advantages of allowing participants to specialize in their areas of interest/expertise, and to involve many more people, ideas, and effort in the operation of the organization. This often gives these boards a level of effectiveness seldom approached in corporate boards

BOARD ISSUES

What does the future hold for corporate governance and boards of directors? Some of the more important issues are likely to be:

- more *objective* boards—appointment of directors who have no allegiance to the company's executives,
- more *active* boards—increased evaluation of boards, and of individual directors, to improve board participation and weed out ineffective directors,
- more involvement of *institutional investors*—fund managers becoming "active investors" rather than speculators,
- changing *proxy rules*—to allow greater investor voice to provide electronic voting of proxies
- more *professional directors*—board members for whom it's a full-time job,
- more *non-CEO* board chairs.

SUMMARY

The board of directors can, and should, play a significant role in the success of their organization.

Chapter 16—Board of Directors

Boards of publicly-traded companies, are legally charged with fiduciary responsibility for the operation of their companies; a serious responsibility. But company executives should view their boards not as potential impediments, but as valuable assets, and should staff them with members who have experience and expertise that can add significant value to the company and its operations.

While boards of privately-held companies and non-profit organizations may function primarily as advisory boards, board members can, here again, be valuable assets, who should be selected for the kinds of experience and expertise they can bring to the organization.

Although we may not currently operate at the executive level of our organizations, understanding how boards of directors are supposed to work, and how they do work, can be important to us in at least two ways: providing insight into how effectively the organization we work for is being led; and insight into any potential employer we may consider in the future.

There are effective boards and ineffective boards and, to a large extent, board effectiveness is dependent on how the CEO of the organization utilizes the board and its members. When you see a board that largely rubber-stamps whatever the CEO wants, you should ask yourself whether or not that CEO is running the company in his own interests or those of the owners. If he's running it to serve himself, you should ask yourself what kind of future the company has.

But if the board isn't afraid to challenge the CEO, there's a good chance that she sees the board as a company asset, and is using it and its members to serve the best long-term interests of the company.

How its board is utilized is often a good reflection of what kind of leadership a company has, and a pretty good indicator of how bright its future may be.

PART IV
STRATEGIC RESPONSIVENESS

The implementation of a strategic plan—putting it into action—is not the end of strategic management. It's actually the beginning, because a strategic plan is not a finished product—it's only a starting place. We know from experience that no matter how well we plan, we can't possibly consider *everything* that might happen. When we implement a plan we should *expect* things to go wrong; expect to make changes. So, after *planning* and *implementation* the third part of strategic management is *performance evaluation*—knowing how well the plan is working and when it's time to change it. The chapters in this section discuss how to *allocate resources*, how to *measure performance*, and how to *manage the change* that is inevitably part of strategic management.

Chapter 17

DECISION MAKING

"Heaven helps not the men who will not act."
(Sophocles, 495-405 B.C.)

In the first chapter I suggested, as the most important qualities of leadership, vision, commitment, understanding people, persuasiveness, integrity, decisiveness, and a sense of responsibility. Although one can debate which quality is *most* important, unless he is decisive—able and willing to make timely decisions, even with minimal information—a leader doesn't lead.

Decision making is the process of making choices; choosing between one course of action and another, or between several possibilities. The objective is to select the best course of action in a particular situation. And decision-making is almost always about identifying and solving problems.

RATIONAL DECISION-MAKING

Rational decision-making involves systematic analysis of a problem and its underlying causes, following a logical step-by-step process, then implementing the decision through rational actions. Although making decisions through a completely rational process is seldom possible in rapidly-changing organizational environments, it is a useful model for teaching managers the *ideal* way to make decisions: logically, rather than emotionally. Rational decision-making usually involves at least seven steps:

1. *Problem*—identify the *problem*: what is happening that shouldn't be happening? The difficulty here is that what we initially see as a problem often isn't the problem, itself, but a *symptom* of the real problem.
2. *Root cause*—determine what's *causing* the problem. Peter Drucker (1966) suggests we begin by determining if the situation is generic or an exception. He describes four degrees of generic vs. unique situations:
    A. Generic, across all organizations—the occurrence is only a symptom of a systemic problem (most problems are of this type.) An example would be inventory decision—how much to inventory to stock vs. the cost of carrying it.

B. *Generic, but unique to the organization*—something that may happen frequently in organizations, but never before to this organization. For example, an offer to merge with another company.
C. *Unique*—a truly unique, one-time event. For example, a multi-state power failure.
D. *Unique*—a first-time event, but one that may be a sign of things to come. For example a multi-state power failure that's unique, but an indication of a deteriorating infrastructure Drucker says we should begin by always assuming the problem is generic, and that the current situation is simply a symptom of the real problem.

3. *Goals*—clearly specify what needs to be accomplished. How will we know when the problem has been resolved? What outcomes can we expect?
4. *Optimal decision*—determine, in advance, the ideal outcome. What would be the *best* possible decision? Then, even if we have to settle for less than the best decision, which is often the case, we will have something to compare it with.
5. *Alternatives*—what are some possible solutions for the problem? Developing viable alternatives requires ideas and opinions from a variety of sources—the more diversified the better. The best alternatives come from dissention and disagreement, not consensus.
6. *Selection*—choose the alternative that comes closest to the optimal decision.
7. *Action*—implement the decision; make it happen. Until it's executed, a decision isn't a decision, it's just an intention.
8. *Feedback*—continuously assess the results you're getting against those you had expected.

In this process, steps 1-3 identify the problem and its causes, 4-6 develop a decision, 7 implements the necessary actions, and step 8 analyzes their effectiveness.

INDIVIDUAL DECISION-MAKING

The fundamental difference between decision-making by individuals and decision-making in organizations is the number of people involved in the process. As individuals, we can go through every step of the decision-making process by ourselves, if we choose, without seeking help from anyone else. But organizations generally involve more than one person, although the decision, itself, final selection of the best alternative, usually falls to a single person.

No matter how it's done, or where, decision-making is based on how people think, how they develop alternatives, how they consider consequences, and how they assess risk vs. return. And the way we make decisions isn't always the logical, seven-step sequence previously described.

Programmed Decisions

Some decisions, for example, are programmed, in the sense that we have standard procedures for dealing with certain types of situations. These are usually repetitive situations; things that we deal with regularly or periodically; decisions that we make almost without thinking about them. (e.g., stopping at stop signs, boiling eggs, getting our oil changed.)

Non-Programmed Decisions

These occur when we face new or unusual situations, for which there are no existing procedures. Each case must be decided on its own circumstances. (e.g., responding to a call for help, breaking a fall, making an impromptu speech.)

Intuitive Decisions

In areas in which we have a lot of experience, our subconscious mind retains vast stores of information that can be invaluable in helping us make decisions. This information is often so thoroughly embedded in our subconscious that we make decisions automatically, without thinking about them. Our instincts and our reflexes take over for us.

It's interesting to note that often decisions that are made quickly are often just as good as those made slowly and deliberately. We make them so fast, based on minimal information, that we don't take time to second-guess ourselves. In this process, we use our intuition in place of the information we don't have.

That's why it sometimes pays to go with our first impulse, and let our subconscious make the decision. As long as we monitor the results so we can quickly change or fine-tune the decision, this can be one of the best ways to make effective decisions.

Bounded Rationality

When thinking about how decisions are made, we often assume it's a logical, rational process designed to arrive at the one best decision—the optimal decision. But most of the time we don't operate that way, primarily because the human mind doesn't have the capacity to consciously consider more than a few facts at one time.

Our subconscious memory is believed to retain everything we've ever seen, heard, read, felt, smelled, or experienced. It's like a massive data bank and, theoretically, has the capacity to support *rational* decision-making, by allowing us to consider every possible alternative. But, unfortunately, our subconscious won't let us access what we want, when we want it. For example, do you ever have trouble recalling a person's name? Of course you do; we all do. But, sometime later, when we're thinking about something else, that name will invariably pop into our mind. That's how our subconscious works; it's always there and always working, but not necessarily on *our* schedule.

So, since we can't always utilize that magnificent store of information when we need it, we have to rely on our short-term memory, with its limited data-processing capacity. That's why we usually settle for *bounded rationality*—a decision-making capability that falls far short of optimal decision-making.

So whenever we have more than just a few alternatives, we don't even attempt to consider them all. Instead, we go through them systematically, one by one, rejecting some and setting others aside for further consideration, until we have a few that look as though they *may* solve the problem. At that point we stop searching, and begin reviewing those we've set aside, finally selecting the best of that group.

Although it might have been possible to find an even better solution if we continued our search, once we've spent what we feel is all the time we can afford on searching we decide that what we have is "good enough," and don't look any farther. This is called *satisficing*—we aren't able to optimize, to select the *best* solution, so we have to be satisfied with one that's *good enough*. (When done in organizations, this is often referred to as the Carnegie Model of decision making.)

Consider, for example, how we choose what to wear. At one extreme is the person who doesn't want to be bothered with that decision, and buys only white shirts and one color of slacks. His decision is easy: any shirt will go with any pair of slacks. (And maybe he gets a volume discount on his shirts, to boot.)

At the other extreme is the person with blouses and skirts in a variety of colors. If she has, for example, 12 different blouses and six different skirts, there are 72 possible alternatives to consider. How does she choose? Certainly not by considering every possible combination; she'd never make it to work. So maybe she selects a blouse first, then the skirt that goes best with it. Using that method, she only has six possible alternatives, and a manageable decision.

What does all this mean? Simply that most of the time we're better off choosing one of the first alternatives that will solve the problem, rather than spending additional time searching for the best possible solution.

ORGANIZATIONAL DECISION MAKING

Organizational decision making can be affected by anything that goes on within the organization, or anything that influences it from the outside. Some major factors are the organization's structure, its culture, how mechanistic or organic it is, and how centralized or decentralized its decision-making process is. An interesting analogy is that its decision-making process is the brain and nervous system of the organization. (Daft, 2007)

Daft describes four primary types of organizational decision-making processes:

Chapter 17—Decision Making

Management Science Approach

This approach is used when problems are mathematical or statistical in nature, and have too many variables to be solved by individual decision makers. It is most effective when the problems and variables are quantifiable and measurable.

Carnegie *Model*

Primarily applies to non-programmed decision-making, in situations where there are no precedents, procedures, or decision rules to reduce the time managers spend searching for optimal solutions. It involves the concepts of *bounded rationality* and *satisficing*, previously described in more detail under *Bounded Rationality*.

Incremental Model

Based on the theory that major organizational decisions are often accomplished through a series of small decisions, over time, usually involving considerable trial and error, and multiple approaches to the primary problem.

Garbage Can Model

Developed to explain decision making in rapidly-changing organizations; perhaps especially relevant in learning organizations, where multiple decisions are being made simultaneously, often without coordination among them. While the Incremental and Carnegie models focus on how a single decision is made, this model is looking at all of the decisions being made in an organization.

ESCALATING COMMITMENT

Escalating commitment occurs when a person or an organization continues to invest in a failing effort, even after it becomes obvious that it isn't working. A classic example is the gambler who keeps doubling his bets hoping that one win will recoup all of his losses. Following are discussions of several theories about why people get trapped in this kind of situation.

A tendency to find excuses for negative outcomes that result from our own decisions. It's easy to become trapped by our unwillingness to admit a bad decision, and to invest additional time, effort, and money in a desperate attempt to salvage the situation and prove that our decision was right, after all. Perhaps it can be chalked up as a cost of preserving our pride.

The fear that changing our mind, or our decision, will be seen as inconsistency, or indecisiveness. This perception may be reinforced by an organizational culture that values the status quo, and is threatened by change. In such circumstances, we may feel that our career will be jeopardized if we don't stick with our original decision. So, to avoid being seen as "wishy-washy" we do whatever it takes to make our decision come out right.

Then there's the pressure of sunk costs. The more time, effort and, especially, money, we have invested, the more we're committed to that course of action, and to doing whatever will make us feel it wasn't wasted.

One way to avoid escalating commitment, and its waste, is to identify, in advance, the point at which we will abandon a decision; the point at which its probability of success will be in serious doubt. Then we must be willing to bail out or change course, no matter how much we stand to lose in sunk costs. Instead of thinking about how much we've lost, we should think in terms of how much we'll save by not continuing to invest in a losing effort.

SUMMARY

Making decisions is one of the most critical success factors for individuals and organizations. Many companies and individuals fail to reach their potential because of their inability to make effective decisions, or because of their inability to make *timely* decisions.

A decision doesn't have to be the *best* decision to be effective. A decision's effectiveness depends on several things, among them: 1) proper identification of the problem; 2) a solution that will solve the underlying cause(s) of the problem; 3) a decision made in a timely manner; and 4) a course of action implemented quickly and effectively.

The Problem

It's been said that when a problem has been correctly identified it's half solved. This illustrates the importance, and difficulty, of separating the true problem from its symptoms.

Root Cause

Once the problem has been identified, it's essential to determine what's causing it—its source—because only by eliminating the underlying cause can the problem be solved, once and for all. Failure to identify the root cause invariably results in treating the symptoms rather than the problem, and the problem will ultimately crop up again.

Timely Decisions

One of the most important things to remember about making decisions is that, most of the time, *any decision, even a poor one, is better than no decision*. The biggest time-wasters in decision making are trying to sort through too many alternatives, and trying to find the *best*

Chapter 17—Decision Making

solution. Usually choosing an *acceptable* alternative (rather than waiting to find the best one), then implementing it quickly, will result in an effective outcome.

Quick Implementation

A timely decision has little value if it isn't implemented quickly. Timely implementation not only solves the problem earlier, but also gives the opportunity to quickly examine the effects of the decision and take any corrective action that may be necessary.

Decision-Makers

Decisions in organizations often involve getting opinions from many people, but no matter how many are involved in the process, the final decision is usually the responsibility of one person. And that's the way it *should* work. Trying to make decisions by consensus invariably slows the decision-making process, sometimes with disastrous results.

On the other hand, any boss who makes major decisions without seeking the input of others is passing up the opportunity to have multiple alternatives to choose from, and risks sending the message that he/she knows it all, and needs no help.

A much more effective approach is to ask as many people as practical for their help in identifying the problem, and their opinions about how to solve it. The leader should then choose what he/she feels is the best approach, and challenge the rest of the participants to ensure that it is implemented successfully.

Decision-making should never be about trying to reach consensus. Dialectic discussion is invaluable, including the disagreement it generates, but once the decision is made (usually by a single person, not the group) the discussants need to join together to support it enthusiastically. This results in better decisions, particularly where there is significant uncertainty and/or complexity. And there's considerable added value from giving participants the opportunity to offer their opinions, and from the understanding they gain of what was decided and why.

Decision-Making as a Learning Process

The more decisions we make, and the faster we make them, the more opportunity there is for making errors, mistakes, wrong decisions. But that's how individuals and organizations learn. So the fact that we make mistakes shouldn't be a concern; what *should* be a concern is how well we learn from them. If we recognize that nobody *wants* to make mistakes, we can be confident that most of the time people won't make the same mistake twice. And we can be confident that they will learn from their mistakes.

And tolerating mistakes is a good way to reduce the risk of escalating commitment, since decision-makers will find it easier to revise or reverse their less-effective decisions, and see less need to defend and justify them.

The more we allow people to try things, and make decisions, the more they and their organizations learn, and the more innovation the organization will experience.

Chapter 18

RESOURCE ALLOCATION/BUDGETING

The way we allocate resources will have a major affect on our success. To make sure that our strategy has the best chance for success, we must make sure that our resources (e.g., people, money, equipment, space, information, knowledge, time, and energy) are used where they can have the biggest impact. It is a fact of life that most of us (organizations and individuals) will *never* have enough resources to do everything that we would like to do, so we have to make choices, choices of *what* we want to do, and in what *order*.

For a strategy to be successful, and to achieve our major goals, every part of the organization must have enough resources to carry out its piece of the plan, but the most critical activities must have first priority to get the resources they need, even if other activities have to do without. We must, for example, must make sure that any activities that are essential to our distinctive competencies have access to the resources they need *before* activities that are less essential. This means that lower-priority projects may have to make do with less than they need, or wait longer for what they need. Although it is easy to understand why this concept makes sense, making it work in practice is *not* easy. It takes hard-nosed management to make sure that resources are allocated in a strategic manner, because those whose resource needs are denied or delayed will invariably resist, and some will go to great lengths to get the allocation decision reversed or amended.

Take, for instance, a new strategy that requires a major re-allocation of resources, giving some managers more people while reducing the staffs of others. Those managers who have been given more responsibility and the additional people to carry it out will undoubtedly be pleased with what they view as a positive career step. But those with less responsibility will likely see it as a demotion, a backward step in their professional careers, and their reactions are likely to be quite negative. They may go to great lengths to convince their superiors that this is a bad move for the organization. Some will inevitably become so frustrated that they leave the company, or worse, remain and become negative influences within the firm. The possibility of this happening can be reduced or eliminated by properly preparing the affected managers. They should be informed, well in advance, of what is to come, who will be affected and how, and why it is important.

By the time we begin allocating the resources that are necessary to implement our strategies, every department, work group, and individual should know exactly what objectives they are expected to achieve, and what resources will be required to achieve them. The activities that are undertaken to achieve these objectives should become the primary focus of the efforts of everyone in the organization, and all of the organization's resources should be allocated in the way that best supports those activities.

Not only should our resources be budgeted based on the action plans for achieving our objectives, we should *deny* resources to any activity that is not part of meeting those objectives. In other words, *nobody* in the organization should be doing *anything* that doesn't contribute to meeting the organization's goals. This means that we should not allow "...because we've *always* done it" to be an excuse for continuing to do something that is no longer part of our action plans. It also means that any ongoing activities that are important to the organization (e.g., maintenance, training) must be included in objectives at some level, to ensure that the necessary resources are provided for them. This process is similar to "zero-based budgeting," in which an organization's budget is developed anew each year, rather than simply updating and revising last year's budget. People should justify, each budget cycle, everything they do and why they do it. Organizations that *don't* follow such a policy, which might be called "zero-based resource allocation," are almost certain to continue performing some activities that no longer add value to the organization, simply because nobody questions whether or not they are still necessary.

In an earlier chapter we discussed the importance of having only a *few* major goals, no more than five or six, and the necessity of prioritizing them. The importance of this should now be clear: since we will never have enough resources to do everything we would like to do, the fewer objectives we have the more effectively we can allocate our resources and to make sure we accomplish the most with what we have.

Another important consideration is making sure that we don't overlook those operations that provide crucial, yet sometimes invisible, support for the organization, sometimes referred to as *critical support systems*.

If, for example, being a low-cost producer is important to our competitive strategy, cost accounting and inventory control systems may be crucial to maintaining and evaluating our efficiency. Or if we rely on the dependability of manufacturing processes to make sure that products are always available when the customers need them, machine-maintenance capabilities will be very important to our success. And any organization that knows that people are the key to its future success will rely heavily on competencies in recruiting, training and development. Every organization has systems like this; systems that they may not often think about, but that are essential to their ongoing success. It may be an information-distribution system, a series of policies and procedures which help maintain organizational culture or, in the case of an airport, a baggage-handling system. Although these systems are not high-profile or glamorous, without their support higher-visibility functions are likely to become high-visibility *malfunctions*.

Finally, and perhaps most essential to assuring the effectiveness of resource-allocation, are our incentive and reward systems. They must be designed and administered to reward *only* activities that are essential to achieving pre-set objectives and to withhold rewards from any activities that are not.

SUMMARY

One of the greatest difficulties in implementing a plan is making the *right* things happen. Any organization can make things happen, but only one that has a deliberately-developed strategic plan and implements it effectively can be assured of accomplishing the *right* things. So the real key to strategic success is *implementation*.

Even the best strategic plan is worthless if it is not implemented effectively. Effective implementation, of course, means that we do, in fact, achieve the major objectives that we have set for ourselves. And the key to that is making sure that *every person* and *every activity* follows the strategic plan. That means that we can't have people doing what they've always done, or what *they* think should be done, or following any agendas that are different than those of the organization. We must keep everyone focused on what the *organization* needs done to achieve its major activities. How do we do this? How do we focus everyone's attention and effort?

A major force, and one of our most powerful forces, is the way we allocate resources. If we *do* provide resources for something, it *will* get done, and if we *don't* provide resources for something, it *won't* get done. It's really as simple as that—simple in concept, but *not easy* to make happen. Not easy because sometimes managers don't have the conviction and fortitude to enforce it, by saying "NO," and sticking by their guns when they meet resistance. It requires removing friendship and favoritism from the decision-making process and making sure that we are all driven by the strategic plan and what it has outlined as the best course of action to assure the ongoing success of the organization.

Chapter 19

PERFORMANCE EVALUATION (Feedback)

"A true critic ought to dwell rather upon excellencies than imperfections, to discover the concealed beauties..."

(Joseph Addison, 1672-1719)

Once we have the right people, the right culture, an organization structured to help people work together, and leaders and managers who will make it all work, it is time to begin strategy implementation: taking the actions and beginning the activities that will make our strategic plan a reality. It is important to remember that at the time we develop new strategies we *think* we know how they will work, but we can't be sure until we've tried them.

So before implementing our plan, let's refer once more to the "wheel of learning" (Figure 21). Reflecting back on the strategic planning process we've just completed, we began by asking ourselves the *question* "How can we accomplish our mission?" To answer that question, we moved to the second step and developed a strategic plan: our *theory* for how to answer the question. Now we're ready for the third step: *testing* the theory, which requires implementing our plan. But before we begin implementation we should look forward to the fourth step: *reflection*. Reflection means reviewing how the test went: what worked, what didn't, and what we learned. But how will we *know* what worked and what didn't? Somehow we have to be able to measure the effectiveness of our implementation process; how well it's actually working. This doesn't mean just looking at it *after* it has been completed, but also monitoring the plan *while* it is being implemented, while there is still time to change it.

This requires a way of measuring the *progress* of the strategy and improving it. An effective feedback system will allow us to continually monitor the process and quickly make any adjustments that are necessary to correct it, or any that we believe will improve the process. Since measurement is the key to effective feedback, we will need to develop *measurements* for each of the activities and outcomes that are most important to us.

But we don't have to start from scratch; we actually laid the foundations for measurement when we translated organizational objectives into lower-level objectives throughout the organization. Although organization-level objectives are the ultimate measure of organizational effectiveness, some of them will not be completed until too late in the process to help us monitor the early stages of implementation. So for short-term feedback we will have to rely on lower-level objectives, particularly individual objectives, because the people doing the work are likely to have the best sense of how things are progressing, especially those things over which they have direct control. They know when they are on schedule, and generally have a good awareness of what might prevent them from *staying* on schedule.

From an organizational point of view, we should make sure we measure performance in each of three areas: inputs, outputs, and the transformation process. Most performance feedback systems focus on the organization's internal *transformation* process, because there is the greatest opportunity to correct minor nuisances before they become major problems. But measuring *inputs* is also crucial, because it ensures that we are hiring the right people and training them properly, and that we are receiving the materials and equipment that we need, when we need them, and that they are of the desired quality. *Outputs* of course, are the final measure of organizational effectiveness although, in many cases, they can't be measured until after the fact, when it is too late to help improve the process; when quality has already been compromised.

What we choose to measure is very important. For many years financial results were the primary measures of organizational effectiveness and, in many organizations, the *only* measures. Advocates of strategic management had, for years, insisted that financial measures, alone, were not sufficient to provide the feedback necessary for processes to be managed in the most responsive manner. Their concerns were largely ignored until they received reinforcement from quality improvement programs, which insisted that every activity in an organization could, and should, be measured continuously. These programs emphasized that the key to continually improving quality is to continually measure the effectiveness of all processes. More recently, the idea that we need more than just financial measures of organizational performance has been reinforced by the "Balanced Scorecard," a framework that "translates an organization's mission and strategy into a comprehensive set of performance measures..." (Kaplan and Norton, 1996:2)

This model suggests measuring organizational performance from four perspectives: financial, customer, business process, and learning and growth. The *financial* perspective measures primarily long-term objectives including, for example, sales, return on investment (ROI), return on equity (ROE), economic value added (EVA), and revenue. The *customer* perspective addresses the organization's desired customer groups and might include measuring customer satisfaction, customer retention, and market share. The *business process* perspective is directed at the organization's internal processes and how they add value. Measurements might include any of an organization's processes, such as product development, manufacturing, inventory, and distribution. And the *learning and growth* perspective focuses on the skills and abilities of members of the organization. This generally includes measuring the effectiveness of training and development programs, and providing gap analyses of those areas in which important capabilities seem to be lacking.

Strategic Management and the Balanced Scorecard share the perspective that organizational performance cannot be measured effectively by just looking at financial information; the organization must be examined from several different perspectives and at all levels. We must be aware, at all times, of how the organization is doing in terms of: acquiring *inputs*,

Performance	Measures
Inputs	
Money	Debt, equity
People	Recruiting effectiveness
	Retention/turnover
Materials/equipment	Cost
	Quality, consistency
	On-time delivery
Transformation	
Product development	Development time
	Number of new products
	Innovation
	Success rate
Production processes	Quality, consistency
	Productivity
	Cost
	Rework
	Inventory—in-process
	— finished goods
Employee development	Training—hours/employee/year
	Education—number of employees involved
	— average education level
	Promotions
Budget	Income, expenses
Outputs	
Sales	Sales volume
	Market share
	Returned goods
Customer satisfaction	Customer satisfaction
	Repeat customers (customer retention)
	Market share
	On-time deliveries
Financial results	ROI, ROE, EVA
	Cash flow, revenue

Figure 23. Performance Measures

performing the *transformation* process, and providing *outputs*. An important part of evaluation is staying in touch with how well we are meeting the expectations of both *employees* and *customers*. Are we able to find, attract, and retain the employees we need? And how well are we satisfying our customers? Figure 23 shows examples of measurements, grouped by inputs, transformation, and outputs.

Although every organization will have different categories in each area, *inputs* will generally include several ways of measuring the organization's ability to acquire the people and materials it needs. *Transformation* will require measuring the efficiency of the organization's processes and activities, and determining how well employee development efforts are going. And *outputs* will include indicators of sales effectiveness, customer satisfaction and, of course, financial results.

Corporate performance is usually measured based on outputs, while departmental and individual performances are based on measures of inputs and transformation.

The most important thing to remember about measuring organizational performance is that the measures, themselves, have little value unless and until we use them as guides to *improving* performance. The only reason we measure is to keep track of how we're doing, so that we can learn how to do it better. To make that happen in the most responsive and most effective manner, we need to make sure that *everybody* in the organization knows what their personal performance indicators are, as well as those of their department and the organization as a whole. In addition, everyone should be charged with *quickly* spreading the word any time they see something that isn't going according to plan, so that the situation can be corrected immediately.

This way the entire organization will be continually moving around the wheel of learning, constantly reflecting on how well it's doing and using that information to find new ways to do it better. Then, as we implement our strategic plan the organization is continually learning how to do things better and revising the plan accordingly. This process has two major benefits: 1) it makes the strategic plan dynamic, constantly evolving, becoming more effective; and 2) it makes the organization truly a learning organization.

Summary

Doing anything without knowing *how* we're doing is like flying blind—we don't know where we are and therefore have no idea what we have to do to get to where we're going. To make the course-corrections necessary to arrive at our destination, we must have feedback—a flow of information that helps us compare how we're *actually* doing with how we had *planned* to do. Feedback is actually performance evaluation. In implementing strategy, as in traveling, we can only achieve our objectives by continually monitoring our progress; measuring where we *are* at any time, and comparing it with where we *thought* we'd be at that particular time, then making any changes that are necessary. Two things are important for effective performance evaluation: 1) measurements; and 2) information.

Chapter 19—Performance Evaluation (Feedback)

Evaluating performance means comparing *actual* performance against *expected* performance. This requires *measuring* actual performance and comparing it against a pre-set standard (*expected* performance). Measurement requires quantification (i.e., how much? of what? by when?).

Comparing actual performance against expected performance requires two kinds of *information*: 1) actual performance, at any point in time, and 2) the standards against which performance is being measured.

Once we have the necessary measurements in place, and a flow of information that allows us to compare actual performance with expected performance, we can constantly monitor performance and correct or improve it as necessary to keep the implementation process on course. This is a crucial part of successful implementation.

Chapter 20

MANAGING CHANGE

"Nothing endures but change."
(Heraclitus)

The world in which we live and work is constantly changing, and as it changes it affects how we live and how we do business. This means that to manage strategically we must know how to manage change. When the world around us is changing we can do one of three things: resist the change, change with it, or try to influence how it affects us. Although the third option may look a bit ambitious, our discussion of External Analysis (Chapter 5) describes a number of ways it can be done, so we won't repeat them here. Instead, we'll concentrate on the other two: changing, and resisting change, and the advantages and disadvantages of each.

RESISTING CHANGE

When confronted with change, the response of many organizations is similar to that of many people: they tend to resist it, at least initially. Why? Robbins (1990) offers five reasons that *individuals* resist change:

1. *habit*—we get used to doing things a certain way and resist changing those habits;
2. *security*—we feel safer in a familiar situation than facing the prospect of a new and relatively uncertain one;
3. *economic*—we fear that the change will affect our income;
4. *fear of the unknown*—what we *know*, even if we don't particularly like it, is generally less threatening than the uncertainty of what we don't know; and
5. *selective information processing*—we hear what we want to hear, and we hear it in the context of our own experience and perceptions.

You'll notice a common thread among those concerns: uncertainty. Change represents uncertainty, and most of us are more comfortable staying in a familiar situation, as long as it is not totally unbearable, than trying something different. We get used to operating in a "comfortable rut" and as long as our situation doesn't get too uncomfortable, inertia is likely to keep us there. In short, it's easier to keep doing what we've been doing than to do something different. When we're sitting, we have a strong tendency to stay seated. When we're walking or running, it's easier to keep going than to stop and start up again or to change direction.

But it isn't just individual resistance that makes introducing change difficult. *Organizations* reinforce our individual change-resistance in several ways (Robbins, 1993):

- *structural inertia*—our selection and formalization processes "fit" people into certain slots in the organization, and imply that those positions are permanent;
- *group inertia*—peer pressure is sometimes so strong that even a person who is willing to change feels pressured to resist;
- *threat to expertise*—the change may look threatening to the importance of specialized individuals or groups, threatening their value to the organization;
- *loss of power*—our decision-making authority, a form of power, may be threatened by the proposed change; and
- *resource allocation*—the resources that we currently control may be threatened by the proposed change.

And there's one more we should add to Robbins' list: *arrogance*—the mindset of an organization that is impressed with its own success. The longer an organization is successful the more those within the organization are likely to see it as immortal and guaranteed to continue that success in the future. Peter Drucker describes the risk of this mindset with the proverb, "Whom the gods want to destroy they send 40 years of success"(1993).

So it stands to reason that organizations, like people, are more likely to oppose change than to embrace it. But resisting change isn't always bad. It can provide a kind of organizational stability, making it less likely that the organization or its people will be bounced around by a turbulent environment, or by uncertainty, industry fads, or indecisive decision-making. Although an organization with strong internal resistance *can* be influenced to change, it usually only succeeds through a deliberate, well-thought-out process, rather than a response to *arbitrary* attempts at change.

On the other hand, change resistance can be bad when it becomes too deeply embedded in an organization's culture. When that happens, the organization may resist change so adamantly that it becomes a pawn of its external environment and the uncertainties it presents. Then, rather than controlling its own destiny, the organization lets its future be determined by fate, and organizational decline is almost certain to follow. That's the basic difference between planned and unplanned change. Planned change is initiated in support of a deliberate strategic plan, and is generally implemented well in advance of when it is needed. Unplanned change is often *forced*, for example, by an external crisis that puts the organization at risk, or by a strong internal coalition trying to serve its own purposes. Although most organizations are likely to face a crisis at some point, those that manage strategically are more likely to anticipate the crisis and act *before* it reaches a critical point, while others will delay acting until *after* the situation becomes critical, and then have to *react*.

Studies have shown that more than half of all organizations fail within five years of their founding, and only one out of every ten survives for more than 20 years. Failure to see the need for change, and failure to change are surely major contributors to such a high mortality rate. Although resistance to change isn't necessarily bad, it can be devastating if it results in failure to change when change is absolutely necessary.

LEADING CHANGE

The effectiveness of an organization is influenced by how dynamic it is in changing, developing, and improving. An organization or individual that is not moving forward might as well be moving backward, at least with respect to its competition. The more turbulent its industry the more dynamic the organization must be just to keep up, and the most dynamic organizations are generally those that develop cultures that will *lead* change, rather than resist it. How can we develop such a culture; one that embraces and leads change? Fombrun (1992) suggests three internal systems that organizations use to change their cultures: reward systems, educational systems, and socialization systems.

As individuals, most of us respond to *rewards* and punishment in predictable ways: when we have been rewarded for doing something we will *do it again*, and when we've been punished we will *avoid* doing it again. With this in mind, one of our first steps in leading change should be to make sure that our reward systems are designed to *reward* those people who do what we want them to do and to withhold rewards from those who don't.

Additionally, our employee *education* and *training* systems should be designed to reinforce what the organization is trying to accomplish, and the direction in which it intends to head. They should help people understand how achieving the organization's objectives will make them, as well as the organization, more successful in the future. In other words, we should make sure that everyone in the organization understands the strategic plan and what they have to do to make it successful and what that success will mean to them.

Socialization involves introducing employees to the organization's culture and practices, and helping them understand its values, history, and philosophy. Rituals, legends, and symbolism are important parts of the socialization process, and can be very effective in introducing change. INC Magazine (February, 2002) gives an example of a deliberate act of symbolism that took place at Steuben Glass in 1933. Steuben, a subsidiary of Corning Glass Works, made colored glass tableware and decorator pieces. The firm had been struggling, so its president decided to change to the production of higher margin products. To make a point of this change and Steuben's new business focus, the president and a member of his staff deliberately destroyed thousands of pieces of the old inventory by throwing them onto the concrete floor of a warehouse, an action designed to leave no doubt in the mind of any Steuben worker that things would be different in the future.

At Wal-Mart, Sam Walton deliberately developed a culture that would facilitate change, and constantly reinforced that culture by encouraging employees to suggest new ideas for ways the company could improve. And Wal-Mart is just one of many organizations that are now tapping into the creativity of their employees by encouraging them to participate in continuous improvement, quality circles, and similar activities.

Employees' attitudes toward change are strongly influenced by how clearly they understand *why* change is being made and what advantages it offers them and the organization. Helping people understand the need for change is essential if we want to develop a culture that will embrace and facilitate change. That understanding requires knowing the answers to five questions:

1. *What* is driving the change?
2. W*ho* is initiating the change?
3. W*hat* must be changed?
4. *How* will the change be accomplished?
5. *When* will the change take place?

What is driving change? Although there are many possibilities, some of the more common drivers of organizational change are changes in:

- the organization's *strategy*—a new strategy often requires changes in the organization's structure and in how resources are allocated;
- organization *size*—growing pains frequently lead to the need for changes in organization structure;
- *technology*—introduction of new technology can change how we do things, and the skills and capabilities required;
- *environment*—changes in the organization's external environment that are driven, for example, by new competitors, changes in pricing, product introductions, strategic alliances, or new legislation;
- *power*—a shift in power within the organization, especially at the top, can cause dramatic change, particularly when the change is made in response to a crisis.
- *competition*—a competitor's change in strategy that forces the organization to change its strategy.
- *organizational life-cycle*—as the organization evolves through different stages of its life-cycle, its strategies will likely change accordingly.

Who is initiating the change? Most often change is initiated by organizational executives or managers, or by specialists or consultants who are called in as advisors. Our willingness to support change is strongly influenced by how legitimate we feel the initiator's motives are. If we believe the motives are self-serving rather than designed to serve the interests of the entire organization, we are more likely to resist the change than support it. Trust can have a major influence on our attitude toward change, particularly on how legitimate we feel the reasons for change are. In fact, sometimes consultants or outside experts are brought in just to provide that legitimacy.

What must be changed? We should help people understand, before the change, what must change, in terms of people, structure, technology, and processes. *People* changes may include changing the culture, or part of it, as well as the types of skills, capabilities, and expertise that will be most important in the future. *Structural* changes are often the most far-reaching and

Chapter 20—Managing Change

frequently involve changes in authority, responsibilities, reward systems, procedures, and resource allocation. *Technological* changes may include new equipment, new expertise, and changes in job responsibilities and assignments. Organizational *process* changes are likely to affect communication patterns, coordination of activities, and decision-making.

How the change will be accomplished and *when* it will take place are questions that will be foremost in everybody's mind. To the extent possible, we should encourage the people who will be affected by the change to help determine *how* it should be done. This is one of the best ways to get them to *support* the change, rather than resist it.

When the change will take place will be determined by at least two issues: 1) when does it *need* to take place? (i.e., Is there a deadline?); and 2) the answer to "*how* will it take place?" (i.e., to a large extent, the method we use will determine what things will need to happen and when they will have to happen.)

Regardless of *what* changes will be required and *when* they will have to take place, the details of the plan for change should be outlined as far in advance as possible, particularly to those who will be involved and those who will be affected.

How will the change be accomplished? It is often useful to make change a three-step process: *leaving* the current phase, *entering* the new phase, and *reinforcing* the new situation.

It can be helpful if we make the transition from the old to the new a well-defined process, in which *leaving* the old and *entering* the new are both highly visible. Similar to a right of passage, this process should signify the end of life as we have known it and the beginning of something new.

Leaving should signal that, although the old way was good for its time, that time is over now. *Entering* the new situation includes answering three of the previous questions (i.e., *What is driving the change? Who is initiating it?* and *What must be changed?*), then assigning responsibilities, what each of us will need to do to implement the change. *Reinforcing* includes revising any policies and procedures affected by the changes, changing the reward system, and continually communicating what needs to be done and why it is important to do it. The most common reinforcement techniques are:

- *persuasion*—identifying the need for change; letting internal and external experts present various ideas for how the change might be made; and then asking those who will be affected by it to choose the ideas they feel are best;
- *participation*—involving those who will be affected by the change in determining how it should be done;
- *intervention*—convincing those who will be affected by it that the change *is* important, and *why;*
- *edict*—top management tells those who will be affected what the change will be.

Studies show that *persuasion* is the most widely used; almost twice as often as the second choice: *edict*. However, *intervention* had the highest success rate, at 100%, followed by *participation*, at 84%, and *persuasion*, at 73%. *Edict* was successful just 43% of the time, which shouldn't surprise anyone who understands people. Human nature is such that most of us are more likely to understand and support something in which we have been involved than something that we have simply been ordered to do.

A major reason organizations resist change is that most of them, particularly large organizations, have been designed for efficiency. In our quest for efficiency we usually standardize activities to make them more routine; rely on formal documentation for governance policies and operating procedures; manage by top-down decision-making; and administer reward systems that discourage risk-taking. All of this is done in the interest of maintaining control; a fundamental goal of bureaucracy. Bureaucratic organizations depend on "sameness" for their consistency, and they discourage, either explicitly or implicitly, most attempts to change something or to do something differently. In these organizations management may actively avoid change because of its cost, disruption of the status quo, and possible loss of control. But all organizations must ultimately change; if they don't they are not likely to survive.

When it comes to making change happen we have two basic options: make *incremental* changes—gradual changes, as necessary to keep up with changes in the external environment, or *dramatic* change—make it happen all at once. This kind of dramatic change also happens when an organization delays making changes until it is in crisis, then does it all at once as an impulsive reaction. Managers in bureaucratic organizations often delay change until it is absolutely necessary; "Organizations are characterized by long periods of inertia, punctuated by brief periods of dramatic and comprehensive change that culminates in a very short period of change." (Robbins, 1990: 404) Robbins suggests that managers prefer it that way, since they have power in the current structure that they may not have in a new one. Whether we choose to make change incrementally or in large steps, the important thing is that we *choose* to change rather than having it forced on us. And a key to making change a conscious choice is anticipating the need for change; seeing it coming well in advance.

A good tool to assist us in anticipating when we may need to change is the Organizational Life Cycle (Figure 18). There are two stages of the life-cycle in which change is likely to be most critical: *growth* and *decline*. Both cause organizations to change, one for positive reasons, the other for negative reasons, and both are important to organizational success. But let's look at each of the stages.

In its *infancy*, an organization is fighting to survive long enough to demonstrate the value of its products or services. During that period it is likely to be changing almost constantly, as it learns from its experiences and adapts to its environment. If it succeeds it will enter into a period of *growth*. As it evolves from a start-up to a small company, then to a mid-sized and ultimately a large organization, change will be an ongoing part of its existence. During these early periods in the organization's life-cycle, organization members are more likely to take the need to change for granted because they realize that's how the organization survives and establishes itself. But once it becomes sufficiently large and successful, and enters its *maturity*, the organization is more likely to rest on its laurels, confident that its future is finally assured. From this point on change may seem less urgent; after all, we've made it haven't we? "If it ain't broke, don't fix it." And during this stage it is likely to perhaps almost impercep-

Chapter 20—Managing Change

tibly gradually change from a change-driven culture to one that is increasingly resistant to change. The organization has reached adulthood and is more likely to become set in its ways.

So after having gone through numerous growing pains, each of which was remedied by making the necessary changes, the organization reaches a point where changing no longer seems as necessary; in fact, it may seem downright *un*necessary. Part of the reason may be that, as it grew larger the organization became more bureaucratic, and the status quo became more attractive than continuous change. In any case, the organization evolves from one that was constantly changing to one that now seeks stability. And with stability comes inertia. When it was growing the organization's natural state was dynamic, *ever* changing; now its natural state becomes static, *never* changing. From this point on, the organization is likely to resist changing until it is forced to by a crisis. In the process it becomes a *reactive* organization, one more likely to act in response to what happens *to* it, than proactively making things happen *for* it. And once the inertia of stability takes over, the organization's progression to the final stage of its life cycle, and organizational *decline*, may be inevitable.

Once it reaches the decline stage the organization may no longer have a choice of whether or not to change; it may be *forced* to change. And then the questions become: "What kind of change?" and "How much?" and "Will even that be enough?" It's now also faced with *negative* change. Changes that we make to support organizational growth generally create "nice" problems because we understand that they are an essential part of growth, a good thing. On the other hand, changes that are necessary for survival are often brought about by failures of the organization and its management, and are much harder to accept by those affected. Managing the type of change required by organizational decline is much more difficult than managing the change caused by growth

Managing change during a decline frequently leads to downsizing the organization, one of the most traumatic and demoralizing actions any organization can take. Downsizing is made more critical by the knowledge that how we go about it lays the foundations for future trust or mistrust between the organization's leaders and its members. It's not so much *what* the organization does to downsize, but *how* it's done that makes the difference. We won't attempt to cover the complete details of the proper ways of downsizing in this book, but one issue is too important not to mention. Since every downsizing affects people, how those people are treated is critical to the long-term effects of the process. Those who survive a downsizing often feel guilty because they still have jobs while some of their friends have lost theirs. Organizational managers can either add to their guilt or ease it by how they treat those who are laid off. If surviving employees see their departing friends being well treated, including assistance in finding new employment, they will not only feel less guilty, but will also be reassured that they, too, will be treated fairly if the same thing ever happens to them. One other key to rebuilding trust is to do the downsizing *all at once*, not in stages. Make the cuts large enough that you can assure the survivors that this will only happen once, so there will be no more. When it is done in stages, nobody will ever be sure that there won't be more to come.

SUMMARY

In the environments in which we live and work, change is inevitable, and an important part of being successful, as individuals and as organizations, is how *we* change to become more effective in the new environment. We *know* that change will come; we just don't know when, how, or where. But we can, by watching trends, see things happening that are likely to affect us in the future. Trends in areas like demographics, the economy (national and global), legislation, and technology are not difficult to see, and can often be seen well in advance. Being aware of them will allow us, and our organizations, to make incremental changes well in advance, so that we can reduce the probability of suddenly being faced with a crisis.

And that's really what strategic management is all about: *Planning the organization's future and the actions necessary to achieving it, while being prepared to react to unanticipated events in an organized manner.*

REFERENCES

Bennis, W., Biederman, P. W., 1997, *Organizing Genius: The Secrets of Creative Collaboration*, Reading, MA: Addison-Wesley Publishing Company

Block, P., 1993, *Stewardship*, San Francisco, CA: Berrett-Koehler Publishers

Bluedorn, A. C., 2002, *The Human Organization of Time,* Stanford, CA: Stanford Business Books

Bower, M., 1966, *The Will to Manage*, New York, NY: McGraw-Hill

Brown, J. S., 1991, "Research that Reinvents the Corporation." *Harvard Business Review*, January-February, 1991, Boston, MA: Harvard Business School Press

Christensen, C. R., Andrews, C. R., Bower, K. R., Hamermesh, R. G., Porter, M. E., 1982, *Business Policy: Text and Cases*, Homewood, IL: Richard D. Irwin, Inc.

Cohen, M. D., March, J. G., Olsen, J. P., 1972, "A Garbage Can Model of Organizational Choice." *Administrative Science Quarterly*, 17 (March), Ithica, NY: Cornell University

Colvin, G., 1997, "The Changing Art of Becoming Unbeatable." *Fortune*, New York, NY: Time, Inc.

Csikszentmihalyi, M., 1990, *Flow: The Psychology of Optimal Experience,* New York: Harper Perennial

Daft, R. L., 1998, *Organization Theory and Design*, Cincinnati, OH: South-Western College Publishing

Deal, T. E., Kennedy, A. A., 1982, *Corporate Cultures*, Reading, MA: Addison-Wesley Publishing Company

De Geus, A., "Planning as Learning." *Harvard Business Review*, March-April 1988, Boston, MA: Harvard Business School Press

Drucker, P. F., 1966, *The Effective Executive*, New York, NY: Harper & Row, Publishers

Drucker, P. F., 1986, *The Practice of Management*, New York, NY: Harper & Row, Publishers

Drucker, P. F., 1993, *Post-Capitalist Society*, New York, NY: Harper Business

Drucker, P. F., 1993, "A Turnaround Primer.", *The Wall Street Journal*, Feb. 2, 1993, New York, NY: Dow Jones & Company

Drucker, P. F., Dyson, E., Handy, C., Saffo, P., Senge, P. M., 1997, "Looking Ahead: Implications of the Present." *Harvard Business Review*, Boston, MA: Harvard Business School Press

Fombrun, C. J., 1992, *Leading Corporate Change*, New York, NY: McGraw-Hill

Garvin, D. A., 1993, "Building a Learning Organization." *Harvard Business Review*, July-August 1993, Boston, MA: Harvard Business School Press

Hambrick, D. C., Fredrickson, J. W., 2001, "Are You Sure You Have a Strategy?" *Academy of Management Executive*, Vol. 15, No.4, Briarcliff Manor, NY: Academy of Management

Handy, C., 1990, *The Age of Unreason*, Boston, MA: Harvard Business School Press

Handy, C., 1997, "The Citizen Corporation.", in Drucker, P. F., Dyson, E., Handy, C., Saffo, P., Senge, P. M., "Looking Ahead: Implications of the Present.", *Harvard Business Review*, September - October, 1997, Boston, MA: Harvard Business School Press

Hedley, B., 1977, "Strategy and the Business Portfolio." *Long Range Planning*, London, UK: Pergamon Press

Hill, C. W., Jones, G. R., 1998, *Strategic Management: An Integrated Approach*, Boston, MA: Houghton Mifflin Company

Kaplan, R. S., Norton, D. P., 1996, *The Balanced Scorecard: Translating Strategy into Action,* Boston, MA: Harvard Business School Press

Kolb, D.A., Rubin, I.M., McIntyre, J.M., 1984, *Organizational Psychology: An Experiential Approach,* Upper Saddle River, NJ: Pearson Education, Inc.

Maslow, A. H., 1998, *Maslow on Management*, New York, NY: John Wiley & Sons

McGregor, D., 1960, *The Human Side of Enterprise*, New York, NY: McGraw-Hill

Mintzberg, H., Quinn, J. B., Voyer, J., 1995, *The Strategy Process,* Englewood Cliffs, NJ: Prentice-Hall

O'Neal, D., 2006, *If Not Now, When?* Bloomington, IN: AuthorHouse Publishing

Porter, M. E., 1980, *Competitive Strategy*, New York, NY: The Free Press

Prahalad, C. K., 1993, "The Role of Core Competencies in the Corporation." *Research/Technology Management*, November-December 1993, Washington, DC: Industrial Research Institute, Inc.

Robbins, S. P., 1990, *Organization Theory: Structure, Design, and Applications*, Englewood Cliffs, NJ: Prentice Hall

References

Rokeach, M., 1973, *The Nature of Human Values*, New York, NY: The Free Press

Senge, P. M., 1990, *The Fifth Discipline: The Art and Practice of the Learning Organization*, New York, NY: Doubleday/Currency

Taylor, F. W., 1947, *Scientific Management*, New York, NY: Harper Brothers Publishers

Thompson, A. A., Jr., Strickland, A. J. III, 1998, *Strategic Management: Concepts and Cases*, Homewood, IL: Richard D. Irwin, Inc.

Tushman, M. L., Anderson, P., 1997, *Managing Strategic Innovation and Change*, New York, NY: Oxford University Press

Wheatley, M. J., 1992, *Leadership and the New Science*, San Francisco, CA: Berrett-Koehler Publishers

Woodward, J., 1980, *Industrial Organization: Theory and Practice*, New York, NY: Oxford University Press

Index

acquisition, 65, 66, 67, 69, 70
advertising, 23, 24, 43, 55, 81
agricultural sector, 7
authority, xvii. 7. 104, 107, 109, 110, 117, 119-120, 122-123, 130, 178, 181

backward vertical integration, 62
Balanced Scorecard, 172
basic strategy, 55
behavior, 87, 89, 91, 94, 138, 143
benchmarking, 22
boards of directors, xvii, 149, 153, 154, 155
Boston Consulting Group, 71
boycott, 40
brand loyalty, 28, 30, 32, 49, 55
budget, 24, 168
buffering, 48
buyer power, 29, 90

capabilities, 15, 35, 37, 43, 73, 82-83, 87, 91, 9, 100, 108, 115-116, 130, 139, 141, 168, 172, 180
Cash Cow, 71
cash flow, 23, 71, 72
centralized decision-making, 129, 137
change, xv, xviii, 4, 6, 7, 14, 18, 25, 30, 32, 43, 55, 56, 57, 65, 66, 67, 74, 89, 104-106, 119, 129, 138, 150-152, 157, 161, 164, 171, 177-184
closed systems, 45
commitment, xiii, 4, 5, 17, 21, 24, 90, 91, 93, 96, 111, 144, 159, 163, 164, 165
commodity, 54, 55
communication, xvii, 62, 92, 104, 106-107, 117, 119-123, 126-127, 181

competition, xiii, xvii, 27, 30-32, 35, 38-39, 41, 43-44, 50, 53, 55-60, 65, 74, 75, 82, 90-91, 98, 104, 106-107, 121, 123-124, 145, 179-180
competitive advantage, v, xvii, 8-9, 15, 29, 33, 35, 37-38, 42, 44, 47, 53-55, 57-58, 61-62, 64-65, 69, 74, 76, 80, 88, 122, 129, 139, 143, 145-147
competitive analysis, xvi, 27, 34
competitive brands, 49
competitive disadvantage, 37-38, 64-65, 83, 88, 129
competitive strategy, xvi, 43, 53-54, 56-57, 70, 91, 107, 134, 138, 168
competitive success, xv, 139, 147
competitors, xiv, xvi, 9, 15, 22, 27-35, 37-40, 42, 44, 53-61, 65, 73, 78, 31-82, 88, 91, 145, 180
conflict, xvii, 6, 89, 91, 103-107, 110, 126-127
consolidate, 32
consolidated industry, 30, 56
contingent strategy, 70
continuous improvement, 22, 179
contracting, 65
control, xvi, 5-6, 9-10, 22, 27, 37, 44, 45-56, 51, 53, 62-65, 77-78, 89, 92, 93, 99, 106-110, 115, 123, 128, 131, 149, 152, 168, 172, 178, 182,
coopting, 50
copyrights, 61
corporate strategy, xiii
cost variations, 76
cottage industries, 142
co-workers, 14, 20, 96, 98-99
creativity, 91, 105, 130, 138-139, 141, 144, 179
critical support systems, 168
customer satisfaction, 14, 72, 73, 99-100, 116, 172, 174
customer service, 13, 18, 59, 71-73, 90-91

customers, xiii, xvi, 9, 13-16, 18, 21, 23, 27-30, 32, 35, 37-43, 45, 47-49, 53-63, 68, 71-73, 8-88, 90, 108, 111, 116, 122-124, 128, 134-137, 142, 145, 18, 173-174
cyclical, 41, 48, 68, 71

decentralized decision-making, 104, 129
decisiveness, 5, 159
decline stage, 183
declining market, 32
defensive strategy, 60, 71
demand, 18, 22, 27, 42, 48-49, 55, 59, 61, 68, 80, 108
demographics, 14, 46, 184
development, 51, 54-55, 61, 71, 76, 122, 130, 135, 142, 18, 172-174
distinctive competence, 8, 15, 34, 37, 42-43, 58, 90
diversification, 68, 69
diversify, 63, 68, 69
divestiture, 69, 70
Dog, 71
downsizing, 48, 183

economies of scale, 5, 33, 50, 55, 64, 65, 75, 79, 80-82
economy, 28, 46, 87, 184
education, xiii, 6, 14, 46, 173, 179
emergent strategies, 53, 54
employment sectors, 7, 8
empowerment, 110
entry threat, 28, 90
esteem needs, 95
ethics, 88
evaluation, xviii, 15, 144, 154, 157, 174
exit strategy, 65
expectations, 174
expectations, xiv, 5, 9, 14, 22, 38-44, 63, 67, 72, 91, 174
expected performance, 175
experience curve, 33
experience, xiv, 29, 33, 43, 46, 50, 63-65, 74, 90, 99, 100, 106-107, 113, 128, 135-136, 141, 144-146, 155, 15, 161, 166, 177
explicit knowledge, 146

export, 79, 80
external analysis, 27
external analysis, xvi
external environment, 27, 38, 44, 45-47, 50, 51, 53, 5, 90, 104, 107, 178, 180, 182
external locus of control, 8, 89
external strategies, 47

feedback system, 171, 172
feedback, xvii, 171, 172, 174
first-mover strategy, 61, 62
focus strategy, 58, 68
follower strategy, 61, 62
forward integration, 62, 63
forward vertical integration, 62
fragmented industry, 30, 56
free-riders, 64
functional structure, 121-123, 125, 128-130
functional structure, 135
fundamental strategy, 55, 56, 57, 58
future, xiii, xv, 1, 9, 10, 18-20, 23, 42, 47-48, 51, 55, 64, 75, 83, 90, 96, 104, 116, 123, 129, 138, 143, 154, 168, 178-180, 182-184

gap analysis, 43
geographic market, 58
global strategies, xvii, 82
globalization, 46
goal incompatibility, 104
goals, xiii, xiv, xvi, xvii, 1, 6, 10, 16, 17-25, 27, 37, 43, 53-54, 73, 89, 91, 93, 96, 98, 103, 105, 115, 119, 126-127, 137, 139, 167-168
good performance, xv
governance, 149-154 182
government regulation, 90
government, vi, 6, 18, 39, 46, 81, 90, 110
greenfield investment, 66
growth stage, 31, 71, 128
Growth/Share Matrix, 70, 71

heterogeneity, 104, 106
homogeneous, 106, 107

Index

imitator strategy, 61
implementation, xvii, xviii, 74, 85, 157, 165, 169, 171, 175
incentives, xvii, 25, 89, 93-94, 96, 98-99, 109-110, 146
individual objectives, 171
industry life-cycle, 31-32, 128
industry life-cycle, 56
industry sector, 7
industry structure, 56
infancy, 30, 31, 56, 128-129, 182
inflation, 78
information asymmetry, 108, 145
information technology, 145
information, v, xiv, xvii, 35, 45, 47, 73, 90, 104, 108-111, 115, 117, 119-122, 125, 145, 147, 159, 161-162, 167, 172, 174-175, 177
innovation, 6, 55, 61-62, 74, 91, 105, 130, 133-135, 138-139, 142, 144, 147, 166
inputs, 29, 45, 58, 62, 68, 115, 120, 133, 135, 137, 151, 172, 174
inspiring people, 4
integrity, 5, 92, 159
intellectual property, 61
internal analysis, xvi, 27, 37, 43
internal locus of control, 8, 89
internal strategies, 47
international markets, 78, 83
international strategies, 75
invention, 142

job satisfaction, 96, 142
job security, xiv, xv, 96, 152
joint venture, 50, 65, 66, 68

knowledge, 1
knowledge, xiii, xvii, 1, 6, 8, 15, 37, 43, 45, 85, 92, 99, 108, 110, 114, 120, 125-127, 130, 133-136, 141-143, 145-147, 167, 183

leaders, 3-5, 8-10, 23, 33, 60-61, 71, 88, 123, 138, 141, 171, 183
leadership characteristics, 3, 5
leadership, xvi, 3-11, 54-58, 62, 73-74, 80, 90, 130, 146, 155, 159
leading change, 179
learning curve, 33, 61, 81, 98
learning organization, 143, 144, 146, 163, 174
learning, xvii, 10, 22, 33, 38, 61, 81, 98, 121, 141, 143-147, 163, 171-172, 174
learning-curve effects, 34
licensing, 50, 61, 63, 79
local-content, 76, 77
location, 14, 15, 43, 55, 80-81, 136
locus of control, 89
long-term objectives, 105, 172
loss-leader, 71

major objectives, 169
management hubris, 38
management, vi-vi, xiv-xvi, xviii, 5-10, 20, 38, 40, 42, 87, 92, 99, 104-105, 107, 111, 115-116, 123, 125, 142, 149, 152, 153,157, 167, 181-183
managers, v. xiv-xv, 8, 46, 82, 91, 98, 100, 103, 106-107, 111, 123-127, 131, 149, 151, 154,159, 163, 167, 169, 171, 180, 182-183
manufacturing technology, 136, 137
manufacturing, 8, 14, 23, 224, 33, 55, 67, 66, 76, 78, 80, 82, 109, 122, 127, 130, 134, 136, 137, 142, 18, 171
market segment, 14, 23, 59
market share, 21, 28, 31-32, 57, 59-60, 65, 71, 82, 90, 172
market, 14, 21-23, 27-29, 31-32, 45, 53, 55-62, 65, 70-71, 75, 79-82, 90, 97-98, 100, 108, 114, 122, 124, 126, 130, 151, 153, 172
mass production, 135
matrix structure, 129, 130, 135
meaning, xiv, xvi, 13, 19, 89, 93, 151
measurements, 22, 171, 174, 175
mechanistic organizations, 130
meetings, 21, 23, 100, 114-115, 152, 154
merger, 65-68, 70

mission statement, 13, 16
mission, xiii, xiv, xvi, 6, 9, 13-16, 18, 19, 25, 27, 57-58, 73, 89, 91-92, 101, 119, 149, 171=172
monetary rewards, 94, 96
money, xviii, 1, 9, 14, 25, 33, 41, 43, 45, 56, 61, 69, 71, 73, 87, 93, 96, 99, 101, 104, 108, 147,151, 163-164, 167
monopoly, 29, 56, 90
moral principles, 88
multi-tasking, 19, 20

needs, xiv-xv, 4, 6, 9, 13-16, 18, 21, 24, 27-28, 38, 43, 48, 53, 54, 55, 57, 61, 62, 64, 65, 75, 79-80, 93-96, 101, 108, 120, 123, 126, 128, 129-130, 136-137, 143, 160, 165, 167, 169, 174, 181
network centrality, 108, 109
non-monetary rewards, 101

objectives, xiii, xvi, 13, 17, 82, 89, 94, 101, 103, 106, 109, 119, 120, 126-127, 147, 167-168, 171, 174, 179
obstacles, xvi, 4, 11, 28
offensive strategy, 60, 71
open systems, 45
opportunities, vi, 10, 18, 27, 33, 39, 46, 48, 50-51, 53, 61, 79, 96, 99, 125, 142,
options, 6, 42, 48, 182
organization form, 123, 127, 128, 129, 137-138
organization structure, 104, 120, 122, 126-131, 1335, 137-138, 171, 180
organization theorists, 8, 130
organizational efforts, 20
organizational incentives, 98, 99
organizational learning, 143
organizational life-cycle, 180
organizational memory, 146
organizational objectives, 106, 139, 171
organizational outcomes, 39
organization-level objectives, 171
organize, xvii, 73, 120, 138-139, 151
organizing, xiv, xvii, 119, 123

outcomes, xiii, 6, 13, 17, 19, 24, 39, 73, 89, 92, 94, 101, 111, 131, 160, 163, 171
outputs, 15, 35, 45, 48, 62, 68, 120, 126, 133, 137, 151, 172, 174

participative management, 104
patents, 43, 61
people, v, xiv-xv, xvii-xviii, 3-10, 15, 19, 23, 25, 35, 37-38, 42, 45, 47-50, 55, 61, 63, 64, 66, 67-68, 72, 73, 85, 87, 89, 91-92, 93-94, 96, 97-100, 104-110, 113-116, 117, 119-121, 124-131, 134-135, 137-139, 141-144, 146-147,154, 159-160, 163, 165-166, 167-169, 171-172, 174, 177-181, 183
performance standards, 96, 98
physical environment, 46
planning, xv-xviii, 9, 13, 18-19, 53, 73-74, 129, 157, 171
politics, xvii, 46, 107, 109, 111
portfolio, 70, 71, 73, 80
power, xvii, 104, 107-110, 25, 29, 39-40, 90, 92, 128, 142, 151, 160, 178, 180, 182
practical knowledge, 141
predict, 27, 46, 51, 129
predictability, 46
price, 28-31, 41-42, 49, 54-56, 59, 65-66, 72, 91, 106, 108, 134, 153
prioritize, 13, 17-20, 104
prioritizing, 20, 168
productivity, 41-42, 78, 98-99, 109, 130, 142
products, xvii, 9, 13, 14, 18, 21, 23-24, 28-31, 35, 38, 45, 48-49, 53-63, 64, 69-72, 76-79, 82, 87-88, 90, 91, 99-100, 122-123, 126, 134-139,145, 168, 173, 179, 182
proprietary, 61, 74, 79, 145
proxy system, 150, 152
quality improvement, 172

Question Mark, 71
quotas, 76, 77

rationing, 48
relationships, xvii, 14, 42, 45, 72-73, 120, 133, 152

Index

resisting change, 177, 178
resource allocation, xv, 104, 168, 178, 181
resources, 1
resources, xiv-xviii, 1, 9, 14-16, 18-19, 24-25, 37-40, 43, 45, 47, 54, 65, 73, 75, 79, 87, 89,104, 108-110, 113, 116, 117, 120-121, 125-127, 139, 146, 152, 157, 167-169, 178, 180
responsibilities, xvii, 11, 19, 24, 46, 91, 109-111, 114, 117,119-120, 124, 126, 150, 153, 181
responsibility, 5, 19, 66-67, 72, 88, 120, 122, 126, 130, 139, 149, 151, 155, 159, 165, 167,
result, xiii, xvii, 3, 6, 10, 15-16, 17-21, 41, 47, 62, 65, 68, 92, 96, 100, 104, 111, 113-114, 122-124, 130, 142, 144, 149, 152, 163, 165
results, xii-xv, 6, 22, 32, 89, 115. 121-122, 144, 160-161, 164-165, 172-174, 179
rewards, xvii, 40, 61, 91, 93-94, 96, 98, 100, 106, 110, 120, 168, 179
risk, xv, 15, 17, 25, 61-62, 66-69, 79, 107-108, 124, 126, 160, 165, 178
rivalry, 27, 90
routine tasks, 100, 114-115

sabotage, 41
Scientific Management, 142
self-actualization, 94, 95, 96, 99
self-discipline, 20
self-knowledge, 141
service sector, 7
service technology, 136
services, xvii, 9, 13-14, 18, 29-31, 35, 38, 45, 48-49, 53-58, 60-63, 70-72, 76, 79, 88, 90, 99, 111, 123-124, 136-137, 139, 182
signaling, 60
social responsibility, 88
stakeholders, 35, 38-42, 44, 88, 110
Star, 71
start-up, 65, 66, 182
stewardship, 110
stockholders, 66, 69, 149, 151, 152
strategic alliances, 65, 79, 82, 180
strategic intent, 139
strategic issues, 18, 19

strategic management, v, vi, xiii-xviii, 27, 54, 66, 73, 85, 119, 133, 141, 157, 172, 184
strategies, xvi-xvii, 18, 27, 29, 31, 34-35, 37, 43, 46-48, 50, 53-58, 60, 69-73, 80, 91, 139, 149, 167, 171, 180
strategy formulation, xvi, xvii
strategy implementation, xvii, 73, 117, 171
strengths, 3, 27, 34-35, 37-38, 4353, 90, 110
substitutes, 28, 90
success, v-vi, xiii-xiv, xvi-xviii, 14, 17-20, 22,-23, 25, 29, 37, 39, 44, 45, 50, 55, 59-61, 63, 74, 83, 85, 87, 91, 94, 96, 99, 105, 109, 111, 113, 126-127, 130, 139, 147, 154, 164, 167168, 169, 178-179, 181-182
sunk costs, 56, 164
super-ordinate goals, 105, 126
supplier power, 29, 90
suppliers, 29, 39, 41-42, 47-48, 63, 65, 71, 76
supply, 24-25, 27, 55, 71, 81, 90
survival, xiii, 32-33, 57, 107, 183
sustainable competitive advantage, 35, 38, 42, 73, 80-81, 139, 145
switching costs, 49

tacit knowledge, 146
talent, 1
target market, 14
tariffs, 76, 77
task interdependence, 104
technology, 33, 37, 43, 46, 73, 75, 79, 82, 87, 104, 107, 120, 125, 133-137, 139, 146, 180, 184
testing, 79, 144, 171
theory, v, 4, 8, 99, 144, 163, 171
threats, 18, 27, 46, 48, 50-51, 53
threats, 27
time management, xvii
time, v, xiv, xvii-xviii, 1, 3, 5, 7, 11, 16, 17-21, 23-25, 33, 39, 41-43, 45-47, 49-50. 53, 56, 58-59, 61-62, 63, 66, 71-73, 82, 87, 94, 96, 99-101, 104, 106-107, 111, 113-116, 121, 123-124, 126, 129, 131, 133-137, 144-145, 147, 157, 161-165, 167, 171, 173-175, 181
trade policies, 76, 80
tradeoffs, 25, 83, 113

transformation process, 45, 63, 120, 125, 133,136-137, 171, 174
trends, 46-48, 50-51, 184
trend-spotting, 46

uncertainty, 5-6, 46, 48-50, 61, 65, 104, 131, 145, 165, 177-178
uncertainty, 61, 65
underperformance, 93
unions, 39, 65

values, 37, 87-92, 97, 105, 131, 153, 163, 179
vertical integration, 59, 63, 64, 65

virtues, 10
vision, 131, 159
vision, 3-6, 9

wage program, 97, 98
wages, 39, 41, 78, 96-98, 100, 114, 134-135, 151
weaknesses, 3, 10, 27, 34-35, 37-38, 43-44, 53, 60, 121
workplace, 46, 98-99

zero-based budgeting, 168